East Kent Within Living. Memory

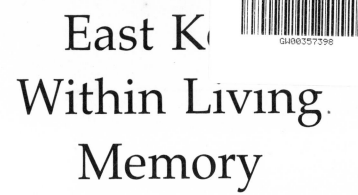

Compiled by the East Kent Federation
of Women's Institutes

Published jointly by
Countryside Books, Newbury
and the EKFWI, Canterbury

COUNTRYSIDE BOOKS
3 Catherine Road
Newbury, Berkshire

ISBN 1 85306 248 0

The cover photograph shows cherry pickers
at Bredgar in about 1900.

Designed by Mon Mohan
Produced through MRM Associates Ltd, Reading
Printed in England

Contents

Acknowledgements

East Kent Federation of Women's Institutes would like to thank all the members, their families and friends and the East Kent Institutes who have contributed such fascinating material for this book. We know what a very great deal of endeavour went into their entries and are only sorry that it isn't possible for every 'memory' to be included – the book just could not be large enough for that – but every contribution has been greatly valued. It has been such a very worthwhile project for the East Kent Federation of Women's Institutes and has been entered into with much enthusiasm.

By noble efforts most members managed to get their contributions typed but for some this proved impossible. Our thanks go to Mrs Pam Keen who so cheerfully and willingly solved the problem, involving her in many hours of work with the handwritten scripts. Our thanks also to Mrs Mavis Stewart for her attractive line drawings and to Mrs Judith Moosuddee and Hazel Jones for the County Map.

List of Contributing WIs

Contributions were received from the following East Kent Women's Institutes:

Abbey, Aldington, Alkham, Appledore, Ash with Westmarsh, Ashley with Studdale, Barham with Kingston, Bethersden, Birchington, Blean, Bleangate, Boughton under Blean, Brabourne, Bredgar, Brenzett & District, Bridge with Patrixbourne, Broadstairs, Capel-le-Ferne Evening, Castle Green, Challock Lees, Charing, Chaucer, Cheriton, Chilham, Cinque Port of Hythe, Cliffsend, Cliffsend Evening, Cliftonville, Deal, Denton Wootton & Swingfield, Doddington & District, Folkstone, Godinton, Godmersham with Crundale, Greenstreet, Grenham Bay, Ham Street with Ruckinge, Hastingleigh with Elmstead, Hawkinge with Acrise & Paddlesworth, Herne, Hernhill, Kennington, Kingsnorth, Little Chart, Lower Hardres with Nackington, Lydd, Lympne, Lynsted with Teynham, Middlemarsh, Minster in Sheppey, Minster in Thanet Evening, Mongeham & Ripple, Monkton, Murston, Newchurch, Newington, Newnham Valley, Nonington & District, Northwood, Orlestone Evening, Painters Forstal with Ospringe, Preston with Elmstone & Stourmouth, Ramsgate, River, Rodmersham, Rodmersham Green, Rough Common, St Dunstan's, St Margaret's-at-Cliffe, St Martin's, St Nicholas-at-Wade with Sarre, St Stephen's, Saltwood, Sandwich, Seabrook, Seasalter Cross, Sellindge, Selling & District, Shepherdswell, Singleton, Smarden, Smeeth, South Street, Stanford with Postling, Stone cum Ebony, Stowting, Stubbs Cross, Sturry, Swalecliffe with Chestfield, Temple Ewell, Thanington Without, Tilmanstone, Tollsford, Tunstall Afternoon, Upchurch, Walmer, Westwell, Whitfield, Whitstable, Wingham, Woodchurch, Woolreeds & District, Word in Worth, Wormshill, Wye.

MARGATE • BROADSTAIRS

Manston

Minster

RAMSGATE

• Herne

Sarre

lean

• Preston

• Richborough

ANTERBURY

Wingham

• Sandwich

Chilham •

Barham

Deal

Godmersham •

Wye •

Tilmanstone

St. Margarets at Cliffe

Elham

DOVER

Brabourne

Alkham

ingsnorth

reet

Hythe •

FOLKESTONE

• Lymphe •

Dymchurch

CITY

LVER

• New Romney

Lydd

Dungeness

Foreword

'Living Memory' takes many of us back to the Second World War and a few of us to the War before that. Add on the stories told to us so often by our elders and personal recollection stretches to the turn of the century. We recall here in East Kent the days when the horse and cart were commonplace and we lived with the outside privy, the copper boiler and Reckitt's Blue. Children walked to school down country lanes and most of the girls then worked on the farm or went into service.

East Kent had its own peculiarities; the hop gardens attracted thousands of pickers from London's East End but chiefly from the surrounding villages, who relied on the work each year from all the family to buy their winter clothes. Our long coastline bred fishermen and the famous Whitstable oyster and the equally famous Margate and Ramsgate holiday landladies – perhaps, also, the infamous Romney Marsh smugglers. A coal industry was started between the wars, flourished to dominate complete districts and now, suddenly, is gone. Here, too, we received back the men from the Dunkirk beaches, watched the Battle of Britain over our heads, prepared as best we could to resist German invasion and ducked as the Doodlebugs, rumbling overhead, were shot down around us.

Yet, with all this and the Channel Ports with their age old to-ing and fro-ing across to the Continent, we have always been and still are, a collection of rural villages scattered around a market town and an old Cathedral city. It is most noticeable how many of our contributors to this book are writing now from the same village – or thereabouts – as that in which they spent their childhood 50 years ago.

It is timely, as the Channel Tunnel with its motorways, high-speed rail links and development areas open around us, to record for our grandchildren how we lived then. It may be that they will dismiss our claim of 'Ah, happy days' and say with Walter Swinburne that 'Time remembered is grief forgotten.' Perhaps; but let them be aware that recalling these times has given very real pleasure to the many people that have shared in the making of this book.

Celia Armitage
County Co-ordinator for the
East Kent Federation of Women's Institutes

TOWN & COUNTRY LIFE

SOME TOWNS AND VILLAGES
REMEMBERED

A blacksmith at work in his forge in a Canterbury lane; dockyard workers swarming through Sheerness on their bicycles; elderly ladies in black being pushed along the Leas at Folkestone in bath chairs; watching the oyster boats go out at Whitstable – just some of the memories of the 1920s and 1930s that now seem long gone. Here are just a few reminders of life in towns and villages in days gone by.

WHITSTABLE 1920

'Whitstable was a great place of interest in my younger days, as there was the harbour, the railway, the oyster fishing fleet of smacks, the boat builders, boating lake, golf course, and in the summer lots of swimming.

We had three shipbuilding yards and in the 1920s one caught alight, and you can imagine the sight that was. We, my pals and I, would go to these yards, as they repaired all the barges, oyster smacks and rowing boats. They had a very long shed, about 40 ft long, at the side of the building, into which they would put planks of timber to steam the wood so that they could shape them to the outline of the various boats. All sorts of repairs were done and we loved watching them working.

As you may know, the native Whitstable oyster was famous all over our country and overseas. There were about 150 oyster boats (smacks or yawls) which used to go out every day and dredge for the oysters. As there were two tides a day these boats would sometimes be used twice a day. There were three to four men to a boat and sometimes I would be lucky enough to be able to go on these trips. When the men returned to the oyster stores at the horsebridge, the oysters were put into various deep wells, according to size and year.

If you go down to the horsebridge today you may still see the outlet pipe sticking out of the sand at low tide. This let all the silt from the washing sheds out into the sea. Also at the horsebridge, sometimes the barges would anchor just 50 ft offshore, and when the tide went out you could see the horses and carts go down to the

St Margaret's-at-Cliffe in the 1950s – no road markings or traffic signs, no television aerials, and it was still safe to walk in the middle of the road!

barges and unload them. The wooden storage sheds were in Harbour Street, which is where they stored, mostly, grain of all sorts. We would sometimes help push the carts at the rear, to help the horses pull the loads up the slope at the horsebridge, and run down to the store sheds and watch them unload. Inside the shed you could see rats as big as cats watching you, up on some of the beams over your head. We used to throw big stones at them – with not much luck!

Now, the harbour was a very interesting place, with local fishing boats, cargo boats, yachts, and smacks and barges. There was also the railway train that came from Canterbury (the old Crab and Winkle line). The train would bring goods for various places around the country, and the cargo boats and barges would load up the empty trucks and then the train would go back full. They also had passenger trains from Canterbury. The fare was fourpence and trippers would come to the seaside all white looking and go back sometimes very red faced. As we were there all the time we were pretty brown (lucky me). There were two turntables on the harbour, and these were used for turning the trucks to different tracks. Sometimes we would push at the rear of the loaded trucks to help those very strong shire horses pull at them, because once

11

the engine train had left Whitstable there were only these horses to move them.

In 1929 the sea froze solid for six weeks and you could walk out to the fishing smacks and back. What fun. I felt like the good Lord, walking on the sea.

Mum liked cockles, jellied eels, a large crab, and most wet fish and it was great fun to walk to Seasalter and go out to the mud as the tide went out. That is the best time to get your cockles, when a lot of them are still on top and the others which go under the mud you can still find as they leave a faint discolouring on the mud surface and you use your fingers to lift them, sometimes even your big toe! Oh, what days.

You could catch lobsters. Now lobsters also go out with the tide, and they feed as they go. Two of you go on a very calm day, one beats the very edge of the water (nearest the beach) and the other one is a good 50 yards further out to sea, and when the lobster hears the noise on the sea surface he makes for the open sea. That's the time to cut him off. In one hand you have a piece of wood, that's to hold his tail down, and in your other hand a sack, that's to put him in. The tail can give you a nasty sting.

On a calm hot day skate would float on top of the water and I have been out in a rowing boat, with some of my mates, to catch them when the boat quietly glides up behind them. That's when the two oars are shipped onto the boats, and one oar is used to scull the boat. Up in the bow of the boat one leans over the top and glides a big hook up under the skate; that's the tricky part. If you are lucky you can, with an upward lift, hook the skate and with help from the others you can get him into the boat, but beware the tail!'

ISLE OF SHEPPEY 1920

'When I was growing up in the 1920s and 1930s on Sheppey, the island was a very different place. Sheerness was a bustling, lively town with the dockyard its main workplace. To see the swarms of dockyard men on bicycles sweeping home through the town at midday dinnertime was a regular sight.

Clustered around the central town clock were a number of shops, mostly grocers. They included The World's Stores, Home and Colonial, Lipton's and The Maypole. My mother favoured the International, where, seated at the counter, she would give her weekly order to an attentive assistant. For some reason she always purchased her butter from The Maypole, where my sister and I watched in fascination as smart young men in spotless white aprons, hair slicked down with Brylcreem, performed wonders with two wooden, carved butter pats.

Sometimes we were allowed to visit the shops near late closing on a Saturday evening. I can still see, against the twilit sky, the row of white gas lamps flaring outside Ted Ancell's Bazaar on the corner of Beach Street. The rather dim interior was like Aladdin's cave, presided over by the Ancell family.

Then there were the drapers' shops: Featherstone's, Godwin's and The Bon Marché, their smart young lady assistants clad in neat dark uniform dresses, black, brown or navy, set off with dainty white collars and cuffs. I was most in awe of the cashiers, seated with some dignity behind their glass-surrounded cash desks, dealing so efficiently with money in the little metal containers whizzing busily along on the overhead rails. The Bon Marché was an old building with sloping wooden floors, glass roof and a large, black coke stove in the centre which glowed with heat in the winter, trying to combat the many draughts.

Woolworth's was the largest store in town, with its low counters, assistants in dark red dresses, and everything under sixpence!

My first visit to the cinema was to the Hippodrome in the Broadway, opposite the post office. It had started life as a music hall and the decor and red plush seats remained. The usherettes patrolled the aisles regularly, with spray cans. I can smell that airspray to this day! We were never allowed to go to the only other cinema, The Oxford, known locally as "The Fleapit" for obvious reasons.

The long summer holidays, when the sun always seemed to be shining, were spent mostly on the beach. Sheerness was a popular seaside resort then, with trippers from London coming in droves on the train and crowding the beaches.

As we lived in what was then called Marine Town, quite near the seafront, my mother and her neighbours boosted their small incomes by taking in summer visitors who wished to stay for a week or more. Some of our regular families returned year after year.

On Sunday mornings we walked home from Sunday school sedately along the seafront, clad in our white socks, ankle strap shoes, best dresses and panama hats with strict instructions *not* to go on the beach!'

CHILHAM 1920

'Many years separate the 1920 cottage residents from the commuters of today in the village of Chilham where I grew up. Most people worked on the farms and smallholdings or in the shops or as craftsmen with a trade. My home was lit by oil lamps and drinking water was drawn from a deep well which took two men ten minutes to fill one bucket. Water for washing came from a rainwater well at the back of the garden and was pumped up to the kitchen, where a copper was used for heating the water.

All children walked to the school from the age of five taking their lunch; we used to meet the postman who walked from Chilham station up to our hamlet.

Transport was by horse and trap, railway and bicycle. A local carrier brought shopping from Canterbury or Ashford and on a Saturday took passengers in his van to Canterbury for sixpence return. Local deliveries were made by the butchers, grocer, baker and haberdashery, and a fishman walked from Faversham pushing an old pram with the fish in. The dairy farmer brought the milk in a horse-drawn milk float.

Shops in the village included bakers, butchers, grocers, hardware, sweets, newsagent and a post office. A corn miller lived in the house by the mill, and a cobbler mended boots and shoes. There was a hairdresser and a dressmaker, a saddlemaker and two music teachers. Competition for trade was high with tradesmen coming round from nearby villages. In the draper's shop a packet of pins was given in lieu of a farthing change.

The church was in the main village and the two hamlets had small mission rooms where Sunday services were held. Social events took place in these halls with the altar closed off by huge doors, when we had whist drives, dances and socials.

The village doctor and the district nurse and midwife lived in the village and most babies were born at home.

Most farms were arable with hops, fruit and dairying. Cherries and plums were picked by men as few women went out to work except at hop picking time. Hops were picked by hand and pickers came from London, Ashford and Folkestone. They lived in huts near the hop gardens. Their arrival changed the village during their six week stay. Hops were dried in the oast houses and we used to take large potatoes to be baked in the hot ashes in the evening.

The forge of the local wheelright, farrier, smithy and undertaker was a place of interest for all the children, seeing horses shod and watching when the smith had a "firing" day. The large waggon wheels made by the carpenters had the outer iron rims put on by the smith and many people came to watch this event. All coffins were made by hand, farm tools and implements made and repaired.

Cinema shows, dances, whist drives and socials were held in the village castle hall by kind permission of the castle owners Sir Edmund and Lady Davis. At Christmas time they provided a tea party with each child being given a present chosen from a list given to the school, of books, toys, dolls etc.

A Sunday school outing to Whitstable by waggon and a picnic lunch on the beach was an annual event. A very special treat was to go to Canterbury by pony and trap to meet my grandmother who lived in Bekesbourne; we had afternoon tea in a restaurant, which we thought very grand. The annual Flower Show and Sports Day was an event which all villagers attended and joined in the activities. Entries for children included a collection of wild flowers, an egg and spoon race and a three-legged race. Prizes were money, five shillings for a First.

The outbreak of war brought many changes to rural life but in the 1920s our village was a place full of pleasant sounds, simple pleasures and timeless ways.'

CANTERBURY 1930

'We lived in a small cottage in St George's Lane (where the bus station is now) from 1925 until 1932.

The lane led off the main street, with The Coach and Horses pub on one corner and a furniture shop on the other. It was a very narrow lane with terraced cottages along one side and a few houses on the other side, which was mainly taken up with Jennings Printing Works (they also printed the *Kent Herald*) and the long wall of the Simon Langton boys school. We could also see the playground of the Simon Langton girls school from the front bedroom window and it was a delight to me to watch the girls playing or rehearsing for special events, one of which I remember was "Merry England" which provided colourful costumes and happy dancing.

There was a hop oast in the lane, which stood empty most of the year but just before hop picking time, two elderly men would move in, clean it up and light the two furnaces down in the cellar. The two men spent hours sitting by the furnaces and sometimes they would bake potatoes in the fire for us. When hop picking started, they opened up the top doors of the oast and let down a big hook which the hop-cart man wrapped around the hop sacks on his cart and they were hauled up to the top door and swung inside. Later they were emptied into a small doorway and fell on a canvas floor above the furnaces to be dried (I can still smell the hops and sulphur as I write). Sometimes we were allowed to ride on the hop cart, which we loved, but once or twice the horse bolted so we had to jump off in a hurry. When dried, the hops were put into six ft pockets (sacks) and pressed down hard, then tied with two ears at the top, to await the storage horse and cart. We were also allowed to play in the oast if we behaved ourselves, so on wet days we had concerts, with a big bag of dressing-up clothes, and we sang and danced and recited poetry to the others, or anyone that would come and watch. We also played games with our dolls.

There was a forge in the lane and it was interesting to watch the smith shoeing the horses. He would heat the shoe up to red hot and hammer it into shape, then pick up the horse's hoof onto his leather aproned lap and fit it on. This again is a smell I will always remember.

A dressmaker lived opposite us and she used me as a model for some of her customers' children's dresses and in return she made me some lovely dresses. This dressmaker had a parrot who mimicked her and some of her customers so that we often heard Laura (the parrot) saying "Oh no – really?" then laughing raucously, and sometimes we didn't know if it was the parrot or the lady.

Above the dressmaker lived an old lady, and woe betide any children playing underneath her window as she often opened the window and emptied the contents of the teapot or chamber pot out into the street!

We were lucky to have the cattle market just near and we spent hours looking through the railings at the animals and listening to the auctioneers and farmers. The sheep and cows were often driven on foot to the market and this was a sight worth watching, especially when a frightened animal dodged the drover and ran all over the place. After the market had finished, the market place was hosed down and the Salvation Army held a service there. This again was of great interest to the children of the lane.

The Dane John Gardens were quite close to us and if a bigger girl came with us, we could play there. We loved the autumn when the leaves were lying around – we would gather them into piles to make the outline of rooms of houses to play our "Mothers and Fathers" games (not many boys would play though). Cricket Week would be like fairyland in the Dane John, with all the coloured lights strung from tree to tree right down the avenue. The concert parties and military bands entertained from the bandstand and the fountain played. We were all well behaved – we had to be, or the Beadle would very soon turn us out of the gardens.

Once a year the Roman Catholic community had an open air service on the Dane John, then a procession would wend across St George's Terrace and I particularly loved to see the little girls in white dresses, strewing flower petals on the ground.

I mustn't forget the colourful old Italian lady (Mrs Coia), who sold ice cream from a barrow outside the Dane John gardens and opposite, just under the Riding Gate bridge, was a little sweet shop

16

where we could spend a halfpenny on one or two of so many lovely sweet things. This was a Saturday morning treat.'

'I lived in 9 Blackfriars Street in the city of Canterbury in the 1930s, where the river passed by the back of the houses. Before my parents lived there it was used as a public house named The Maid of Kent. The river was well populated with both brown and rainbow trout and at an early age I would go fishing in our boat. The river was deep in the 1930s with Denne's Mill holding the water back.

Our next door neighbour, my father and I went fishing round the Westgate Gardens and we bought a pint of cockles for bait; I was only eight years old at the time and got rather bored so started to eat them. They tasted so nice that I ate the lot. My father was very cross when we had to come back because we had no bait. When I got a bit older I used to row the boat on my own. Just below the Friars Bridge there was a large wooden building where they treated sheepskins, called "Greens"; the smell was not to be desired. When I rowed by I saw there was an iron grating where the river flowed through and under the grating were large eels' heads sticking out. I would drop a big fat juicy worm on a hook in front of them and pull them out into the boat. Sometimes their heads were so large I couldn't get them from under the grating and they got away. I used to sell them to MacFisheries, where the manager would say, "Where did you catch them, sonny?" – I would reply "the Stour". He paid me one shilling and sixpence a pound for them; it's a good job he didn't know where I had caught them.

One day I was fishing under the other side of the King's Bridge in the boat, hoping to catch a trout under the flats at the back of the Eastbridge Hospital. I was sitting quietly concentrating, when a window from one of the flats above opened and out came a bucket of potato peelings and water all over me; they closed the window not even knowing I was there. In those days everyone threw anything they didn't want into the river. Sometimes we would get lovely flowers, geranium heads from the Greyfriars Nursery. I didn't have to buy any balls, they were always floating down.'

FOLKESTONE 1930

'On Sundays we wore our best clothes and were taken for a walk along the Lower Road or the Leas. Men stood in a rank with bath chairs for hire on the Leas and elderly ladies, always in black, would be wheeled in the sea air for the good of their health. Sometimes we would be allowed to listen to the band at the bandstand.

Hundreds of people strolled along the Leas and the Promenade during the summer season. There were many photographers on the Promenade and if you were snapped you could see the proofs displayed the next day on endless boards, and if you wished you could order copies from the kiosk.

The Folkestone Regatta was held each summer and crowds of people sat on the beach to watch the boating and swimming races at high tide. The pier was crowded also and the Slippery Pole was a great attraction – there was a purse of money to be won by the man able to negotiate the height of it without slipping down. The day ended with a wonderful firework display. In those days it was only ten shillings and sixpence to go to France on the cross Channel boat, and four shillings and sixpence to travel to London by steam train.'

ASHFORD 1930

'Tuesday was the highlight of the week in the market town of Ashford. I used to sit in the window and watch the farmers walk in from all over the county with their flocks of sheep, cows, pigs etc, through the centre of the town, the odd animal being chased back after straying round the corner. Some farmers had to have overnight rest places to complete the long journey. The market was the centre for a variety of stalls, from food to clothing and drapery, where the farmers' wives would do their shopping.

The milkman brought the churn straight from the farm to the door and measured out your requirements of milk into your jug. Boys delivered fresh bread from the bakery daily. The fishermen brought their freshly caught fish on a barrow door to door, and shrimps were very popular to buy. Shopkeepers used to have errand boys to deliver their goods, and the errand boy race was quite an event in the town to find the fastest lad. At Easter time orders were given to the baker for hot cross buns and they were left on your doorstep, still hot, at seven o'clock on Good Friday morning.'

SHOPS AND SHOPPING

Going shopping was often a special event, since so much day to day produce could be delivered direct to the door by the roundsmen and delivery boys who were a part of the street scene in towns and villages throughout East Kent. Shops, commonly family concerns, were at the heart of the community, and so too were pubs, where a great deal more than drinking went on!

A DRAPER'S IN FOLKESTONE

'My grandfather lost his job in London and couldn't find any work, but he had a well-off son in law, who set him up in a draper's shop in Folkestone in about 1908. My mother, father and aunt all worked in the shop. Mother looked after the baby and children's wear, my father did the dress materials, curtaining, sheets and blankets and Auntie did ribbons, lace and insertions. An assistant had the vests, socks, stockings, knickers and combinations to look after and another assistant took care of knitting needles, wool, cottons, embroidery silks, buttons, poppers and hooks and eyes. Upstairs was millinery, run by two assistants and a small room where alterations were made. My grandfather manned the desk.

Everyone in the shop worked very hard and for long hours. The shop opened at 8 am and closed at 7 pm except for Fridays and Saturdays, when it didn't close until 8 pm on Fridays and 10 pm on Saturdays. Wednesday it closed at 1 pm. On Christmas Eve it stayed open until 10 pm, and there was always someone who came in at the very last minute before closing time.

During the First World War many Belgian refugees came into the shop. Most didn't speak English, so it was sign language for what they wanted. After the war the shop did very well for a time, but by 1928 things were beginning to get worrying. Mother and Auntie used to go up to Copestakes in London to order new stock (my father had died by this time and my grandfather was suffering with his heart). Trade began to decline fast as the recession took hold. First, the millinery department and workroom were closed and the three assistants there lost their jobs. Then the girl who sold the materials etc went. Soon the assistant who sold knitting wools and tablecloths and tray cloths to work disappeared. Wonderful value for money were these ready to work cloths. I've still some of them in use now.

They were in Irish linen, stamped with a design. The 36" × 36" cost 1/11¾d and the 48" × 48" cost 3/11¾d. When you paid for them you were given a row of pins instead of the farthing change.

In those days things were sent out on approval to see if the people really liked them. My brother and I often took these parcels to people's homes on Saturdays or in the school holidays.

My people fought very hard to get better conditions and earlier closing for shops. I think they would have been very upset to see the later closing times coming back and shops opening on Sundays.

By 1932 only my mother, aunt and one assistant were left and the shop only just supported them. By 1939 only my aunt and one assistant remained. Then in 1940 loudspeakers could be heard on the streets at night asking anyone who could to leave the town, and my aunt and her friend went to Reigate and found a small shop where they sold baby clothes. The shop in Folkestone suffered quite a severe bomb blast.'

BAKEHOUSE DAYS IN CANTERBURY

'My parents established their bakery business shortly after the First World War. At first they had two shops; one in Northgate, and the other in Station Road West, Canterbury, but no ovens. The bread was baked in brick ovens on what is now part of the Sainsbury's site, and taken back to the shops by handcart. Before their marriage, Mum lived and worked at the Station Road shop, and Dad in Northgate, but later they concentrated on the Northgate shop and soon after I was born closed the other one, though I was often wheeled up St Dunstan's in a pram loaded with bread!

Hygiene was not such a fixation with people then as it is now, and some of the things we did would be frowned upon today. In common with most households, we did not have any running water upstairs, but used a jug and washbasin on a stand. The bakehouse had a cold tap over a drain (no sink) and a tap from a tank of water heated by the ovens, which had to be filled by hand. In the yard there was a stone sink and cold water tap for washing the bakehouse things, and the privy in the corner. It wasn't until much later that the Health Inspectors insisted on a sink in the passageway so that employees could wash their hands properly after paying a visit! Even the "kitchen", the room between the bakehouse and the shop, where we ate, rested and prepared the teas served out front, had no sink. Washing up was done in a bowl, and the weekly wash in two baths (one zinc, one enamel) on the kitchen table, before being hung up to dry in the attic (the yard was barely big enough to hang your smalls!).

Saturday night was bathnight. Three or four old jam tins, full of water, were placed in the oven to heat (the bakehouse ovens never went out) and the bath set out on the bakehouse floor. Unlike most folk, who kept their bath in the yard or the porch, ours was kept on a hook on the side of the oven, so it was always warm and you didn't have to chip ice out of it in winter before you could get in. Naturally we all shared the same water, with me going first and Dad last – I often think it's a good job we weren't a big family.

I can't remember a time when we were without at least one cat at home. Dad didn't like them in the bakehouse, not because they were unhygienic, but because he was afraid of standing on one and sliding across the floor on a feline roller skate! Once, however, one of the cats did make a sortie into forbidden territory. When the day's doughnuts had been fried, the lid was left off the fryer to allow the fat to cool. Nobody's quite sure what happened, but the cat ended up in the oil and had to be fished out, greasy and indignant. Such was our abhorrence of waste in those days, I shouldn't think we even changed the oil!

We didn't only sell home-made bread and cakes in the shop, but basic groceries and provisions: packet tea, cocoa, biscuits, soups, and even Omo and Surf. On the counter were tall glass jars of Rowntree's fruit gums, chocolate bars in display cabinets, and scales and little paper bags for the loose sweets. Mum served behind the counter, and was helped at various times by Cynthia, Mercy, Connie, and occasionally by me. Mrs Hilder prepared the cake tins and did the weighing-out in the bakehouse, and the delivery boy took orders round in a handcart or by bike. Dad made all the bread and cakes himself, pastries being his speciality: curly cream horns, jam puffs as big as cushions, and flaky, melt-in-the-mouth Fleed cakes, as light as air. There was something for everyone, from Belgian buns at a halfpenny each (seven for threepence) to wedding cakes at £2 10s 0d complete with decorations!'

THE WHITE SALE IN DOVER 1920

'January was special, for not only was it my birthday month, it was also White Sale time.

My Aunt Kate lived opposite us; she had been a governess and we children held her in awe. She was very kind, very "proper" and, having no family of her own, she took a great interest in me, the youngest of the family. So, in January she took me with her to replenish her linen in the January White Sale. It was a great treat. We went by train from Deal to Dover Priory station and walked down to Hattons in the main shopping street.

21

We were welcomed at the door by the floor walker, who escorted us to the Linen Department. A chair was placed for "Madam" and another for me. I was even helped up onto it (I was not yet five). The assistant was called, the most senior who was free, for all serving was done in strict order of seniority, and when we were quite comfortable the gentleman drifted away (or so it seemed) to welcome the next customer.

I felt very important as I sat very still while the sales business began. Great rolls of sheeting, fine linen for undies, Dorcas pillow slips and Osman towels. I loved the fresh clean smell and watched fascinated as rolls were thumped over and over on the counter and what seemed like miles of material was measured off. Watch and learn was the motto, and children seen not heard was the order of the day. I was treated like a lady, I felt like a lady, and when the buying was done I felt proud and tall as I took Aunt Kate's hand and we were escorted to the door and thanked for our custom.

Then, joy of joys, the crowning treat of the day. Tea and cream cakes in Ogdens Tea Shop. Aunt Kate even let me pour the tea if I was very careful. Then back to the train and home again.'

THE DOVER CO-OP 1920

'The River Co-operative Society was established about 1879 by a foreman papermaker. Some of the papermakers put a small amount a week away into a fund to bulk buy a chest of tea and a few other commodities. These were then sold at a cheaper rate than would be paid in a shop. The first shop was in Lower Road, River and is now a newsagent's and sweet shop. Later when a bigger shop was needed it moved further along the road to Dover; the present Co-op Stores is on the same site. A bakery was converted from the adjoining building. The Co-op for the whole area was known as River and District Co-operative Society until the Second World War, when it became Dover and District.

When my father was working in the grocery department, it was an oblong shop with counters down two long sides where groceries were served and across the short end, opposite the window and entrance door, was the provisions counter. This is where all butter, lard etc was in a large block and was patted into the desired weight. Cheese and bacon were also served on this counter. Just inside the main door was a partitioned-off office with a sort of pigeonhole where the cashier sat. Connecting this to each position on the serving counters was a wire contraption with a little round container. As each purchase was paid for at the counter the money and check were put into this container, a lever pulled and it travelled along the wire to

22

The staff of the River (Dover) Co-op on their annual outing in the early 1920s – by Co-operabanc!

the cashier. Any change was returned to the customer the same way. Regular customers had a notebook where they recorded all purchases for the week, then paid at the cashier's desk on Saturday.

At the back was the store room. Each Monday, as this was a fairly slack day, the staff would weigh up and package sugar, flour, spices, dried fruits and so on, sufficient for the coming week – they hoped!

All the bread for the Dover area was baked at River and the baker's carts and horses were stabled across the yard from the main building. The practice was for the stableman to clean the stables each morning and stack the manure in a corner of the yard. Each man on the staff was allowed to have this for his garden or allotment for a week at a time, provided he moved it himself. As my father had suffered a dislocated hip, and limped, and our allotment was up a hill, I had the joyful task of "helping" not only to load the wheelbarrow but also to pull it by means of a rope tied to the front while Dad pushed. Most of the boys in the village had home-made barrows (soap boxes on wheels) to go round collecting dung from the village streets. Being rather a tom-boy, I also had a "dung barrow".'

THE ROUNDSMEN AND DELIVERY BOYS

'The future looked bleak for my father, approaching the end of his school days in 1920, and as one of a large family with parents struggling to make ends meet working in the fields, he was more than anxious to make his contribution. Then, unexpectedly and to his great delight, just before his 14th birthday he was offered the job of a milk roundsboy, to be given the opportunity to open up a new round in a country area. He left school at once, with two months of the term still to run, and was taken on trial at a few shillings a week.

In a very short time he was given his own three-wheeled handcart with pails and measures and, in his own words, was as happy as a sandboy! He was out every day at three o'clock to meet the four o'clock milk train at Gillingham station. Then after delivering two churns of milk to the dairy he would load up his own cart and set off on his round. He walked the round twice every morning. First it was the orders, leaving cans at the doorstep and collecting empties, then back to the dairy to fill up again, ready to start the second round. This was the bit he liked best, yodelling "Milk-o", filling jugs as they were brought out and having a bit of a chat. At midday he returned to the dairy to cash in, clean up the cart and wash all the utensils in scalding soda water. Everything had to be thoroughly cleaned, rinsed and dried before he was free to go. A hard job indeed for a 14 year old.'

'My first job on leaving school at 14 in 1928 was selling papers at the Open Golf Championship at Royal St George's Golf Course at Sandwich. I wore a peaked cap with *Daily Express* on it – this was the only daily paper at the championships. The pay was fabulous at ten shillings a day, and there was no golf on Sundays.

My next job was as a roundsman for Roses Supply Store Ltd, Sandwich. They delivered groceries etc from Dover to Whitstable, including the whole of Thanet. I went out, for example, on Mondays to Richborough, Westmarsh, Preston, Wingham and Ash. I would deliver the order and pick up next week's order together with last week's payment. During the summer months when the housewife was out to work in the fields I knew where the key was kept and I would go in and get the money and order.

Roses supplied all grocery items, pharmaceutical goods, decorating supplies and even beehives complete with everything for the beekeeper. Some country folk had primus stoves so a special rack on the van held these items. Only Roses had special racks for carrying paraffin – Pratt's two gallon cans were used.

The competition for this trade in Sandwich was intense with three other private grocers' stores as well as World Stores and the International East Kent Ltd. At Michaelmas farmhands would change farms and if you could find out about the changes you tried to get in touch with clients who were moving to your area and guarantee a delivery on the day they moved in.

Roses covered such a vast area they often acted as messengers between families who lived in different districts.

Roses supplied groceries to the lookers on the Marshes. These were employed by the Earl of Guildford, who owned the marshland. Local farmers paid him for the services of the lookers, who looked after their livestock grazing there. They were paid twice a year so we collected the money owing to us twice a year. They lived in small cottages on the marsh, quite remote from anyone.'

'My first day at work as a greengrocer's errand boy in 1937 seemed quite simple. Put the tradesman's carrier cycle outside the shop in Bellevue Road, Ramsgate, sweep the floor, and polish the brass scale pans and weights (two sets). Meanwhile Mr Birch, the greengrocer, would set off on the first of two rounds with his order book. Being new, I was neither prepared nor allowed to perform such advanced work as serving customers, but with the first sound of the shop door bell the ample and homely Mrs Birch would descend the three steps from the living room and deal with the customer. By this time she had got her two young sons off to school.

Edwards and Bugden, 'Hythe's leading grocers' in 1930. Delivery boys such as the lad on the right were a familiar sight before the Second World War.

25

When Mr Birch returned with the orders, he showed me how to make them up – weighing so many pounds of potatoes and making newspaper parcels of them; apples to polish and bag up; bananas, peas, oranges, greens of all sorts, the odd tin of beans, peas or fruit, and many other items were all carefully chosen, inspected and wrapped. The cycle, old but serviceable, was the type with a deep carrier over a small front wheel. Into this fitted a very large basket. When this was piled up with orders, and Mr Birch had staggered out of the shop and placed it in the carrier, we fell to packing another smaller, but still large basket, with the remaining orders, and when this was full it was placed on top of the first, so that the bicycle was very top heavy and extremely cumbersome.

Being a seaside town, Ramsgate had its fair share of steep hills, some of which were much too steep for a heavily-laden cycle, so I adopted the standard errand boys' method – arms across the handlebars and leaning far forwards to keep the load moving. This was slow progress of course, but it was quite pleasant to do this in company with other lads on similar work, chewing a bar of chocolate and sympathising with each other on the hard parts of the job in bad weather, or trying to outdo each other on the quirkiness of our customers. Of course one tends to remember the happy times, but there must have been the bad times as well, chiefly the weather – rain and wind mostly, the enemy of the cyclist. For rain, a cape was the only thing, but then it would shed the water onto your legs, so leggings were also necessary. In cold weather, mittens were far more efficient than gloves, the fingers being the worst part in cold weather.

There was a sort of camaraderie among errand boys, probably because they were, after all, a lowly subservient few, subject to the whims of employer and customer, and mistrusted by the odd policeman on account of their circus tricks on their tradesman's cycles! One of the many institutions, like jobbing gardeners, horse-drawn milk floats, bakers pushing handcarts, and shrimp sellers on bicycles, overtaken by progress.'

PUBS: FISH, TOLLS AND TIMBER

'My grandfather, my father and three uncles were all fishermen. We lived on the edge of the river Medway and, according to the tides, we used to run down to the pier with a white enamel bucket to get anything that was going – lovely fat pink shrimps, young crabs, dabs, smelts, the lot! My dad cooked the mussels himself on our big kitchen stove and always put an onion in the saucepan to kill any poison. He cooked sprats for us in an oval iron frying pan; he used to say that when their eyes turned white, they were cooked.

When smelt were in season a gentleman used to meet my Dad's fishing boat and take some boxes of smelt back to London. We found out afterwards that he was from Buckingham Palace and that smelt were King George V's favourite fish. The man continued coming for many years.

My grandfather had a fish shop, and I loved to go round and curl newspapers into cones for selling shrimps at twopence a pint. Over the gas bracket hung dried eels, made into rings by putting their tails down their throats. Mothers used to come for miles to ask for one, as grated ". . . they were sure to cure whooping cough."

My mother and father were also licensees of the Railway Tavern and Imperial Hotel, from 1911 to 1935. The name Imperial Hotel was added to it in 1844 because the Emperor Napoleon and Empress Eugenie and the Prince Imperial sat in the gardens and had refreshments whilst waiting for a train to take them home to Chislehurst where they were living.

When King George V and Queen Mary celebrated their Jubilee in 1935, HMS *Scimitar* was moored in front of our pub. At nightfall, they switched on all the lights making the ship a fairyland silhouette. Its searchlights picked out landmarks on the shore as well.

Sometimes 4,000 ton boats used to moor near us, with woodpulp, monkey nuts or staves. When the cargo was nuts, we would wait for the stevedores to come ashore as they always had some in their pockets, which they would give to us.

We had a big Club Room in our pub, with two fireplaces and in the winter my mother would have them both lit and big fires going by midday for the stevedores. She would put salt in dishes, cut up big onions and huge chunks of bread and put them on the tables. These were all free, but they had to pay for the cheese. That, with a pint of mild for fourpence, was their dinner. With a packet of Woodbines for twopence and their cheese, the lot cost one shilling.

Two regular customers of ours were John Henry, the comedian, on his way to Margate to do a show, and A. P. Herbert, the author. He would spent hours talking to the skippers of barges, getting their knowledge for his next book.'

'Our village of Stone is situated in the Isle of Oxney. Until the 15th or 16th century it really was an island and even today it is surrounded by rivers. Until about 1936 there was a tollgate by the Oxney Ferry Inn.

Everyone entering the village had to pay a toll of a halfpenny for foot passengers, other prices varying from animals to cars and charabancs. Sheep and cattle were charged for separately. Everyone paid to go out of the village but had a free passage back. We had to ring a bell by the gate and someone from the pub came out to unlock the gate and let you through, not a very nice job on a wet and windy day.

The brewery of Leney & Sons owned the tollgate and they were very much against taking it away. The bus company ran a bus to Ashford four times a day and they wanted the gate removed, and they eventually came to an agreement and the gate was taken down. A list of the toll charges can still be seen outside the inn.'

'In the early 1900s publicans often acquired land from their clients. The farmers were often big drinkers and gamblers. When they got into debt they paid off with land. There were at least three strips of land in the Alkham Valley which are known to have changed hands like that, one being known as Drunken Meadow.

The woods were properly tended and used, there being annual wood auctions at the village pub, The Marquis of Granby. The hard woods such as oak were left standing but soft woods were cut and cleared about every ten to twelve years. The woods were divided into cants. The farmers bought cants at the pub auctions, and used saplings and brush for stakes and binder fencing, while wood cutters cut the faggots for fires.'

'I was born in 1920 and brought up in The Rose and Crown, Beach Street, Deal. The pub originally sold Flint's beer and my father was known as "Flint" Roberts.

We lived on the seafront at Deal, and these were the days of spittoons with sawdust in – which frequently smouldered when people put their cigarettes out in them and which we had to douse with water. Our customers were in the main fishermen and local people, with visitors in the summer. Later, when the Betteshanger mine opened in the 1930s, many of the miners would come in.

My father owned a motor boat which was kept on the beach opposite our house. The notorious Goodwin Sands lie off Deal and many ships went aground there, especially in rough weather. On these occasions a maroon would be fired to call out the lifeboat, and one or two motorboats would also put to sea in the hope that some salvage work would be available. As these boats had a shallow draught, it was sometimes possible to take an anchor over the sands, the idea being that the ship might be able to pull itself off the sands without the help of tugs, which cost a great deal of money. Many's the time a maroon would be heard and, on going into the bar, there would be a row of pint glasses, no customers, no landlord, no oilskins hanging on the stairs – they were all off to the ship wrecked on the Goodwins, maybe to stay for 24 hours or more. Sometimes their efforts were successful, but many ships broke their backs and the evidence is still there today.

On their return from such a trip, the beach needed to be prepared for the boat to be hauled up. There would always be many willing hands to dig out the beach, and there were woods to be placed in position for the boat to slide over. These were large planks, well greased (usually with old dripping) and a rope attached to pull with. A capstan was used to haul the boat up, with four or five men to go round and round until it was finally above high water line. Later a winch driven by an engine was used.

On the outbreak of war in 1939 a contraband area was established which made merchant ships anchor off Deal until clearance was given for them to proceed. Many of these had deck cargo of fruit and other perishables, which of course quickly rotted. My father would take the shipping agent out to the ships in his boat, to see if any provisions were needed. One day he came ashore with bunches of Canary bananas and was immediately told that as he did not have an import licence they must be thrown away. As the bananas were still somewhat green, he got the local Medical Officer of Health to declare them unfit for human consumption. They were the last bananas I ate for over five years.'

THE VOLUNTEER FIREMEN

'The working day was long for most men and shopkeepers like my father worked from 8 am to 8 pm with an hour for dinner and for tea. On Christmas Eve, many stores were still open well past 9 pm. Somehow my father found time to be a voluntary firefighter. Brass buttons and helmet were the order of the day, and I earned many a sixpence by making them shine with the aid of Brasso. Fire-alarm bells were fitted over the stairs to alert Dad when there was a fire, and a maroon was fired at the station. No matter what time of the day or night he never failed to respond and was off on his bike before you could say knife.

Usually it was a haystack or chimney fire. Besides fighting fires, firemen were expected to have a good knowledge of first aid and to assist the ambulance service if needed. With the outbreak of war in 1939, these voluntary firemen were incorporated into the National Fire Service and had to fight a different kind of fire.'

'Belgian born, I had realised that in marrying an Englishman and going to live in what was to me at that time a foreign country, there were bound to be some difficulties. Different manners, customs, the language, etc. No! The great problem I encountered initially was the currency. Coming from the Continent and decimal coinage, sterling was a complete mystery: "tanners", "bobs" and "quids". To say that it was double Dutch would be quite wrong. Double, or even treble Dutch I could have coped with – that language being a variant of Flemish, one of my mother tongues, but this was "Multi-Gibberish"!

I can remember being told by a stallkeeper in the market that something cost, as he said, "Nine-'een an' eleven free". What did this mean? Nine-'een was probably nineteen, and eleven free. Did this mean that the cost was nineteen but that eleven were free, so that one paid eight? Or did it mean nineteen plus eleven = thirty and three (could it be *three*?) made thirty-three. In any case – eight or thirty-three what? Bobs, tanners, quids? I felt just like the King of Siam when he said to Anna, "It's a puzzlement". So many things had a three-farthing ending – groceries, clothes, etc. One finished up with a purse full of farthings.'

LIFE ON THE COUNTRY ESTATE

Far removed from the life of the towns was that of the workers on the country estates, such as this account written by a gamekeeper's daughter who lived high on Barham Downs.

'My early childhood was spent with my parents in a cottage on the ridge of Barham Downs, high above the A2, carrying now a constant flow of traffic from Dover to Canterbury and on to London. But before the First World War it was a peaceful area. My father was a gamekeeper, the eldest of six brothers, all of whom were keepers, like their father who worked for Earl Kitchener at Broome Park. We lived on the estate belonging to the Marquis of Conyngham, whom we never saw, as the land was rented to farmers and the shooting rights to private consortiums.

My father's work consisted mainly of producing pheasants and partridges for shooting parties in October through to February. This meant that vermin like stoats and weasels had to be kept under control, as well as rabbits who destroyed the outside of the cornfields and took bark from trees. Father used to be up at the crack of dawn in the summer, walking miles round the woods and meadows, inspecting nests etc. We usually had four dogs – a Labrador, two terriers and a spaniel, and these had to be fed, exercised and, above all, trained. There were outbuildings at the cottage, especially for the animals, for storage of food and a large stove for cooking.

During the winter keepers often had rabbit shoots, where several would join with some of the farmers to reduce the rabbit population; some were sold, others shared out and some given to farm workers, for a rabbit made a very tasty meal. As I grew older my father and I used sometimes to go rabbiting – nets would be placed over the holes, ferrets would be put down into the ground and eventually the rabbits would appear, to be caught and quickly killed. Any who tried to escape would be caught by the terrier.

Spring was a busy time because this was the rearing of the birds, when eggs were purchased from the game farms and put under the broody hens to hatch. If a nest in the wood or in the hedges was spoilt and abandoned by the hen bird, my father would collect the eggs and put them to hatch as well. The little chicks were lovely and would become very tame. Eventually they would be moved into the woods, or partridges would probably be placed on the edge of a meadow, so that they could shelter if a hawk should be hovering overhead. Sadly, some of these had to be shot as did jays, crows and magpies. Gamekeepers used to have a graveyard, a pole fixed between two trees, on which the dead vermin was hung, rather a gruesome sight.

The great days were those of the shoot, when the gentleman who rented the area would come with his guests and other keepers and other dogs. The beaters would come first, and would be taken to the edge of the first drive – spread out, carrying sticks to beat and make a noise to scare the birds. My father would give them the signal when to start walking slowly forward. Meanwhile the guns would have taken up their positions behind the butts – a shelter to hide them from the birds. These had been made beforehand by the keeper. Once the birds were up in the air they could fly at a remarkable speed, especially if it was windy, but a good shot could still bring down a number of birds. At the end of the drive the dogs, usually retrievers, were sent in to find the dead birds.

There would be a break for lunch and the host and his guests would come into our kitchen where his kitchen staff had worked in the morning to prepare things like jacket potatoes. My sister and I used to watch all the excitement from indoors and one great day the host, who was a Major in the army and was stationed at the barracks in Canterbury, had brought as a guest Prince Harry, Duke of Gloucester, uncle of the Queen, for the day. We were very excited, but only saw him in the distance. We often wished we had marked the chair in which he sat!

Our cottage was small, with no running water or lighting. My father had to fetch fresh water from the local manor house, about a quarter of a mile away. He would put wooden yokes over his shoulders, with chains attached and two buckets, and go to the Manor, to collect what was really a very small amount of water for four people and it was a chore to be carried out quite often. We had oil lamps and candles for lighting and wood and coal fires. We were able to collect a great deal of wood from close by, a job we really quite enjoyed – we needed plenty because clothes were boiled in the copper and father needed to make fires for cooking dog meals. We also helped with black-leading stoves, whitening steps, feeding chickens and helping in the garden. If anything was needed we had to walk to fetch it. No milk was delivered and we walked to local farms to collect it and also lovely farmhouse butter. We kept our own chickens, all to be fed, my mother had several hives of bees, and we grew all our own vegetables and quite a lot of fruit. We walked miles in the woods and fields and knew where to find the best blackberries, walnuts, chestnuts, mushrooms and wild strawberries.'

CHURCH AND CHAPEL

Sunday was a day of rest when work and play alike were frowned on in many families, and church, or chapel, and Sunday school filled the hours. There was always Sunday dinner and tea to look forward to – and the annual Sunday school treat, a high spot in children's lives when holidays were few and far between. But religion could also sometimes prove to be an indication of social divisions.

SUNDAY WAS A SPECIAL DAY

'Mr Jacobs and his sons kept a fish and chip shop down the High Street in Minster in the 1930s, next door to Miss Bacca's restaurant.

On Sunday mornings Mr Jacobs Junior could be seen in a clean white coat and apron, pushing a tradesman's barrow, also covered with a spotlessly white cloth. Under the cloth were freshly cooked pink and brown shrimps and winkles. Sometimes he had cockles and mussels too, all about one shilling and sixpence a pint. He could be heard calling his wares about the time people were coming from morning church. Out of the houses came his customers with their bowls and dishes, to purchase their favourite Sunday tea.

After cooking a hot roast dinner over a solid fuel stove all morning, it made an easily prepared tea with bread and butter, home-made buns, and sometimes a trifle. What a feast!'

'When I was a child in Saltwood in the 1920s Saturday night was bathnight and that day it was also my job, as eldest child, to see that clothes had all their buttons on, elastic was in the knickers and there were no holes in the gloves, all ready for Sunday, for on Sundays very little was allowed to be done. It was a real day of rest and quiet. We wore our best clothes only on that day or on special occasions. We had high button-up boots, using a button hook to do up all the buttons. We also had gaiters.

My mother cleaned Saltwood church and part of her duty was to see to the church paraffin lamps. Every Saturday we took our lanterns, comprising a candle in a glass frame, and went in the dark to the church. It was rather scary as owls hooted and there were no lights. In the church there were about six suspended rings with four oil lamps on each. These were let down, the glass cleaned, wicks trimmed and bowls filled with paraffin. On Sunday evening we went before the service and topped them up again. We stayed to the service but always at the back of the church, never mixing with those better off than us. I can still smell the odour of the paraffin which always hung over the church.

Another duty was to launder all the surplices belonging to the choir – about twelve boys and twelve men. The garments were laundered about four times a year for festivals etc. They were boiled, starched and ironed. When the ironing was carried out we children were not allowed near. Mother placed a sheet on the floor with the ironing board in the middle. The flat iron was heated on the gas ring and rubbed over with a candle covered with a cloth to clean off the soot. The surplices, all beautifully starched and ironed were then taken back to the church in large wash baskets.

Once a year the church was spring cleaned. What a mammoth task that was! My father brushed the walls down, and all the felts and hassocks from the pews were taken outside the vestry and beaten together with the matting from the floor. Pews were then scrubbed and polished. Mother used a long mop head which had extending handles. I used to play hide and seek under the altar. Outside the church was a yew tree and we played with the berries, using them in games with our dolls, though we knew they were poisonous and on no account to be eaten.'

GENTLEMEN AND OTHERS

'Hythe after the First World War was on three levels. Officers connected with the small arms school lived on the hill, tradespeople lived over their shops in the High Street and the workers lived in rows of cottages going down to the sea, and there was no communication socially between the three groups. Officers went to church; their domestic staff sat at the back behind the gangway. In the early 1900s St Michael's (commonly called the "tin church") was built, so the lower classes could go to church without feeling uncomfortable in the "presence of their betters". The middle class were Methodist or Congregationalists and the working class Salvation Army!

My father, a builder who had built a lot of the hill houses, was still "trade". Next door to us in Station Road was a "gentleman" with daughters of our age. They would reach over our fence and take our fruit – but said "We can't talk to you, your father's in trade". There were several private schools in Folkestone for "the daughters of gentlemen". We went to a Methodist school.

My father employed a lot of workers. Mother would help the families in times of trouble but it was not done for us to associate with the children. They went to the Methodist Sunday school but it would not have been the thing for us to attend.

Motors were few. At chapel the late Lord Wakefield and my father were the only two owners. Chapel members thought it "sinful" to use a car on Sundays.'

SUNDAY SCHOOL

'Church was an every Sunday occasion, with Sunday school first at 10 am followed by church at 11 am, then again Sunday school in the afternoon. Best dresses were the order of the day with hats and white crochet gloves for the young girls.

The highlight of the year was the annual outing to Whitstable, having tea at the Continental Hotel. The excitement at the first shout of "I can see the sea"; the fun on the swingboats on the front; a little money to spend in the amusements – and then tea! Paste sandwiches, and fancy cakes in little paper cases, the latter making excellent paper missiles for the choir boys to flick at the rather prim Sunday school young ladies, who in turn were very often first class shots. They were days when growing up took its time, and we were still children at 13.'

'We attended Sunday school regularly every week. This would be some 70 years ago and how eagerly we looked forward to the annual summer treat. Although the village was only five miles from the sea, the getting there was a lengthy business, with a two mile walk across fields to the halt on the "Crab and Winkle" line to wait excitedly for the little train with the famous Rocket engine to come puffing along from Canterbury, its starting point. As it pulled into the Tyler Hill Halt, all clambered into the carriages, and we were on our way to the seaside. A little walk from the station at Whitstable and we were on the beach and into our paddling shoes.

Then there was the amusement arcade to visit, and of course we had to have a go on the swingboats, and lastly a tea of bread and butter and shrimps, and a bun. What a good thing we had been up and down on the swingboats first. All too quickly it was time to go home, but still there was the excitement of travelling back in the little train as it chugged its way through the wooded area to the Tyler Hill Halt. Our walk back across the fields was a little slower than that of the outward journey, but we arrived home tired but very happy after our annual Sunday school treat.'

'On Sundays we went twice to Sunday school. The morning session was "open school" in the church hall. We learned hymns and listened to readings and fidgeted during the calling of the interminably long register. I wonder where Lionel Moon and Lavinia Jones are now. After the register we formed twos and walked to church. During the service we counted all the ladies wearing veils over their faces and all the men with beards, and we swapped texts and cigarette cards. Release came during the hymn before the sermon, when pew by pew we filed out.

The afternoon session was held in the school – in classes, and we copied out summaries of the lessons from the blackboard. We could earn five marks each week, one each for punctuality, good conduct, taking Bible and Prayer Book and for reciting the week's collect from memory. At intervals we were invited to attend at the vicarage to select a prize. I loved spiders; watching their activities

I could stand still for long periods. Until forbidden at school, I collected and carried them around in my pockets. One prize day, there on the vicar's table was a book entitled *Spiders and Scorpions*. I grabbed it quickly and took it to the vicar. "Oh dear," he said, "this one needs 1,000 marks and you have earned only 750. You must look for something else." For me there was nothing else, and when I had stood disconsolate for some time, hugging the precious book he realised it, and suggested that I ran home, showed it to my mother and asked her for threepence. Away I sped. I have the book still. It has 84 pages, pencilled "1/6d" written inside the front cover and the inscription "Awarded for 750 marks gained + 3d payment".'

'The Wesleyan Sunday school treat was a much looked forward to event at Lydd. The children lined up behind the banner outside the chapel in New Street, then marched to Mr Charles Bass's field at Tourney Hall. It was the custom to stop and sing a hymn at various houses. "How many more stops?" the children would say. "When are we going to have tea?"

After the tea and races, the great event was scrambles. Mr George Bayley would throw monkey nuts and sweets into the air. This was the time for children to show all the love and kindness they had learned about throughout the year, as they pushed, shoved, kicked, bent fingers back, and stamped, but there was no reward quite so satisfying as a retrieved pink fondant which had been trodden into the ground of Charlie Bass's sheep field!'

GETTING ABOUT

From horse-drawn transport to the first buses and cars and then even to aeroplanes, our means of getting about have changed dramatically this century. Not only have new skills had to be learned, but we have had to come to terms with the speed at which some of these new inventions could travel!

HORSE-DRAWN

'In the 1920s there was no public transport for the country folk so they made their way to the towns by foot or cycle. Some living far out across several fields were allowed the use of a horse and cart, but this was often a young and frisky horse that only the husband could drive, so shopping days were limited. Children had no transport to school, so if more than one had to be put on Mum's cycle they did not attend until one could manage a cycle of their own, and ride the many miles to the nearest school, Brenzett. This is what happened to me. I started school at nearly eight years old, having a brother a year older, my mother could not manage the two of us on the main road (A259) on her own cycle.

There were other children in the village taken to school by a local farmer, who carried his own three girls and a few more in his pony and trap; these were older children and went to another school in New Romney. In 1925 there was a fatal accident on the way home from Brenzett school, after several children climbed onto the back of a timber-tug carrying wood from Hamstreet to New Romney. A little girl fell off and a wheel ran over her; the man did not see her as he was walking in front with the horses that were pulling the "tug".

There were very few motor cars on the A259 those days. I well remember the Foden lorry driven by steam, with its fire underneath at the front; the Trojan red van, "Brooke Bond Tea", chuffing along at a slow pace; and the district nurse driving her three-wheeler, all open at the front showing the workings of the engine and fascinating to us children.

There were only a few farm carts drawn by horses on the main roads. They used the lanes, which were only beach tracks with grass growing at the sides and middles chewed up by the horses' feet. One had to be careful when cycling along the lanes, as they were very narrow and rough.'

'My grandparents lived at Great Everden Farm, about a mile uphill from the centre of Alkham. Granny used to walk down across the fields to get the landau to go shopping in Dover. It was run by "Two Fisted" Miller and it carried four passengers. I think it cost fourpence in about 1900. "Two Fisted" Miller also brought the landau out from Dover on Sundays to run pleasure trips.'

'My mother used to take me up to the West End of London quite a bit when I was a small child (about 1907), and I was frightened out of my life when she took me across some of the wide roads. It was all horses with carts etc and so many of them going up or down the road. I was quite small and some of these horses looked huge to me. Mum used to dodge in and out of them like magic, dragging me with her, but she would say, "Come on, Rene, this way, they will think we are 'Country Cousins', the horses won't hurt you." But I was not so sure; it seemed as though I was enveloped in hot steaming breath and great big hooves. The people who lived in London got used to dodging in and out of the horses and anyone standing hesitating on the kerb was called a "Country Cousin". Of course, Mum's dresses were very full in those days, and I was glad I did not have to hold up a huge lot of my dress to save it sweeping the pavement or road. It was not so bad for the dresses when it was dry weather, but when it rained the pavements were very muddy.'

ROAD REPAIRS

'My father was an agricultural engineer and owned a stone quarry near his premises at Hillyfields, Gravel Castle Hill, Barham. This entailed the grubbing of stones by local labour, to be transported by skip trucks on a rail to a hopper which dumped them into a lorry waiting below. They were then delivered to various points at the roadside locally.

"King" Miles was a local man whom I remember wearing dark glasses and using a rake and hammer to break the flints, measuring them by the yard. The roads were repaired with these, watered in and rammed down by steam rollers. These were very handsome and bore the crest of East Kent (ie a brass horse on the boiler to match the brass around the funnel). The driver needed to get up steam very early in the day. The water cart would come behind to bind the flints in. These flint roads were very bad for children's knees and many of us experienced gravel rash. Nurse would come dressed very grand in her neat uniform complete with starched apron. Her bicycle had a skirt guard. After bathing the knee she would use iodine and her fee was sixpence.'

FROM BLACKSMITH TO ENGINEER

'When Dad was twelve years old, in 1914, he left school and worked for his father on his smallholding, working with horses. When he was 17 he decided to broaden his horizons and skills by leaving the family business and going to work at the local Wingham Engineering Company. There he learned to be an agricultural blacksmith, making all sorts of tools including very heavy implements like ploughshares.

As he progressed with his firm he also learned to be a fitter for the very large steam driven lorries called Sentinels. Sentinel was the actual trade name of the vehicle manufacturer, but the lorries were only known by this name. These enormous lorries eventually took over from the horses and drays used by breweries. They were also

38

used on the roads carrying the grit and tar barrels at the time when the roads were resurfaced by men with tar-buckets and shovels. He also had to help repair and clean the steam rollers and engines, which were used in road repair, getting right inside the working parts to find the cause of any trouble.

By the time the Second World War broke out Dad was also doing electrical welding. He was employed at a very large Army depot stationed at Wingham, repairing tanks and lorries for the troops. He was also an instructor at RAF Manston, teaching all types of welding and metal repairs to the aircraft fitters. He stayed at the engineering works until he retired, when he became the village bicycle and motor cycle repairer. He had his first motorbike at 14, in the days when they were belt-driven. During the time we were growing up he had a motorbike and sidecar, but when Mum got to 50 he bought a Morris 10, our very first car. That was quite something in those days, and so was the next one, a brand new Triumph Herald. That was the time when most people's mode of transport was either the bicycle or the local bus.'

THE FIRST BUSES

'When the buses came in at first, everyone jumped on as quickly as possible, for if it started off before you got to the top, you had quite a job to balance yourself and had to hold on to the rails. On every seat there was a mackintosh cover, which you had to pull right over yourself if it was raining, and I remember how frightened people were at the speed the buses went.

We moved to Bexley Heath when I was about six years old in 1910, and here trams were very new. There was a steep hill on the way to Woolwich, and we used to come down this at quite a pace (or so it seemed), but before we got to the bottom we had to stop, as clouds of smoke used to come up from the driver's seat. He would stop and put this out and then we would proceed on our way.'

'When a bus service started from Saltwood to Hythe it made it easier for villagers to do their shopping in the town or visit the cinema. In the 1930s an enterprising firm started a bus service to Sandling Junction, as it was then called, from Hythe and Saltwood. This was a unique service as the bus called at your door by prior arrangement for most trains. This was most useful, as good as a taxi but much cheaper.'

'Buses in Folkestone were frequent and very efficient in my youth, but when my father first went there from Lydd he had to walk

The early buses, such as this Partridge bus of 1928, were a boon to country dwellers.

home to visit his mother as there was no transport at all. This would have been around 1900 when the top end of the Leas was still open country with corn growing in the fields. Later there was Carey's horse bus and my mother and sister used to visit relatives at Dymchurch. I think the horse bus went from Hythe, with still a fair amount of walking involved.

I can recall the Cambrian and Silver Queen buses in Folkestone before East Kent had the monopoly, also a small private concern run by Sergeant Bros. In snowy weather we often had to disembark at Killicks Corner and walk up Dover Hill to The Valiant Sailor if the road was bad. A very early memory is of going to Lade, at Dungeness from Lydd over the shingle before there was a hard road, in the brewer's dray. This had large wooden wheels to get over the pebbles and made for a very uncomfortable ride! We were visiting my uncle who had a herring hang and this was about the time the Romney, Hythe and Dymchurch railway came into being. The carriages were little more than trucks, with no glass in the windows but my cousins and I thought it was lovely. The track went over the beach between the fishermen's houses and the sea and they should have been compensated but never were.'

THE FIRST CARS

'Today it is unimaginable that one could be charged for speeding at twelve miles per hour!

A close friend remembers his father being so charged for speeding on the downward run from Canterbury into Littlebourne. At the bottom of the hill a policeman jumped out from a hedge and put up his hand and waved the motorist down, exclaiming that twelve mph was outside the speed limit. Without today's technology two gentlemen of the law were involved – the first giving a signal from the top of the hill when a car passed a given point, whilst the second was positioned at a set distance at the bottom of the hill with a good watch. This happened in 1907.'

'The following is taken from my father's pocket book dated 1920, when he was a young police constable:

"I stood at the junction of Cherry Garden Avenue and Shorncliff Road and heard a car coming in the distance towards Folkestone. By the high humming noise the engine made I could tell the car was travelling at very high speed. In a few seconds I saw a large motor van tearing along at very high speed and giving no warning of his approach. I stepped into the road and shouted and whistled for him to stop. The car slowed down for a short distance then gathered fresh speed and continued for Folkestone.

"At 1 am I saw the car at the GPO Folkestone and told the driver I should report him for a summons for driving a car at a speed dangerous to the public, which I estimated to be 25 miles an hour, at 8.55 pm. He replied, 'I heard someone whistle and thought they wanted a lift!'

"Defendant was fined £2, 24th February 1920." '

'In 1953 my Mum and Dad bought a car. It was a little Hillman and I can even remember the number – AXA 27. My Dad's mum lived in Twickenham and occasionally we would go and visit her. One Easter we all dressed in our best clothes and set off for London. We followed the A28 and then the A2 right through the middle of Canterbury. The journey was really long and Mum would pack up a breakfast of bacon sandwiches. We would stop in a wood at Laughing Water for a picnic. The A2 was narrow and the countryside went all the way to London. We only used the car for special occasions as Dad used his bicycle for work.'

MOTORBIKE AND SIDECAR

'In about 1919, when I was seven, my father bought a motorbike and sidecar. There were few cars about at that time and I think we felt quite grand! My mother, father, two brothers and I all went for rides together. My mother sat in the sidecar with my elder brother on her lap and my baby brother at the bottom of the sidecar on a cushion. My father wore a heavy mackintosh, and I had to sit on the back of the motorbike and hold tight to his wide leather belt. I suppose we didn't go very fast but I used to get scared and had tummy ache and then Mother would change places and I had to sit in the sidecar, holding my brother.

When I was about ten, my father bought a car. He had one lesson with a mechanic and then off we went. The motorbike was sold but found many years later, dumped. My brother went to a lot of trouble to get it repaired in time for my parents' golden wedding, when my father drove it once more with me on the back.'

BUILDING THE LITTLE RAILWAY

'In the 1920s the Hythe, New Romney, Little Railway was built, opened in 1928 by the then Duke of York, later to be George VI.

I remember my father cycling across the Marsh, as there were no other means in those days of getting to the project. When working on the beach, which it crossed to Dungeness, flat boards were strapped to the men's boots, called back stays, making it easier to walk.

My father stayed on after the opening to be a guard, but found it difficult as he was a very big, tall man.

Captain Howey was the man who had it built. He owned a sports car and would take my father on rides in it, which he enjoyed very much!'

ALTERNATIVE MEANS

'In the winter of 1938–39 Appledore, on the edge of Romney Marsh, had a heavy fall of snow, more than had been seen for many years. Roads in and out of the village were blocked for several days. I was the village baker and it was difficult to do deliveries; one van had to be left in the wagon shed on the Woodchurch Road, the other at the pumping station, after being dug out to do deliveries and finding it impossible to return.

The wheelwright built a large sledge and we placed a 50 bushel basket on it, filled with 50 to 60 loaves, and pulled it to the hamlet of Fairfield. They were very pleased to see it. On the way back a farmer filled the baskets with mutton, as many sheep had been smothered in the snow, so we came home with mutton for villagers who wished to have it.

The snow on the fields was so frozen you could hear the hares running on it.'

FLYING TIME

'The part played by Lympne aerodrome during the Battle of Britain is well known – and it was of course a grass field that never had a formal runway. Soon after the war, around 1947, the firm of Hunting Air Travel opened one of their many flying clubs here, and at about the same time a Wing Commander Kennard (an ex Battle of Britain pilot) also formed a small air charter company. Lack of sufficient business soon prompted Hunting to pull out and the flying club was then taken on by the Attrees, local people whom I seem to remember lived in Berwick Lodge and who were already running a local (social) club.

A noteworthy event at this time was an "aerial outing" when many members of UK flying clubs passed through the airport on their way to a gathering in France. It was essential to land at Lympne in order to clear Customs and for a while the skies were full of light aircraft.

Also in 1948 the late lamented *Picture Post* sent down a photographer to get some aerial shots of David Tomlinson, a well known film star at the time, who brought Valerie Hobson along for the ride.

Jeanne de Casalis, who lived nearby, learned to fly here; and two elderly twin doctors used for months to come over from Brighton at weekends just to be taken up for a session of aerobatics!

However, the continuing lack of business forced the flying club to be disbanded in 1948. Meanwhile the car ferry (carrying *one car* plus a few additional passengers) came into vogue and for a short period operated here whilst Lydd Airport was under construction.

This was at the time a very popular service, a 20 minute flight to Le Touquet. Another commercial venture involved a service to Beauvais; the package offered a coach trip from Victoria to Lympne, a flight to Beauvais and transfer to catch a train into Paris. The overall journey time was only about three hours and was excellent value for money.

Sadly all these efforts came to an end in the early 1950s.'

HOUSE & HOME

THE WAY WE LIVED THEN

Overcrowding in cold rooms with carpetless floors, no running water and the toilets at the bottom of the garden – yet still we look back on our homes of the past with affection. Setting up home has never been easy, but perhaps those years just after the war presented more problems than usual for the young married couples of the day.

THE HOUSES WE LIVED IN

'We lived in an old Elizabethan house in Wye which was a jumble of rooms, passages and inside steps. A pump in the scullery gave a water supply and any lighting was either by candle or oil lamp. The only lavatory was about 30 yards up the garden and, with no flushing, we had a bucket of soil in order to add some after every major use. This was emptied every week in a pit up the garden and soil added, and this, with the cleanings from the pigsty and chicken house, provided the manure for next year's garden crops.

The sitting room (or parlour) was the only room with a carpet, other floors having linoleum. This room was only used on Sundays or when visitors came. The scullery had a large built-in copper with a fireplace underneath, where clothes were boiled every washing day. There were four bedrooms, three along the front and the fourth at the back, a very large one covering most of the distance of the three front ones, all interconnecting with doors. During the First World War this large room contained five single beds and was used to billet five soldiers each time a contingent stayed in the village on their journey to France.'

'Ruby was born in Minster in 1918 and has lived here nearly all her life. Her mother moved to Minster when they opened the first laundry, called the Minster Sanitary Laundry; seven girls who worked at a laundry in Faversham were asked if they would like to work in Minster and they all moved to the village. Her mother did all the washing for a baroness – most of which was black silk underwear.

Her mother married and they lived in the cottages opposite the old school. You entered the house and on the right was the living

Workmen building new cottages before the First World War, each man posing for the photographer with the tools of his trade.

room, with the stairs in front of you. Through the living room was a lean to type of room which was used as the kitchen. There was no heating out there and no hot water. Upstairs there was one bedroom and another in the attic, which is the room all the girls slept in. Ruby was the eldest of eleven children.'

'Furnishing consisted of wooden chairs, made to make you sit upright, round the large kitchen table, with benches used for extra seating. We had large brass bedsteads or heavy wooden ones with spiral mesh stretched across, and horsehair mattresses, plus feather beds which were never turned on Fridays or Sundays. When visitors came (Christmas, for instance) families slept end to end in a double bed, maybe five in a bed. Bedding consisted of bolsters, pillows, sheets and wool blankets. The terraced cottages had washing facilities and toilets shared between two families, in the yard. The boxed toilet seats were scrubbed alternately by mothers and paper was torn into squares and threaded with string. It was our Saturday job after shopping to slit clean paper bags etc.'

'There were certainly no "mod cons" in my childhood in Folkestone in the 1930s. The only form of heating was by open fires lit each morning with a great deal of "drawing" by means of newspaper held taut across the opening. They often went out and had to be relit during the day – some people banked them up with coal dust. A spoonful of sugar was sometimes used to revive them! The toasting fork stood handy nearby and toast and dripping sprinkled with salt was a favourite snack, also toasted bloaters. In the evening during the winter chestnuts were roasted on the bars of the fire or on the coal shovel.

Our homes did not have wall to wall carpeting – mostly linoleum and mats. My mother made her own floor polish from shelack and methylated spirits and she used to sit my sister and me on chairs on top of the wooden kitchen table while she spread it on the floor. Only our mother and father had fireside chairs with a cushion to sit on in the evening, the children had wooden kitchen chairs. There were always draughts under the doors and round window panes which would be drawn in towards the chimney. The wireless was our father's province; it ran on an accumulator which had to be charged frequently at the garage. It often crackled and whined and was mostly used for the news, especially in wartime.'

'From a child's point of view the Forge House at Hamstreet was a wonderful place to live, with unexpected cupboards, steps, odd corners and lovely places to hide. The roof came so far down at the back that by standing on a chair I could easily climb on it, and often sat up there. The working forge was an added attraction. The most unpleasant thing was the smell of burning hoof and hair, when the blacksmith placed the hot shoe on the horse's foot.

Looking back from the view of a housewife and mother, it must have been a nightmare for my poor mum, who was a London girl who had worked for a top fashion designer. There was an electric light in each of the two main bedrooms, that was all. In the kitchen we had to use oil lamps or candles. The overall feeling when you entered the house was of coolness and dark, even in midsummer. The ground floors were brick and very uneven and big old beams held up the ceilings.

There was no entry to the back of the house; everything had to come through the front door, even the coal. In the front door, through the living room, through the kitchen, out of the back door to the shed. After dark, black beetles came out and covered the ground floors. If you had to get up in the night and go downstairs, there were so many you could hear them squashing under your feet.'

STAYING ON THE FARM

'My home in the 1920s was a semi-detached cottage on the farm where my father worked near Maidstone. My grandparents lived in the beautiful Georgian farmhouse, Grandad being the foreman and shepherd. There was a lovely walled garden where Gran spent much of her time growing fruit, especially wall trained currants and pears, and quantities of vegetables.

The farmhouse had several attics where young workers slept, with access from a staircase in the large kitchen. Also from the kitchen was a stairway to a very large cellar which had stone shelves all round the walls on which milk and meats and other foods could be kept very cold, as it was many feet below ground. Opening from the cellar was a slatted doorway into a dim cave-like place where mushrooms used to be grown in earlier days.

Gran used an enormous copper in the corner of the kitchen to boil water for everyday use and for clothes washing. The water was pumped up by hand into a stone sink. The pump was iron, black with a long handle. The place was warmed by a large black stove in a wide chimney place. I don't remember seeing my Gran in any other style of clothing but long black or brown skirts with blue or grey blouses, always long sleeved and usually covered with a floral top half. The farmhouse must have been very cold in winter as the only heating came from the kitchen fire or occasionally from a fire in the living room.

Our cottage was of a later date, with no water laid on and one tap in the passage between the two houses. Much care was taken in winter to try to keep it from freezing. The covering was a large box filled with straw – and usually inhabited by one or more toads.'

SETTING UP HOME

'I was married at 19 in 1936; we put £15 deposit on a new house but when we went to the Estate Office (no Building Society then) they had put the price up £10. We were devastated as that was five weeks' wages. I cried so the agent, a Mr Kelsey, said I could pay him eleven shillings and fourpence a week mortgage and two shillings and sixpence of the rest of the deposit – they gazumped in those days as well and we had no one to help. Out of £2 housekeeping there was 13 shillings and tenpence for the house, one shilling and eightpence for coal, one shilling and sixpence for a dozen eggs, milk and the groceries. Les had ten shillings and he paid the rates, water rates and electricity bills, and any over he saved. We went back to bicycles and used to go camping most weekends.'

'In January 1945 it seemed that the war would soon be over. I was then living with my daughter Judy, aged one and a half years, in a small village in Suffolk. I had been evacuated twice and had moved about ten times. I felt that it was time to find a house ready for when my husband was demobbed.

I knew that there were many empty houses in Deal so I sent for a copy of the local paper. I made a list of houses for sale at £1,000. We had saved £200. I planned to use £100 for the necessary ten per cent deposit on the house and £100 for buying furniture.

In February I left Suffolk and arrived in Deal in a snow storm to view the houses. They were all empty. I was given keys and trudged around on my own inspecting them. It was very cold and depressing but I liked the last house I saw. It was a modern, semi-detached, flat-roofed house with a small garden in the front and a larger garden at the back. Downstairs were a small hall, a medium sized kitchen with a "walk in" larder and a large dining-sitting room. This had windows at each end overlooking the gardens. Upstairs were two double bedrooms with fitted cupboards, a single bedroom and a bathroom. A special feature was a long window which lit the stairs. All the wood was Canadian pine, which gave a warm contrast to the neutral distemper. I loved the modern character of the house and felt that it would be just right for us.

I had to stop daydreaming and become businesslike as I went back to the agents. The house was on sale at £1,050; I made an offer of £1,025. I was delighted when it was accepted.

I next applied for coupons for utility furniture. These enabled me to order a sideboard, dining table and four chairs, a double bed, chest of drawers and a tallboy. I was told the furniture would be available when I moved into the house. I then had to find a solicitor in Bury St Edmunds to arrange the purchase of the house.

Each week I went to Bury St Edmunds' market to buy some of the few household goods that were available and which I so badly needed. I bought six small forks one week and six large knives the next. There was no choice, one had to be thankful to get anything. I was pleased to buy a pair of rush seated chairs, a Victorian nursing chair, a mahogany chest of drawers and a hall table. When the people in the village heard that I was leaving they gave me some of their spare pieces of china, for which I was truly grateful.

By Easter the purchase of the house was completed and I was ready to move. A man with a small lorry agreed to take us and our bits and pieces to Deal. Judy and I travelled in the back. She sat in her pram, I sat beside her on a pile of bedding surrounded by our belongings.

Once we arrived at Deal and I saw the house again I knew I had chosen the right place. We all had a hot drink from a Thermos flask to celebrate our arrival. My daughter toddled into the garden to explore and I helped the driver to get the furniture into position on the bare boards. The utility furniture arrived – all except the double bed! Judy settled happily in her cot in her new bedroom. I went to bed early too (because there was no blackout to screen the lights) and I slept on the floor.

The next morning I had to buy a gas cooker. Then I used precious coupons for curtain material for the wide windows of the big room. Upstairs I cut up bed covers for curtains. I was able to buy a small amount of lino which also needed coupons. The floor which was left bare I stained and polished. Later I managed to buy a secondhand carpet which greatly improved the sitting room end of the big room. The double bed arrived. I knitted rugs for the bedroom floor using surplus oiled wool which was really meant for seamen's sweaters.

Auction sales were being held in many houses. I loved attending these. I did not have enough money to make high bids but I managed to get many useful household items. My favourite buy was a five ft long wooden box with a padded top, covered in patterned chintz. It made a splendid window seat and chest for toys.

My sister and her little boy came to live with us. We lived happily together. We each put 30 shillings a week into the housekeeping purse for food and we ate well. Her husband was demobbed and joined us but he did not settle because we had no comfortable armchairs. He said that he could not relax, so they moved away.

About nine months after I had moved in my husband was demobbed. He was delighted to be home. An elderly lady, who had known him as a boy and admired him for having "done his duty" rewarded him by giving him an ancient leather armchair. He was able to sit comfortably!

His army gratuity helped us to buy more furniture. So, in spite of the limits of rationing and coupons, struggling to pay the mortgage of £5 each month and having no money to spare, we were happily settled in our first home together.'

LIFE IN 1947

'1947 was a very bad winter. At the end of January we had a heavy fall of snow; most villages were cut off and no tradesmen could get around. I was in my last year at Womenswold Primary Junior School. I lived about a mile away in Wollage village, although in these days most people call it "White City" – I never did know why. My elder brother and his friend set off to walk to Barham to our baker, Mr Hills, a distance of three miles, with my mother's clean white pillow cases which they then filled up with bread for the villages and trudged home and delivered to our locals.

I remember we had quite a time off school as our teacher, a Mrs Ridgeway, had moved from the school house into Folkestone, and was unable to attend due to buses not running.

The milkman had got so far in his van and became stuck in a snowdrift between our village and Barfreston, so we children went with our bags and filled them up and delivered some to our village which had 52 houses.

My Dad had travelled down from Derbyshire to find work at Snowdown Colliery due to the depression of the 1920s; my two elder brothers also worked there, which meant the family received an extra amount of cheese because at this period rationing of foodstuffs and clothing was still in force following the 1939–45 war. Mum used to make a vegetable dish which was very tasty with sliced potatoes, onions and gravy.

We used to sort sackfuls of dried peas out for the local shop, removing the black ones; this was usually done on Sunday afternoon sitting round the table. Then, for Sunday tea, Mum would cook a large pan of these peas and we would eat them with vinegar and bread and margarine (seldom butter). If we were lucky enough we might occasionally have a tin of fruit – we always had to have bread and marge with it, which I hated, but I suppose with six of us to feed it helped to fill us up. When our cheese ration had been eaten the boys would then have to take dripping on their bread (if they were lucky) or bread and marge or lard on their sandwiches, which they called their snap to take to the mine.

Washday also sticks out in my mind – every Monday morning Mother would rise early in order to light the copper. This was a round copper, open-topped vessel, set in brickwork in the corner of the kitchen with a fire underneath, a round wooden lid was fitted to contain some of the steam. It would be boiling away all day with all the whites – there would be a large bowl with Robin Starch and a blue-bag for whitening. In those days the men used to have loose white separate collars held in position by two studs. The kitchen walls were always wet from the clouds of steam. On washdays our dinner was always hash – lots of vegetables but little meat. I hated it but I knew if I didn't eat it one of my brothers would and there was nothing else. The pit clothing was always washed out of doors on the back yard in a galvanised tub with a ponch (dolly). This was a round three-legged stool with a handle set in the middle, made in wood. This was banged up and down on the dirty clothing to remove the dirt.

Mother made some of our bread in a Yorkshire oven which was

part of our living room fire – large cakes would be cooked in the roasting tin, also bread pudding which was delicious, and what a treat it was to toast bread on a long fork in front of the fire and have either pork or beef dripping on it.

Dad being a miner, we always had nice blazing fires. One of the ways mother earned some extra money was to help the nurse with births and doing the washing afterwards, also laying out the dead. She always kept a white overall for these occasions so we knew when she donned this she was either off to a confinement case or a laying out. For laying out she would receive five shillings but for births she didn't always get paid, depending on the circumstances of people. Her bed was of the type with brass knobs which unscrewed, in which she would hide her money.

Occasionally we went to Dover or Canterbury shopping. This was a treat for me as we always went for a cup of coffee and a sticky bun. In those days of shortages what I didn't like about it, though, was when one of the bakeries had just had a cake delivery and Mum would always make me stand in the queue in front of her and say: "What was it your Mum wanted, little girl, slab cake?" just reminding me what I was to buy. I used to feel so embarrassed, but I suppose an extra piece of cake did help and there seemed to be quite a few girls of my age in the queue.

Our Christmas dinner was wild rabbit, roasted with stuffing. I'd never heard of turkey. Mum could do lots of things with rabbits; we had them stewed and in pies, as well as roasted with lots of lovely gravy. My brothers had poached these – most people did, or went without. I didn't have lots of toys for Christmas, usually a jumper or something serviceable to wear, but always had a Rupert Bear Annual, delivered by our lovely old paperman, Mr Thompson, who would bike from Barham with his cycle stacked with papers and books, and always had a kind word and smile for us.'

THE DAILY ROUTINE

Pumping water, doing the weekly wash, cleaning the oil lamps, spring cleaning the house from top to bottom, laying and lighting the fires, coping with the 'little house' at the bottom of the garden or in the yard – women's work was never done. With no labour saving devices, and usually no electricity and no running water, the daily routine kept the housewife fully occupied.

SPRING CLEANING

'Without hoovers or any electrical aids, spring cleaning in our big old farmhouse, with large rooms, rambling passages and front and back stairs, started early in the year and would last several weeks.

About mid-February the "help" (a young woman who lived in) and myself tackled the top floor, consisting of the three attic rooms used to store fruit and the usual junk.

Down to the next floor, where the three bedrooms were turned out over the next week or two. Carpets and rugs were lifted and taken out and beaten and brushed, then after salt had been brushed into them, to bring up the colours, they were dragged up and down the lawn. The younger members of the family enjoyed helping with this.

So on to more bedrooms, with lino on the floors to be washed and polished, cupboards turned out, and windows cleaned and summer curtains put up. The days were getting longer and the weather brighter, and it was easier now we were downstairs and could put chairs that had to be brushed outside. Carpets were lifted and taken out on the lawn and given the same treatment as the bedroom ones.

We had now reached the two front rooms – the drawing room and the dining room. A lot of furniture here to be polished, and each room with three long windows to be cleaned and the summer curtains put up.

As these rooms were not in daily use, we were able to take our time and spread the cleaning over several days.

It was a different matter when we reached the kitchen for this is the most used room in a farmhouse and we knew we must get a move on, before the men-folk came in wanting some dinner.

The chimney had been swept first thing in the morning, so there was soot everywhere. After that was cleared up and the range blackleaded and polished until it shone, table and chairs were scrubbed and the floor washed. By evening there were still a few jobs left for another day, such as turning out cupboards and relining drawers, and polishing brass knobs on the big dresser.

At last we have come to the final big push – the scullery with its stone floor, and the copper in the corner that kept us supplied with hot water (as long as we kept the wood fire going underneath). It had to be a fine day when we started on this job so that everything could be put outside. The shelves were cleared of pots and pans, farm boots and raincoats and many other things, all out the back door. All was ready now for one of the farm workers to whitewash the ceiling and walls; after that the floor was scrubbed and by the end of the day everything was back in its place.

So ended the spring cleaning that started early in the year and was finished with great satisfaction early in the month of June.'

WASHDAY

'Washing day with my Grandma and mother about 1926 starts when the copper fire has been lit very early, the water ladled into it by a bucket. The fire goes out – it is relit and eventually burns away brightly. Now out comes the tub and the dolly pegs ready to take the blanket and heavier things in the wash.

The mangle is resurrected from its position as a table, the screw on the top turned until the rollers (big wooden ones) are close so that the maximum amount of water is squeezed out. The wheel at the end, which weighs a ton, is turned to squeeze out the water.

The bath in the sink holds "blue water"; a square of Reckitt's Blue in this ensures that white things are white. Anything woollen is washed in a big bowl which has a dollop of soft soap added.

Now the fun begins – clothes are washed by hand and then put into the copper. The more fragile ones, and there weren't many, were taken out in a short time – mangled, rinsed, put in the basket. All the top sheets and pillow cases are washed, boiled in the copper, put through the mangle and through the blue water, through the mangle again and then folded before putting in the large basket. The starch has been mixed in a big bowl and aprons etc are all put through this before again being put through the mangle.

The dolly pegs are worked hard on the heavier garments then they too go the way of the rest. By this time the room is full of steam and all the human beings are working away like slaves.

Eventually the basket is full and is taken to the garden to be hung on the line. Hope the line holds or the clothes will have to go through the ritual again.

The water is mopped off the floor, the tiles scrubbed, all the utensils washed and some hung on nails in the shed. The copper is emptied laboriously and the mangle is returned to its table state and covered with an oil cloth.

Eventually, as always on washdays, we eat cold meat, sponge cakes and custard! Hope it doesn't rain! Irons put to heat in front of the fire in the range, soon that job will have to be done – but that's another story. Did someone mention automatic washing machines? That's all women were in those days.'

'Monday washday stands out very firmly in my mind. We had a built-in copper and on Sunday evening water was poured in and the fire underneath laid so that all my mother had to do was put a match to it to get the water heated. I think the soap powder used was Rinso but certainly bars of Hudsons and Sunlight soap were bought and laid on a kitchen shelf to harden before use. A scrubbing board was used in a bath under the wooden-rollered mangle, then the laundry went into the copper to boil, and after rinsing went through a final water tinted blue with a Reckitt's blue-bag. Lump starch with a little added borax was mixed to a smooth paste with cold water, then boiling water was added and stirred to make a thick clear paste. This was diluted according to how stiff the articles needed to be – my father's shirt collars very stiff, tablecloths and napkins less so, down to my pinafores and cotton dresses. I loved putting on a clean starched dress, it felt crisp and shiny.'

WATER, LIGHTING AND HEATING

'My mother is 97 and remembers how, when she was a child, it was a common sight to see little girls employed by householders to hearthstone the front step. Mother had ten children and I often marvel how she managed all of us. She had to wash all our clothes in a little scullery, in a stone sink, and then put the clothes through the old hand wringer. It was a hard life without gas or electricity; we always went up to bed with a candle and I remember the old Tilley lamp on the table to give us light and we used to warm our hands round it in the winter. We didn't have a bathroom and the old zinc bath would be put in front of the fire for us to bath every week, two at a time. The loo was in a shed halfway down the garden. My father had to dig a long trench at the bottom of the garden and the bucket was emptied into it regularly and the trench filled in.'

'I was born in 1919 and brought up in the village of Doddington, where as a boy I used to help my grandfather, who was the Estate Manager for the owner of a mansion. He had a variety of duties, some of which were woodreefing (keeping the woods in good condition and preparing them for the underwood sales), training gun dogs, looking after the orchards and the coach roads, and also the footpaths, which had to be strictly maintained throughout the year, and looking after the chickens. One job that I particularly remember was making the gas. This was done by feeding carbide into the top of a large cylindrical container which held water. Gas was then produced, which in turn was forced through pipes to an outside gasometer, and when the gasometer was full sufficient pressure existed to force the gas up to the mansion to meet their need for lighting. About once a month the gas-making cylinder had to be cleaned out with long-handled scoops, which was a very messy job, but this sediment was not wasted; a local farmer would come with his horse and cart and use it to spread on his fields. The carbide was brought to the gas house in one cwt metal drums by the local carrier from Teynham station in his lorry.

The coal came once a year, a whole truck load of it again into Teynham station. A lorry was hired for a week, and I went with Grandfather to help shovel the coal and get it up to the mansion where even the butler and the gardeners had to help unload it into the cellars. And then there was the winter's wood to get, to feed the huge fireplaces. A sawyer would load his circular saw and stationary engine on to a horse-drawn cart and bring it to the mansion, to spend a week sawing logs to be stacked neatly under cover till needed.'

'We lived in a house at Ashford with no hot water system or bathroom and only an outside toilet. Although we did have electricity, we had a gas light in the living room/kitchen and this was lit by pulling down the "on" chain and putting a lighted match or taper into the glass globe. Woe betide you if you touched the gas mantle and broke it, especially if Mum did not have a spare.

We had a cast iron Belle cooking range supplied by Alfred Olby, Builders Merchants of Ramsgate, and Mum had to blacklead this every week. All the cooking was done on this and a kettle was always singing gently on top for general hot water needs. I well remember how thrilled Mum was when a year or so after Dad returned from four and a half years overseas with the army, he replaced this with a brand new range with vitreous enamel finish so she no longer had to do the weekly blackleading. Just a wipe over with a damp cloth was all that was needed.

Friday night was bath night and this meant lighting up the copper for hot water and bringing in the bungalow pattern tin bath from the garden shed and placing it in front of the fire in the range. The water was brought in from the scullery in pails or bowls. In summer, after use the bath was manoeuvred out of the back door and left overnight to cool and then the water used on the garden.'

'We came to live at The Woodmans, Wormshill in 1947. There was no running water and no electricity. Water was used rather carefully, even though there was an underground catchment tank. This used to get very low at times and to supplement the supply there were a large number of tanks around to gather water from the outbuildings and sheds. My father had a petrol engine to generate electricity for lighting; this was a twice weekly performance as my mother enjoyed hand sewing and tatting. We all used candles for lighting our way to bed. Paraffin was used for cooking and the kettle was on constantly, the copper being lit for washdays.

When electricity was installed our first modern appliance was a Morphy Richards Astral refrigerator. Before this I used to cycle to Sittingbourne for a block of ice cream which I carried from the town in a large Thermos flask.'

'When my sister was a baby in 1930, my mother was coming down a steep wooden staircase in the farmhouse where we lived. There was no gas or electric light and we used oil lamps or candles.

This particular evening she had the baby in one arm and was lighting the way with a candle in the other hand, when she stumbled. Rather than drop the candle and perhaps set the house on fire, she dropped the baby.

Luckily no harm was done, except that we use it as an explanation for some of my sister's eccentricities.'

'Nowadays we get water from the turn of a tap, or a push or pull by a lever, but it was not always so, especially in the country. I am now aged 80, but I grew up on a farm on the outskirts of a once small village in the Elham Valley and every drop of water needed in my home and on the farm was drawn from a well, by rope and bucket; cool, clear water.

My father drew the water needed in my home, enough to last all day, with extra on Monday to fill the copper for Mother's washday; extra on Saturday too, which was bath night in my home; if Dad forgot then Mother had to let down the bucket and turn the handle which brought the full bucket up.

The well was in our garden. A wall ran the length of the farmyard and buildings to separate us, a tank stood the other side of the wall near the well and it was the duty of the horsemen, that is the waggoner and his mate, to see that the tank was always full of water as the horses were taken to it for a drink after their work in the fields and before going in to the stables and having their harness removed. There was also a yardman who had to draw what water he needed; there were always pigs in one big yard, so water was needed for their swill.

During the summer months the cattle were in meadows or on the downs, sheep too, and it was the duty of the yardman to keep them supplied with water every day. He used a two-wheeled farm cart called a float, with a brown pony called Kitty in the shafts and three or four large milk churns filled full of water, which had been drawn bucket by bucket from the well; wherever there were animals so water had to be supplied and, during the summer months, it was a full time job for the yardman.

In my home we were brought up to value water and not waste it and although it is now so many years ago I am still careful with my usage of water.'

'It was so easy to postpone getting up on a cold, frosty morning – the bed certainly did pull! One had to break the ice on the ewer before washing, then to muster sufficient courage to venture out of doors for the loo, which was approached through the so-called "sack garden" (my father was a corn merchant) and up several steps to the garden proper! There was mains drainage, but no flush, so a bucket of water did the trick.

Bathing was a weekly event in a hip bath in front of the kitchener fire. Our family shared a water pump with our next door neighbours in their back yard and there was a linking door for access. I recall vividly jumping out hastily and taking refuge in a nearby cupboard when I thought the boy next door was about to come through.

We went to bed by candlelight, so that reading in bed was strictly forbidden. Most of the time there were hasty hidings of books beneath the bedclothes on hearing footsteps approaching on the stairs. We became used to the scuttling in the roof overhead – rats! It was said by predecessors that the boys used to come downstairs to find rats sitting on their bicycle saddles!'

'We had a spring-filled well at our farmhouse on Romney Marsh. In the late 1930s my father wanted to use the spring water and asked the local doctor's opinion, which was that no authority would pass it fit for drinking. Father, not to be deterred, told Mother that when the gipsies came in summer for their annual visit to work in the fields, to give them the spring water when they asked for some.

He said, "If it doesn't hurt them it won't hurt us." It didn't and ever after we drank from that well. Our other well was a rainwater well and collected water from the roof of the house, which must have contained wind-blown debris, dust and lichen as well as bird droppings. Amazingly it never harmed us.

Mains water was laid on in the 1940s when Father paid for it to be piped from a neighbouring farm. Soon after, we awoke to an unusual noise. There was a burst pipe in the bathroom and water was gushing down into the pantry below. Dishes, plates and food were all floating on the wide pantry shelves, not to mention the old brick floor. But there was no carpet or wooden floor to worry about and we just turned off the mains and waited till most of the water had soaked away through the special two-brick hole at the base of the outer wall. Mother said that this hole was the drain away place when the floor was scrubbed with buckets of water and a broom.'

'I spent all my schooldays in Blean with my parents and two elder brothers. We had no mains water or electricity supply. Rainwater was collected at the rear of the house in four large tanks and barrels. Drinking water was drawn from a spring some distance from the house using a yoke to carry a pair of buckets, one from each shoulder. I used to carry the water if my brothers were working or unable to collect sufficient. Summer was the worst time when the rainwater ran out and we had to collect enough extra for washing day to fill the wood-fired copper and several large galvanised baths.'

'Rainwater collected in tanks was used for general purposes such as washing; the well water was very precious and kept for drinking. As the wells were very deep it was not a woman's job to wind up the bucket of water, nor was a bucket drawn often. When we had a new neighbour in the cottage next door at Coldred, the woman attempted to wind up a bucket of water on her own. Tom Hawkins realised the danger and ran out, telling the woman off and applying the brake. The handle could easily have whipped out of control and knocked the woman out or, worse still, down the well.

A part of the garden was set aside for the lavatory "waste". Everyone in the household, of course, knew where it was. However, town people were unaware of the routine in the country, as a young boy visitor was to find out when he visited the farm. He ran right into it!'

'When I married in 1954 I stayed in Preston, moving about 150 yards down the road from Mum and Dad into a large farmhouse divided into two separate homes. There was water laid on, but it had to be drawn from a standpipe and tap on the wall next door to me. My sister got married after me and as next door was empty, she and her husband moved in and we have lived next door to each other ever since. Her husband put cold water taps in each kitchen.

We didn't have electricity for another two years, and until then we had oil lamps, an oil cooker, a primus stove to boil kettles, a coal fire for warmth and an open fired copper for clothes washing, bathing or anything that needed a lot of hot water. As time passed and electricity became more widely available, we gradually acquired all the modern things we had only seen pictures of and read about all those years before.

When we first lived next door to each other and had our children, my sister and I had only outside toilets, which stood side by side. The children used to have quite interesting conversations sitting side by side with only a flimsy partition between them!

In 1976 we had proper bathrooms put into the houses. Until then every time it rained I had to put a bungalow bath and buckets on the landing to catch the rain, as the join between the houses and the scullery leaked like a sieve. Having the bathroom built stopped all that. At one time, before we had the bathroom built and the toilet inside, my mother-in-law came and wanted to use the toilet, so off she went outside. Whilst out there, a rat ran over her foot. It wasn't a laughing matter, but she did look funny with the knickers round her ankles, screaming her head off.

When my husband and brother-in-law, helped by our dog, got the floor of the toilet dug out, they unearthed a family nest of rats, 32, of all ages and sizes. It took three hundredweight of concrete to cover it in. The good old days?'

'When electricity was first installed in the Ashford area the householders were offered five points of electricity in the home at a special rate, but everyone was scared to switch it on. It made them nervous.'

FOOD AND
CALLERS TO THE DOOR

Food may have been plainer in the past, but who could resist Well Pudding or a savoury rabbit stew? Unfortunately, rabbit was sometimes the only meat a family saw – though those who kept their own pig fared somewhat better. The day to day necessities such as bread and milk were brought to the door by regular tradesmen who became almost part of the family.

FOOD THROUGH THE WEEK

'Meals were largely governed by the housework my mother had to do. In the 1920s she cooked with a coal fired kitchen range which entailed cleaning soot out of the flues once a week. The range was kept gleaming with black lead applied with a brush with a final polish with a piece of black velvet! I had a tiny copper kettle which I was sometimes allowed to fill and put on the top to boil.

My mother was an excellent cook and I wonder now how she managed to produce such lovely sponges and cakes and pastry with no other aid to adjusting the oven heat than pushing the damper in and out over the fire. A lot depended on the direction of the wind too.

On Sundays we had a roast joint with home-grown vegetables and usually a fruit pie and cream. Monday would be washing day so no time for cooking and we ate the cold remains of the Sunday lunch with either mashed potatoes (lashings of butter and milk!) or bubble and squeak and the cold fruit pie.

Tuesday was the day for ironing with flat irons heated on the range. If there was any cold meat left we would eat cottage pie or rissoles and a milk pudding baked in the oven.

Wednesday was probably meat pie or pudding, left to cook whilst the downstairs rooms were cleaned, and Thursday was the day for upstairs. No vacuum cleaner, so all the rugs had to be hauled downstairs and shaken and put over the clothes line to be brushed. Usually we ate stewed beef or mutton as this could be left to cook unattended, with maybe another milk pudding. Friday we had fish, and as we lived in Folkestone this was cheap and plentiful and delicious! Mr Waller came round with his pony and cart with fish straight from the sea. The pony, Jimmy, had once been in a circus and if he heard music would rear up and dance. I recall this happening once and the fish slid off the cart. Nobody seemed to care much, it was retrieved and doubtless eaten.

We also had a Mr Fagg who walked from Hythe to Folkestone with a huge basket of bloaters which he sold at four for sixpence. They were the nicest bloaters I have ever tasted – would that we could still have them!

Saturday was make-up day for lunch, perhaps cold meat and salad when in season, and we always had a substantial pudding. My favourite was Well Pudding, a basin lined with a suet crust containing sultanas or raisins and the middle filled with butter and brown sugar, a crust lid over the top and the pudding steamed or boiled. When cut open the sugar and butter ran over the crust like toffee – need I say more!

Most of our food was delivered, orders were given weekly and arrived promptly. Several bakers, milkmen, greengrocers and oil-men with paraffin and hardware came round, and coal and wood was delivered, so there was no need to go far from home for casual shopping. Drapers and outfitters would allow goods to be taken home "on approval" and delivery vans were a common sight with traders vying for the smartest turn-out. Early in the morning a boy came round ringing a bell and calling "Hot rolls" and we had similar sellers of watercress ("Wingham Well watercress"), shrimps and winkles. Many front gardens in Folkestone were decorated with scallop shells which were readily available.

Cousins at Lydd had a fisherman uncle at Dungeness and he had a herring hang where he smoked fish. His freshly caught shrimps still warm from cooking had to be tasted to be believed.'

'The small shops at the top of our road in Welling were a fish shop, cake shop, haberdasher's, papers and sweets, butcher's and general shop. The fishman used to squeeze the herrings to see if there was a hard or a soft roe and the smoked haddock was hung on sticks and you could choose which size you wanted, then they were slid off the cane and yours was taken off. Friday night was our treat of fish and chips – twopennyworth of fish and a pennyworth of chips for five children and threepennyworth of fish and twopennyworth of chips for Mum and Dad, and as Friday night was bath night the last child for a bath went for our supper. The owner of the fish shop, a Mr Dodds, had a large jug on the counter with his beer in, and when it was empty he used to shout out, "Freddie, beer!" and Freddie had to dash up to The Duchess of Edinburgh pub for his refill.

At the cake shop I used to buy twopennyworth of stale cakes to make a trifle. Every Saturday I got Dad's ounce of Nosegay and a packet of cigarette papers, and at the butcher's half a pound of bladebone steak for Dad and a pound of sausages for us children. We bought twopennyworth of ice cream in a cup when the weather was very hot. The general shop had large earthenware jars filled with jam, treacle, pickled onions, piccalilli and pickled cabbage; we used to take basins to get any of these items and the treacle and jam made a lovely squelchy noise when they came out. The muffin man came round ringing his bell on Saturday in the winter, and on Sundays the winkle man used to come round and we would go out to get winkles and shrimps for Sunday's tea.'

JOE GRAY AND DRIPPING

'My mother used to cook sliced onions and potatoes in gravy, sometimes adding sausages, and she called it "Joe Gray", though I never found out why. We had fresh milk once a week on Sundays, the rest of the time we had condensed sweetened milk. It was used for drinks to save sugar in most things. Sounds terrible now. The fresh milk was generally used to make an egg custard tart in an enamel pie dish. We also had Lent Tart, a pastry base with a filling of ground rice and currants. When we had roast meat we had a pudding, probably suet, cooked in the tin with the meat. It was brown and crisp on the outside and soft in the middle. It helped to fill young stomachs – cheaper than meat.'

'Sharsted Court is a large house under a mile from where I lived at Newnham in the early years of the century. They kept a large staff in the days before the First World War. They consumed a large amount of meat and the cook would ask my father, who was a labourer on the estate, to sell the dripping for her in the village, from 12 to 16 lbs per week at fourpence a pound. Beautiful it was! My brother and I delivered it to the regulars and we were often given a halfpenny for ourselves. Also at Sharsted Court they kept cows and had a dairy. They had large pans of milk to skim off the cream for butter and the skimmed milk was sold to the villagers for a penny a pint.'

'We lived in a mining community in the 1930s. We had meat one day of the week and my mother made rabbit stew with dumplings. These were wild rabbits. For a treat we would have roast rabbit on a Sunday. Bread was baked on a Friday and, if we could afford it, cakes. We couldn't wait for teatime, we had warm bread and butter.'

CATCHING EELS

'A very interesting hobby on Romney Marsh for those who liked eels was catching the slippery fish, with a big set net reaching both banks of the petty sewers on the marsh. These nets were weighted by lead one side to sink them into the water, while the other side floated on top with cork. When the cork bobbed up and down it caused great excitement as this meant a catch. There were beaters who drove the fish up to the net. Two of these men beat the water together on each side of the net while two more men held the draw ropes to pull the net up from the water onto the bank. Then it was home again, and the skinning had to be done and it was on with the frying pan and eels for supper. And jolly nice too.'

KEEPING A PIG

'My father kept pigs and chickens at his smallholding at Swingfield but he was unable to kill them himself. A local man would be called on to wring a chicken's neck and my grandfather would come to kill the pig. We had two pigs killed a year, one in the spring and one in the autumn. When the pig was stunned, killed and its throat cut and bled, a pot of boiling water had to be at the ready to treat the skin so that the bristles could be scraped off. The carcase was hung on a hook in the scullery and grandfather would joint up the pig. A special slate tank of brine was kept and into this went the fat pork. My father enjoyed a piece of fat pork in bread and butter for breakfast and my husband recalls that fat pork in bread and milk was eaten by his family. My mother and I washed the intestines carefully inside and out in salt water. Then these chitterlings could be fried for eating. The blood was caught and used to make black pudding.'

'Immediately after the Second World War, my Mum and Dad ran a pig club at Broadstairs with some other people, renting sties from a farmer at the end of our garden. We also kept chickens and rabbits. Dad had been in the Catering Corps so he was able to joint the pigs after they had been killed, and kill and prepare the chickens and rabbits at Christmastime. We always had a good Christmas with plenty of meat.

When the farm became a breaker's yard, Dad built a sty at the bottom of our garden and we kept one pig. We called him Little Pig Anthony. One day he escaped. There were no fences between any of the gardens and I remember my Mum running along the back of Miles Cottages trying to catch him. She had a blanket round her shoulders because she was not very well. After that we didn't have any more pigs.'

'In the 1950s we were still engrossed with feeding ourselves, not only with the next meal or the week ahead, but long term. This fairly newly married couple arrived in the country from city backgrounds, full of enthusiasm to get down to basics. We had a building which would make an ideal pigsty. What better way to ensure Sunday dinners?

We were overwhelmed with advice from the locals and were soon the proud owners of three eight-week-old piglets, sweet and pink and as pretty as puppies. Our bacon coupons were cut from our ration books for six baconless months ahead so that we could feed the pigs, our mouths watering with anticipation.

The first few weeks were easy; the pigs were small, and all you had to do was mix up the meal, bought with the bacon coupons, with water and household scraps. But all too soon that was not enough for the pigs, they were hungry. A vast mound of potatoes was dumped at the back door, all stained with purple as unfit for human consumption. There was an old copper in an outhouse which had been scorned by me (I boiled the nappies in an enamel bucket on the stove, and the laundry brought back shirts and sheets each week in a hamper). This old black copper was filled with cut-up potatoes each day and a small fire of sticks lit underneath. Then the boiled potatoes were mixed with some meal and satisfied our growing family.

My husband enthusiastically sat by the heap each morning before dressing in his office suit, cutting up an ever increasing quantity of potatoes. The pigs came when they were called by name to have their backs scratched, and the children cooed over them.

The neighbours eventually deemed that they had reached the correct size, so the terrible day came when the lorry took them away, with tears from the family and shrieks from the pigs. The next day we went to fetch our half pig. It was a long, heavy pink slab which covered the kitchen table with mountains of meat.

Friends eagerly took charge of the cutting up. The hams and bacon side were soon salted and hung from the kitchen ceiling; the half head and two trotters were put to boil for brawn; pork chops put by for Sunday dinners for a round of neighbours; and a glorious fry up of kidney, liver and chitterlings was on the menu for the next couple of days accompanied by indigestion and waning remorse.'

GLEANING

'After the wheat fields were "mowed" around Canterbury at the time of the First World War, people would go gleaning. My grandparents took the wheat they collected to the local mill, Deanshill. The flour would help make the Christmas cake and puddings. The local bakehouse would bake the cakes. My Grandma always boiled the pudding in a cloth; it included silver threepenny pieces for us children.'

CALLERS TO THE DOOR

'The baker came every day. He had a cart like a large box, with a curved roof that protruded a little in front. There were doors back and front and slatted shelves inside. The box was mounted on two quite large wooden wheels three or four ft high. It had two shafts in the front, between which the baker *ran*, leaning against a detachable leather strap. It gave the impression of a miniature gypsy caravan, pulled by a man, not a horse. The cart was varnished over a light undercoat and, as was the fashion, combed and decorated with curly scrolls and the baker's name. It was supposed to look like genuine light oak. The baker carried the bread to the house in an oblong wicker basket. The bread was often warm when delivered and delicious with butter or dripping. The baker was only a little man with a moustache, but he was exceedingly strong – he both baked his bread and delivered it. How far he came, I have no idea, but I do know there was a hill either way. In bad weather he wore a sack around his shoulders.

The grocer came weekly. He had a much larger, motorised, van with four rubber tyres and a flattish front. It was painted dark red, with buff coloured scrolls, leaves and his name painted on the sides. It had doors only at the back and the grocer could walk down inside

Mr Clarke, baker of Ash, and his assistant in the 1920s. His motorised van is up to date, many country areas still being supplied by horse-drawn vehicles in this period.

to select the required goods, to be carried to the customers in a wicker basket. My mother had a regular order, though if I was lucky I had two ounces of mint toffees. The van had to be started with a large angular crank handle, which fitted into a hole at the lower front underneath the radiator grill. The handle had to be turned by hand, with some physical and often verbal vigour to start the engine chugging.

My grandmother always put a jug on her white painted window sill for the milkman. The top of the jug was covered with a small circular fly cloth, weighted with beads on the edge, then a piece of card, atop of which she put a stone against the wind. The milkman had a little handcart with two low, painted, curved sides. In the middle of his cart sat his milk churn, and hooked on the side of the cart or churn were his measures, gill, half pint, pint and quart. These were metal beakers on long metal handles with a hooked end, for the churns were a good three ft high – imagine dabbling in that for a lost measure.

Getting the milk from the measure into the jug without spilling a drop was quite a skill. Spillages wasted milk and spoilt the window sill. Sometimes the milkman had cream and butter in a large blob. He chopped the butter up and patted it into shape with his crinkly wooden butter patters; then he picked the butter up between his two patters and transferred it to the waiting dish.

My grandmother's milkman called twice a day and his milk was delicious, before the days of pasteurisation, sterilisation, homogenisation etc. My mother said she visited Belgium after the First World War and saw carts like the milkman's pulled by dogs.

Our milkman only called once a day. He had an open sided cart and the slightly curved roof extended out in front, over his high seat, from whence he drove his horse Daisy. A bag of oats was slung under the cart for the horse. At the appointed times the milkman stopped and hung the bag by a long leather strap over the horse's head, so that the animal could have refreshment and the milkman his bread and cheese. He always stopped – or the horse did – at the horse trough for a drink.

Horse troughs – long stone troughs, filled with clean water – were supplied where no pond was available for the watering of horses. Many were built by a Drinking Fountain and Cattle Trough Association and supplied clean drinking water for horses, and in a shallow trough underneath for dogs, and on top for humans, using a metal cup secured on a chain. Some were quite elaborate affairs.

This was not the only refreshment the horse received. He or she knew where to stop to receive offerings and petting. Offerings included apple, bread, stale cake, carrots, biscuits, sweets or best of all lumps of sugar, or toffee, which stuck around her teeth and made her toss her head. She ate all with great relish and no amount of urging from the milkman could budge her until due attention from grown ups and children alike had been given. She also knew which garden hedges were edible. What all this did to her digestion I hate to think, but she always seemed hale and hearty.

The horses were stabled at night behind the dairy shop. They were warm and dry. The ceilings of the stables were so high it was possible to fit small workshops, reached by rickety stairs, above the actual stables. The horses went down a cobbled alley by my grandmother's house to reach the stables and sitting by the fire at teatime in winter, you could hear the clip-clopping of their feet as they passed under the window.

On Saturdays and Sundays Father was always ready with his bucket and shovel to scoop up any horse droppings, for use on his prize dahlias. He did have another daily source of supply of manure, which here I shall not relate – but bear in mind we only had an outside, distant, unlit, unheated loo.

In summer the ice cream man came on his tricycle – his cold box on two front wheels. "Stop me and buy one" was his slogan. He also sold triangular fruit ice lollies covered in a cardboard wrapper for a halfpenny each.

Then there was the rag and bone man – he had a flat cart pulled by a horse and he sat on a high seat in front. He collected anything and he *paid* for his goods. He rang his hand bell and shouted "Any old rags, any old bones", or a version of the same. For children he had supplies of balloons or goldfish, in exchange for jam jars etc. His narrow yard was piled high with everything imaginable.'

'My mother did not live to see the modern superstores, but all the local tradesmen calling at the house at Deal in the 1920s made shopping in town unnecessary, except for special purchases.

Almost a part of social life, Mr Finch the milkman, with his churn of milk, carefully measured the required amount. The baker called daily with his basket of loaves, baked overnight.

The butcher called twice a week for orders and the fishmonger with his barrow. He didn't knock on the doors but everyone could hear him calling his wares. I remember in November, in the evenings, the call of "Deal herrings, 40 a shilling". Mothers would take out kitchen bowls, which would be filled, no need to count. Deal herrings are still a delicacy; not so many are caught now but I still look forward to them.

Another day came the hardware van, drawn by a lovely old horse called Joe. He was white and he knew just where to stop, mainly delivering paraffin for the lamps. He was driven by Jack Dilnot. Mr Knight, the insurance man, called on Saturdays and because I had lost my father he used to give me a penny. Mr Cornelius, the coalman, also called on Saturday and had to carry the sacks of coal through the house to the backyard. I was frightened of him, quite unnecessarily, and would hide in the cupboard under the stairs. Mr Fuller from Northbourne with his van full of lovely fresh vegetables and fruit was another Saturday caller.

Mother's special caller was Mr Wheeler, who called each week for the grocery order. He would sit in state in the sitting room, writing down the list of groceries required which would be delivered the next day.

All these goods were delivered free of charge.'

'Early in 1931 we moved to the new estate being developed in St Stephen's, Canterbury. Until electricity was laid on we lit the house with Aladdin lamps and one of the tradesmen who delivered all kinds of hardware was known as the "oil and colour man". His horse and cart was a sight to behold and the smell of candles and paraffin remind me to this day of his cart with its funnels jingling on a rail at the back and his shout of "Whoa there!" as his horse began to set off as he was still filling our paraffin cans.

Another early morning caller would be the baker's boy, whose bell could be heard at seven o'clock and whose cry of "Hot rolls and muffins" could be heard from far afield. He carried a large basket on his head with a clean sack covering the freshly baked goodies. The farmer would bring round the milk in large churns, in a horse-drawn float with the long-handled brass bound pint measure dangling from it. Our own jugs would be filled with frothing new milk from the early morning milking sessions.'

BIRTH AND DEATH

It is not so long since both birth and death were more likely to occur in your own home than in a hospital or nursing home. A local woman would be called on to help with the birth, and more often than not would also be there to lay out the dead. On one memorable occasion, the doctor came by train! The undertaker was also likely to be a local man, with a family business.

BABIES BORN AT HOME

'My mother was a midwife and nurse in the Lympne area before the First World War. She helped mothers before and after the birth of their babies, and she also helped to lay out the dead. The doctor had a huge area to cover and only a push-bike for transport.

One day, my mother went to the house of a woman whose baby was due the following day, to ensure that everything was ready for the birth. It was a very cold day in November, and my mother went into the bedroom to make sure it was clean for the baby. I heard her yell, and then she ran downstairs and told me what had happened. The woman had tipped all the feathers out of her mattress, so that she could wash the mattress cover. I was told to go home and bring a clean unbleached calico cover to the house. My brother and I had the difficult and ticklish job of trying to get all the feathers into the clean cover. I well remember feathers in my hair, up my nose and in my ears.

My mother not only helped at the birth, but did all the washing and fed the rest of the family for ten days after the baby was born.'

'My only brother was born when I was six years old in 1925. In those days we knew nothing of those events. I was sent to sleep with a friend and my father came to fetch me in the morning, saying Mum had had a "Sunny Jim". I was most upset to find a baby, as Sunny Jims were toys given away with packets of Force Flakes and I would have preferred one of them.'

'Before the National Health Service, in the early 1940s, it was only the well to do who went into hospital for the birth, or if complications were expected. A few months before the baby was due, you contacted the District Nurse, who in my case lived four miles away. She would call in once a month and later more often to take blood pressure etc. A list of articles required was given, which one got ready – cotton wool, nappies, pins, powder and so on. Nurse was more like a friend and so patient, calling twice a day for the first week after the baby was born and then once a day for a week. A friend would come and stay and help look after the family and do the washing for a little while.

Canterbury was being bombed the night my first son was born. Rations were rather scarce, although nursing mothers had an extra allowance of milk. At that time we had no electricity in the house. Very rarely, however, was the doctor called out. We were taught to put the baby out in the fresh air in the pram, well covered of course, every day except when foggy or wet. Cod liver oil and orange juice were also provided as rations. I must say the babies all thrived.'

'My youngest sister was born in 1947, a very cold and severe winter. Because my mother was expecting we were allowed extra coal, this still being rationed after the war, but it had to be fetched from the coal yard in a wheelbarrow. My sister was born at home as most babies were then, attended by the local midwife. Amongst the things needed for the home delivery were: 1) An empty biscuit tin in which dressings, pads and cotton wool were placed and then baked in the oven to sterilise them; 2) An empty paste jar for keeping the thermometer in; 3) A small basin or cup, which could be boiled in a saucepan and kept for bathing the baby's eyes; 4) A crepe bandage for binding the baby's abdomen to prevent a protruding tummy button – none of these would be needed today, even if babies were still delivered at home. The father was not allowed to be present, his job was to see that there was plenty of hot water to bath mother and baby after delivery, and to make the tea; he would also rush to fetch the doctor if he was needed, as we had no telephone.'

THE DOCTOR CAME BY TRAIN

'Picture, if you can, a tiny piece of ground beside a main line railway track (Dover to London) and just outside the mouth of a tunnel. This was Shakespeare Halt, which was at the foot of Shakespeare Cliff (about 300 ft high). It was in one of the four cottages on this land that I lived in 1952. My husband was then a fireman for Southern Rail so we rented one of their cottages for the princely sum of four shillings and sixpence per week.

Our only means of transport into Dover was by train and those that stopped were very few and far between. About four a day each way made regular stops for the benefit of staff. So you see we were pretty isolated. Of course, if you were really energetic, you could walk round the beach at low tide or climb the very steep cliff path, but for me this was highly impracticable as I had two small children.

A few yards up the line was a signal box and the signalman was our only means of communication with anyone in town. Even this was done through the internal system of Southern Rail. There were no such things as ordinary telephones on Shakespeare!

One night in early April 1952 we were awakened by dirt being thrown up at the bedroom window. Hurrying to see what was wrong we were confronted by a very anxious neighbour who said that his pregnant wife was not well. I pulled on a dressing gown and went with him to see what I could do. It didn't take much to see that the poor girl was well on her way to giving birth, despite her protests she had another six weeks to go! It was now past midnight, so what were we to do? The first available train to take her into Dover was not due until 6.30 am, and the first one up from Dover to bring help was even later – about 7.30 am. There was only one thing for it, my husband would have to go along the track to the signal box (no electric lines in those days) and see if he could contact someone in Dover.

What a good thing my husband knew where the key to the signal box was kept, for on that particular night there was no signalman on duty, so the box was closed. However, my husband got through to "Dover Loco" via the special code and asked the foreman on duty to contact Dr Tolland and arrange to bring her to the halt on a special engine. Dr Tolland was directed to the Military Platform where she was helped onto the waiting engine and then brought to Shakespeare Halt. There she was met by my husband who guided her by torchlight to the cottage – 'twas a dark night and there were no street lamps!

I was more than relieved to see the doctor and prepared to hand over my patient when she told me in no uncertain terms to stay where I was because she needed my help. About three hours later a little boy was born to Emmie weighing about four pounds and I thought, "Thank goodness, now I can get back to bed!" *But* the biggest surprise was yet to come.

"I don't think we are finished yet," said Dr Tolland, "there seems to be more to come." How right she was! Twenty minutes later and little Stephen had a twin sister. To this day I don't know who had the biggest surprise, Dr Tolland, Emmie or her husband. However, when we had got over the initial shock of the double births arrangements had to be made to get the three patients to hospital. Once again my husband did his bit. This time the signalman was in the box ready for the early shift. So my husband asked him to contact

"Dover Loco" again and arrange for an ambulance to come to Dover Priory. The ambulance crew were able to come with a stretcher to the Halt on a "stopping train" which left the Priory just after 7 am. This was the train which also brought our milk, mail and newspapers. There was a train going into Dover which called at the Halt at about 8.05 am so the three patients were loaded on this in the guard's brake and on arrival at Dover taken to hospital.

The next day the national newspapers had a highly coloured version of the birth of twins by lamplight in such a remote area a doctor had to be brought there by a specially chartered engine. What they did not know was that we were making history. No babies were ever born there again for where our cottages once stood is the site of the service tunnel for the Channel Tunnel.'

THE UNDERTAKER

'I was born in 1908; we were a small family of four children, but only two survived. Most of our neighbours had six or seven children but it was quite usual for each family to lose one or two infants. In those days the undertakers had special vehicles for infant interments, which unfortunately were common. These were a horse-drawn carriage, with a small glass hearse underneath the driver's seat. All mourners wore black from head to foot.'

'Father was an undertaker from 1936. I used to love helping him get ready, polishing his top hat with a silk handkerchief, keeping the silk lying one way. He wore a white tie and gloves for the funeral of someone under 14 and black for anyone over that age. I loved the secret pocket in his frock coat, in the back split lining, for his gloves.

Pre war it was the done thing to wear black to funerals and mourning for about six months afterwards. In consequence people paid for an insurance policy to cover the cost and set aside a few coppers weekly. My paternal grandfather died in November 1935 and my grandmother six weeks later, so my mother had two claims. As the black clothing was already being worn, the second claim was used to purchase an uncut moquette three piece suite. The cost, if I remember correctly, was £9.

My grandmother used to follow the coffin to the cemetery if there were no other mourners, so that the departed was not alone. One of my holiday jobs was to make small pillows to pad coffins so that bodies did not move when carried. They were approximately ten inches square and filled with sawdust. For this I received the large sum of a farthing each. The coffins were hand made of elm or oak and there was a lovely smell as they were being planed, shaped and fitted together. They were glued for extra strength and we were never allowed near the gluepot, on a gas ring in the carpenter's shop. The coffins were lined with pitch and then this was covered with beautiful silks and satin ribbons. A lace handkerchief would be placed over the face when the body was on show in the family home and lifted for viewing. If for some reason the family did not want the deceased at home, we had them in our front room (no funeral parlours in those days) and my mother could not sleep; nor could she stand the Ashes of Violets spray, used to cover odd smells.

I once filled my brother's hair with shavings from the coffins to make it curly. Did I get into trouble when my mother tried to get it out!'

HEALTH – FROM HOME TO HOSPITAL

At one time even minor operations were performed on the kitchen table at home, and the only illness to have taken most people off to the hospital was the 'fever', infectious scarlet fever or diphtheria. Before the coming of the National Health Service, the local hospital was, indeed, still likely to have the dreaded 'workhouse' connection. New treatments have improved many lives since those early days.

HOME HELP!

'A visit to the dentist was unheard of at the beginning of the century in Alkham. A remedy for toothache was to get some red hot cinders and scatter henbane seed over them, let the fumes go up into the mouth and it would kill the pain.'

'Around Easter time our blood had to be "purified", so it was a case of having to take sulphur tablets or brimstone and treacle, a mixture of sulphur powder and golden syrup. If I had a cough, I was given a dose of the syrup made from onion and sugar left to stand all night. This was quite a pleasant remedy.'

75

'Illness was treated rather differently in those days. I had scarlet fever and was nursed in the night nursery by Nanny; carbolic-soaked sheets were hung over the door and no one but the doctor allowed past them for the six weeks of my strict quarantine. Then, soon after the First World War, my sister had an appendectomy performed in my father's dressing room; a portable operating table was installed, surgeon and anaesthetist arrived plus nurse, and Mother stood on tiptoe on a bank at the top of the garden, in the vain hope of being able to watch the proceedings!

In cases of illness, straw was put on the roads to deaden the sound of passing traffic.'

'I think our parents were very anxious when we were ill; lots of children died as there were no antibiotics and operations were not so successful. My mother would put me to bed if I had a temperature and there I stayed until it was normal for 24 hours. No solid food, and how I hated Bovril and bread and milk! The weather had to be just right before I was allowed out again.

I remember, vividly, having my tonsils out, not in hospital but at home in my parents' bedroom on the scrubbed kitchen table. I think I was about five or six. My father showed me a beautiful doll in a cupboard and said, "If you are a good girl and have your tonsils out, you shall have it." Then I was taken upstairs and put on the table. It was an awful experience, my throat was so sore and I was sick and told the doctor how naughty he had been to make me feel so ill! It was not a very successful operation, done by our own local doctor, who surely had not had much practice. When I was 14 I had to go through the operation again (not on the kitchen table this time), but then they left a swab in my throat and it was very sore again.'

I'M SURE WE OUGHT TO PAY!

'In the late 1940s petrol was still scarce, but there was enough in Granny's old Austin to take us all to Deal for a swim one day. The water was cold, and I kicked out strongly to get warm, felt a blow on my shin and discovered blood pouring from a deep cut, sustained from contact with a piece of wreckage, much of which was scattered on shore and under the water as a result of the war. I was taken to Deal Cottage Hospital, swathed in beach towels, and stitched up for nothing! I was the first person in our family to use the new National Health Service, and well remember my father saying, "I'm sure we ought to be paying for all this," and Mother replying, "Do be quiet, or they might charge us after all!".'

76

THE 'FEVER'

'One of the most vivid memories of my childhood is of the year 1926, when I was all of five years of age. This was the year of the general strike. I started at the village school in Bourne Road, Old Bexley, in September. Just before Christmas I was taken ill with scarlet fever and because it was a very infectious disease I was to be sent to the "fever hospital". I am not sure of its exact location, but I think it was somewhere between Bexley Heath and Barnehurst.

I remember hearing my older sister crying and when I asked my father why he said, "Oh she's fallen down and hurt her knee." What I didn't know was that my mother had just told her that I had got to go away to hospital, and it was Christmas Eve. No one told me of course. I had very loving parents but in those days no one thought to tell children what was going to happen to them.

The so-called ambulance arrived. Believe it or not, it was a horse-drawn brougham! I can remember being wrapped up in a blanket and my Dad carrying me downstairs and out to the carriage. I was laid down on the seat with a nurse opposite although I can't remember what she looked like. Then we were off. I also remember it had been snowing heavily, it was bitterly cold and of course there was no heating in the brougham. It must have been two or three miles at least to Bexley Heath. There is a very steep hill out of the village towards Bexley Heath called Gravel Hill and as the horse plodded up this hill between high banks of snow, I rolled off the seat onto the floor. Some nurse!

I spent six weeks in the fever hospital in complete isolation. Six long, very unhappy weeks. Because it was an infectious illness I had no visitors, although I seem to remember once seeing my mother looking through the window – but that was all.

At the end of six weeks came the big day, I was to go home. A nurse came to my bed, picked me up and dumped me in a bath of very hot water with a vast amount of disinfectant in it. I screamed my head off because it was burning my skin and watched my body from the waist down turn bright pink. She then started to wash my hair. I heard her tut-tutting and she disappeared, leaving me still sitting there howling my eyes out. The next thing I heard was my mother's voice, and a male voice saying, "I know this family and she didn't come in like that." It was the voice of the Medical Officer of Health who also happened to be our family doctor, who had come to approve my discharge from hospital. Evidently I had nits, an awful disgrace in those days. Anyway I was allowed home. I can still see my mother every morning sitting me on our old kitchen table, draping me with a towel and going through my head with a fine nit comb.'

'I was the youngest of five children and was, to say the least, spoilt rotten. One day when I was seven years old, in 1927, my brother was kept away from school with a heavy cold and a slight temperature. I too was not well so the doctor was called in. Dr Rawkins duly arrived, looked at my brother and said he could have the rest of the week off school, then examined me and asked my mother to come with him into the next room, leaving my brother and me in the dining room. Being inquisitive, my brother listened at the door and heard the doctor say, "The little boy can go to school next week but the little girl has a diphtheric throat and will have to go to hospital." Hearing this my brother rushed and told me I had to go to the isolation hospital.

I fell screaming on the floor, saying, "I'm not going to hospital", whereupon my mother and the doctor came rushing into the room thinking I was dying. My mother was in tears and I think by this time I was lying stiff on the floor with my eyes shut. When the doctor saw the state we were in, he told my mother that the only way I could stay at home would be for the family to be boarded out and a sheet hung across my bedroom door permanently dripping with disinfectant and never allowed to dry out. The doctor called periodically, giving me injections in my bottom.'

THE WORKHOUSE IN 1938

'On a bright day at the end of January 1938, my husband George and I arrived in Etchinghill near Folkestone from Surrey. We moved into one of six cottages belonging to the workhouse where George was to work as a nurse. The first four cottages in a terrace were probably built at the same time as the workhouse, or fairly soon after, and were occupied by an engineer and an assistant engineer, a cook and assistant cook. The cooks also baked all the bread. Later a pair of semi-detached houses was built for two male nurses.

In those days the workhouse was administered by the Elham Board of Guardians. It was a rather forbidding looking place, surrounded by a high wall, with a large iron gate only opened to admit vehicles. A small gate in the big one admitted people, and everyone entering and leaving was recorded in a big ledger in the weighbridge office just inside the gates.

The hospital was quite a large one and included a maternity ward where local women, especially the "fallen" ones, could have their babies. Many of these latter stayed on to work, keeping their babies with them, until at the age of three the children were sent to the Cottage Homes at Cheriton.

All the land around the buildings was used to grow produce, as

Despite the Christmas decorations, the spartan look of the old workhouse still clung to this St Mary's hospital ward in the 1950s.

well as much of the area outside the walls and round our homes. A little way down the hill from our houses were the piggeries. Two inmates were responsible for the care of the pigs, and one little old man used to call at the cottages every day after lunch with two pails in a barrow to collect scraps and vegetable peelings etc, which with all the leftovers from the workhouse kitchen were cooked up in a huge copper to feed the pigs. Killing some of the pigs took place just before Christmas, so roast pork was the usual Christmas dinner.

A busy part of the establishment was the "tramp" wards. Every day towards evening the men and women of the roads would make their way through the small iron gate and book in. They were bathed and fed and given a bed for the night. The following day they worked in the garden and fields, and the women helped in the laundry or at a similar domestic task. After another night's rest and breakfast they would leave by a small door in the side wall and set off, usually in the direction of Bridge, near Canterbury where another workhouse would receive them.

In those early days the hospital wards were heated by large stoves right in the centre, which were stoked at intervals by the ward maids. During cold weather the patients whose beds were in the middle of the ward were the lucky ones – those at either end had to shiver!

It must be said that conditions had improved a great deal since the days of Charles Dickens, but people really dreaded the thought of having to go "up the hill". How different it all is now as St Mary's Hospital.'

FROM INSTITUTION TO NHS

'It was a misjudgment of nature which led me to spend a good deal of my childhood in hospital and my story begins in 1938, before the outbreak of the Second World War.

I was my parents' first child and was born with congenital deformities to both my hands and feet. There was a great deal of prejudice then, and my parents found it difficult to cope with the pressures put upon them from people outside the family circle, who lacked both sympathy and sensitivity. I could not have been out of my cradle before medical help was sought, and help then had to be paid for. My father, through the family doctor, was put in touch with a fund administered by the County of Kent Public Health Authority, who ran the Orthopaedic Scheme for the Institutional Treatment of Crippled Children. Through this scheme, it was arranged that I was to go to the Queen Alexandra Hospital at Swanley, which had an annex for children with orthopaedic problems and was linked with St Bartholomew's (Bart's) London.

Swanley was no place for a children's hospital as it was an ideal target for bombardment during the war, so the hospital, along with the staff, was evacuated in 1940 to Stockwood House, Luton, and it was there that I was sent in 1941 at the age of two and a half years. There were no facilities there for surgery so all operations were carried out at the main Luton general hospital. The anaesthetics used then were primitive, and memories of the gas mask, the foul smelling gas and the fear of being put to sleep, haunted me for many years. At the age of five years I was sent home to Kent, because there were no facilities at the hospital for education, having had five operations which were insignificant and my medical records read, "There is no improvement to her condition".

I had not been home many weeks before Dad was consulting the doctor and I realised that my hospital days were not over. There was great excitement, Dad was talking of a revolutionary new treatment, that of plastic surgery. One day found Dad and me on our way to Harley Street to see the renowned plastic surgeon Archibald McIndoe. The consultation did not take long. His entourage of students, all eager to learn his skills, was hanging on every word. What was a problem to me was a challenge to him. He hadn't tackled anything like this before but he could see no difficulties and it was arranged that I would be sent for as soon as a bed became available. Three months after the end of the war, one sunny day in late November, my appointment came, and under the same scheme that had taken me to Luton I was now on my way to The Queen Victoria Hospital, East Grinstead.

I will always remember that day, Dad full of enthusiasm and me with trepidation. We travelled by taxi because the hospital was difficult to reach from my home in the heart of Kent. We walked up the driveway of the hospital, and we could see the asp, the symbol of healing, twining up the staff, shining golden in the winter sunlight. As we continued we met badly injured airmen coming towards us. Those who could walk, pushed in wheelchairs those who could not. Some of them were so swathed in bandages that we could hardly see that there was a human being underneath. We fell silent at the sight of them and with heads bowed we continued to the doorway. So this was the war, I thought, as we entered the hospital.

My first days were spent on tests and it was here that I had my first x-ray. There were blood tests, and a complete record of how my deformities looked was recorded with photography. For the first time it was established that the bone structure of my hands was intact and fingers could be formed. I remember little of the actual operation now, apart from the anaesthetic which held the same terror. A kindly anaesthetist told me a story while it was administered, but I was not fooled. I went home six weeks later with the first incision made. Even then, as young as I was, I went home with hope in my heart.

I regularly attended the orthopaedic clinic at the Ashford Hospital, but another visit to East Grinstead was not forthcoming. I was caught up in the system, although I did not realize it then. The government was introducing a National Health Service. My father was becoming increasingly agitated and letters were being sent, and in due course at the age of ten and a half I was back again for my next session.

There was a marked difference under the National Health Service, the obvious one being that the hospital was crowded. Surgery had come to the masses. There was a small school for lessons which we had to attend, if well enough. There was also a great improvement in anaesthetics; we were given the modern equivalent of the pre-med, which was supposed to relax us, but it wasn't going to fool this veteran.

My last visit was at the age of 13. By that time the National Health Service was well established. A more sympathetic approach was adopted. Therapy was introduced and we were encouraged to take up some form of recreation such as knitting, soft toy making and sewing. I was even allowed to go to the cinema with the older girls, down to the town of East Grinstead, a form of therapy begun

81

by Archibald McIndoe, who believed that, despite their injuries, the badly burned airmen had to be accepted back into society. Counselling for children was still a long way off but when I left hospital the surgeon did come and see me. For the first time I was asked how I felt about my hands, and whether I was pleased with the results. I was told that I could go back when I was older and have cosmetic surgery to make my hands look neater. I never went back. I was so overcome with emotion that I could barely mumble a thank you.'

THE MASS X-RAY

'From time to time, I think about once a year, the Mass Miniature Radiography van used to visit local towns and factories. The adult public was invited to have a chest x-ray without being referred by a doctor. The miniature films were taken without the examinees having to undress or wait around for them to be developed, and the system was very cheap. If anything abnormal was found on the small film, the person was recalled for a full-sized one, and referred to the Chest Clinic for advice and treatment.

It frequently meant that disease was caught at an early stage before too much lung damage occurred, and should it be diagnosed as TB, before the infection was spread to others. Once the drugs were available to treat TB – sometime in the early 1950s – the patients' recoveries were miraculous.

I worked as a radiographer at Keycol Hill Hospital, Sittingbourne, from 1954–59. The majority of the patients were TB cases, although one ward used to deal with other infectious diseases. A short time before I started there, they had opened an outpatient clinic for all types of chest conditions, and it was my job to take the x-rays the Chest Physician required. The x-ray machine was a secondhand one that had been used previously at Lenham Sanatorium. The valves and transformer were contained in a beautiful polished, wooden cabinet. There was a pull-switch, like you'd use to turn a bathroom light on, that made the change-over when you wanted to use the machine in a different mode. On a modern set you'd just press a button, but this old unit turned out very good pictures.

The in-patients, in particular, were x-rayed quite frequently to monitor their progress, and there was time to talk to them. They became almost like friends rather than patients. Some of the treatment consisted of keeping a diseased lung at rest by compressing it with air, either pumped between the lung and chest wall, or into the abdominal cavity. These people had to be checked every week and their air topped up if necessary. The Chest Physician would look at them in a darkened room on the x-ray fluorescent screen. It only took a few seconds each. We would take all the men together and then all the women. One week one of the men came in his kilt. We weren't sure whether he should line up with the chaps or the girls!

Occasionally we'd have a patient admitted who was seriously ill. I remember one young woman who looked like somebody out of Belsen, she was so thin. She had to be brought from the ward to be x-rayed on a stretcher, she was so weak, but once she was on the anti-TB drugs she soon made progress. In the whole five years I worked there I only remember one death from TB.

The Mass Miniature Radiography vans were disbanded several years ago when the incidence of TB declined. Towards the end of the time, we were picking up more cases of lung cancer and other chest diseases. The population has for some years now been vaccinated with BCG against TB as teenagers, and this has no doubt helped to almost stamp it out, as well as better living conditions etc.

Once I read in a women's magazine a letter from "Worried Blue-Eyes", "Is it true that if you kiss a boy when you have a period you will get TB?" What a good thing the answer is, "No".'

THE DISTRICT NURSE

'Life as a District Nurse did not seem to be all it was cracked up to be, but once I had broken away from hospital life I decided I wanted to branch out on my own, and applied to the Queen's Institute of District Nursing (now called Community Nursing Sisters). At Reading I was delighted to be accepted and soon got into the swing of it. I started the training in May 1954 for four months – trainees without midwifery did the course in six months. My reason for choosing Reading was that I knew the area well – thus being unlikely to get lost.

My first few days were spent going round and being shown the ropes by a supervisor, a Senior Nurse, of how the work was carried out and having to, where necessary, improvise, making do with whatever was available in the house we were visiting. The first visit we made was to a little old lady, who agreed to admit she was well over 80 years, living in the most appalling condition in a very damp, dark basement. We were constantly sworn at by a very scrawny, ancient parrot, who obviously objected to us being there.

As time went by, I was let loose on my own, complete with nursing bag strapped to the carrier on my bicycle and carrying dressings, instruments etc. Whereas in hospital everything is at hand, we had to improvise as best we could. We managed in most houses to get a lidded tin or firm-fitting lidded Pyrex to bake the dressings and swabs in – these containers had to be lined with thick white paper. Dressings were cut, hopefully by the relatives, folded, packed in whatever container we found and baked at Regulo Four, top shelf in the oven for 20 minutes. Sometimes they got a bit "caught". For instruments we often had to delve in some unused cupboard to find saucers and cracked cups with no handles, and on these we would place our instruments for boiling in a saucepan on the cooker. On more than one occasion I have lifted the pan off the cooker and drained it, only to find I had drained the potatoes!

Two years after training and passing exams I sadly left Reading and, with luck on my side, discovered there was a vacancy for a trained District Nurse in the area where I was going to live in Kent. I applied for the post, was accepted and met my new colleagues. I was one of four nurses. I had my own set "district" and would meet the same people each day on their way to work. It took some time to get any more than a nod from them in answer to my "Good Morning". Any new work was phoned into the District Nurses' office by the GP, hospital or even the patients themselves. We were allowed to visit the latter on two or at the most three visits without the blessing of the doctor, provided it was something fairly simple. Any doubt about a patient then a referral would be made. Having one's own area the patients and relatives soon got to know "the Nurse" and treated her like a friend and confidante.

As time went by the Queen's District Nurses were absorbed by the Ministry of Health – Districts were no more and general practice attachment introduced. We were then responsible for all the patients requiring care of one, perhaps two, general practitioners. In many ways it was better, but I missed my set area greatly. All equipment was readily available on loan to the patients and also a laundry service was brought in. Incontinence sheets were a wonderful innovation – thus doing away with the red rubber sheets. We delivered these if there was no one available to collect them. One snowy winter's day I was called to see a very small elderly man who had "water trouble". Story had it that he was a retired dentist and when he was still in practice he had to stand on a box to reach the mouth he was treating. I duly called on him, only to find that his family had put nearly all the absorbent Inco sheets across the polished hall so the parquet flooring did not suffer from wet feet trampling across. I very tactfully informed the wife that was not what the sheets were intended for!'

CHILDHOOD & SCHOOLDAYS

TOWN, COAST AND COUNTRY CHILDHOODS

Whether they grew up on town streets, in village lanes or by the sea, yesterday's children had a freedom to wander and explore that is sadly denied to later generations. Happy days, yet they were also a time of early responsibility for some children.

TEA WITH THE ARCHBISHOP

'I was one of nine children, born in an attic without any running water or electricity, with only candles to see by. How did they manage in those days? This was before the First World War and my family lived in Canterbury where my parents were caretakers for over 50 years at Mowells, the solicitors, in Castle Street.

I had a very interesting life with quite a lot of hard work. My father had to sweep the offices each morning and as we children reached the age of seven, we had to follow him round with a duster, carefully so as not to displace any papers. Another of my jobs before I went to school was to polish all the brass on the lovely front door. I also had to whiten the step, then put on a clean white pinafore and be ready to open the door at 8.15 am for Mr Mowell, who travelled from Dover every day.

I went to the city council school half a mile from where we lived, where all my brothers and sisters had gone. I wore black stockings and button-up boots, a long blue skirt with a white blouse and a pinafore (handed down, no doubt). After school we all had jobs allotted to us. I had to go to the dairy in St Margaret's Street, but unfortunately, when I saw the men rolling the barrels down into the cellar at the pub, my thoughts wandered and I broke a few jugs tripping over. Needless to say, that job did not last long!

My father also worked for the Archbishop of Canterbury (five of them in all), as an odd job man. My friend and I had many happy hours in the courtyard of the Palace, where we learned to ride a bike (no traffic then). We also played in the big hall. I well remember the Christmas parties at the Archbishop's Palace. We children were dressed in our Sunday best, not daring to move, as we were taken to the staff Christmas party. There was a lovely tree with presents for everyone, including the grown ups. We had tea with, and served by,

His Grace and his wife. Then afterwards we all went to the chapel and His Grace took a short service. They were days I remember with love and respect.'

HARD TIMES

'Until I was 16 we lived in Dover, and when my father returned from the First World War he found himself out of work for four years.

Times were very hard. With hardly any money, he received a handout of food vouchers, but the food obtained on them was of poor quality. Father tramped the countryside doing farm work where he could, and repairing a few shoes. His own boots had soles like jigsaw puzzles, being made up of scraps of left over leather.

Dad obtained a magic lantern; he made two bench seats, and once a week the kitchen was filled with children to see slides of funny faces etc. It was very noisy but great fun.

On Sunday mornings after Sunday school, he took my two brothers and me, plus four or five other children, on the top of the tram car to Snargate Street. We went up the Grand Shaft (a winding staircase) to the Western Heights to see the soldiers come out of church and follow the band. We always insisted on going down all the steps to the tram car, on top again, and home for dinner.

We were very poor, but Mum and Day played cards and games with us on the kitchen table, and taught us skills. I could sew at three years of age and knitted on four needles at four and a half. On Saturdays, each one of the children were individually given cooking instructions, so that the three of us were able to cook dinner. What a happy and wonderful childhood we had, with loving and caring parents.'

CHILDHOOD IN BRABOURNE

'My earliest memories of Brabourne are from under the hood of a pram, squeezed in beside my baby brother so that my elder sister could sit at the other end. I remember tall waving trees, almost meeting overhead and, after dark, searchlights in the sky, so this must have been pre-1919.

Our roads were stony and nearly always muddy. There were ditches at the side to drain away the water. In spring we gathered primroses, violets and milkmaids from these mossy spots. There were ponds at the foot of hills too. These took surplus water and waggoners let their horses drink here on the way to the fields or the local forge, which was always busy.

We played in the garden and orchard where the yearly delivery of 25 fire-lighting faggots were stacked to enable us to squeeze between them as a play-house. The unused brick-floored stable had the stalls removed and this was our "cottage" to play in when it was wet.

Nearby Subdown and Moors Woods were favourite summer playgrounds, with kingcups and anemones in Subdown, in a fairly deep stream, but the attraction in Moors Wood was the two streams, both springs trickling from the banks of the field, the start of tributaries of the river Stour. They were clear and shallow, rippling over stones, just waiting to be dammed. A handbell rung from home called us to meals.

Entertainments were in the school, always arranged when the moon was at its best. A concert needed a stage, erected out of school hours. For a whist drive a handcart called at homes en route, late afternoon, to collect small tables and any suitable chairs. As our parents were always involved in these activities we went too, enjoying the excitement until after refreshments when we three were put to sleep on the floor of the small room where the refreshments were prepared, on a palliasse (a half-sized straw mattress). At the end of the event this was transferred to the handcart and we, still asleep, were trundled home.'

SHEER HEAVEN

'My mother came from Kent, and every summer from 1936–1954, except for the war years, my sister and I travelled from Scotland with our parents to spend two or three weeks with our grandparents who lived near the parish church in Wingham, near Canterbury. For two small girls from Glasgow the summer sights, sounds and smells of a Kentish garden were sheer heaven. The sun seemed to shine always, and the sounds of bumble bees, grass being mown, and the church bells (which were right next door) epitomised those holidays for me. We spent almost all the time in the garden which consisted of just under two acres. A hen house in the orchard drew us like a magnet. We determined to sit inside it and wait to see a hen lay an egg. After an hour or so, one obliged, and we were satisfied. It wasn't till we started itching and coming up in little red spots that we realized there were other inhabitants of the house beside hens. Those hen lice gave us an uncomfortable night, and we had scant sympathy from the adults.

Hide and seek was the favourite game; crouching in the cool feathery rows of August asparagus, or up in the mulberry tree time stood still. Mulberries were picked by the bucketload, and we had to put on our bathing suits for the job. When it was done our purple-stained bodies were thoroughly scrubbed in the bath before we were allowed to do anything else.

My aunt gave me, aged 14, my first driving lesson in a Morris 8, along a small country road bounded by a high bank on one side and a steep drop into a hop garden on the other. How the little car jerked and leapt along as I struggled with clutch and accelerator. We never expected to meet another vehicle then, not even a bike, and indeed we saw nothing but a farm cat perched on a gate post.

Richborough Castle was the place I always chose for my birthday picnic, because it was such a good place for climbing about on, and rolling down the grassy banks until we were so dizzy we couldn't stand up. The castle wasn't fenced in then; nobody really bothered about it, it was just there and you could come and go as you pleased.

Sandwich Bay was a favourite place where we swam and dug huge forts and moats with grandfather's garden spade – this was serious digging, with all the uncles and aunts and cousins joining in while Granny sat on a rug, guarding the picnic and our clothes. She *always* wore a hat. After the picnic we would hunt for shells, particularly cowries, which were always found in a long wavy strand of flotsam where fine shingle ended and the real sand began. They are no longer to be found – pollution has killed them off. The beach always had large lumps of oil on it which transferred unfailingly to our shoes and socks.'

THE ELDEST CHILD

'For my birthday present one year I received a pair of ankle socks and a sixpenny piece. I cannot recall birthday parties for any of my family. I went to birthday parties but said afterwards that I had "hated" it. I believe I was envious because of never having had one. Jelly was always eaten with bread and butter – I don't know why.

As eldest child I was put in charge of the others and always got the blame if they did wrong or got dirty. I got to be like a little old woman by the age of ten. All eldest children of large families were treated like this.

I wore navy blue serge gym-slips with box pleats to school. On Friday evenings I had to tack-stitch the pleats in place so that Mother could scrub gently down the length of the garment with a soapy nailbrush to remove dirt, then she would press it with a damp rag under a flat-iron heated on the range cooker. The tacking stayed in till the last minute on Monday mornings.

As a member of a large family, I never had a whole apple/orange/ chocolate bar, always a part – half an apple usually, quarter of an orange and two or four squares of chocolate. I longed to have a whole Mars bar!

My cousin died of pneumonia aged five years. I was about eight and no one told me she had died; death was seldom talked about and when it was, it was said that so-and-so had "passed away". When my cousin died, several weeks passed before I asked where Heather was – "She is ill and has gone to hospital to be made better." I got this reply several times and then gave up asking. It left me with a fear of hospital – which once it had got you, kept you forever.

We were brought up to collect the bounty of nature, regardless of the time of year. Wood had to be brought home on every walk, winter and summer, for kindling – and there were chestnuts, cobnuts, sloes, blackberries, crab apples, windfalls in orchards, sometimes crawling with wasps. Nothing was passed by and, if a tree had blown down, a couple of us would drag home what branches we could – to be praised by Mother.'

AT SANDWICH WITH GRANMA

'My grandmother, Annie Pittock, was widowed in 1932. I spent my holidays with her. When I was five or six years old I became the May Queen of Sandwich and was pulled along on a sort of cart with a maypole which the children danced around. Once a year a carnival was held in the cattle market and I remember being dressed up in fancy dress for the occasion and having raspberry juice put on my face because make-up was frowned upon.

My grandmother was a very proud lady. She always wore long skirts, either black or navy blue, summer and winter, with a three-quarter length jacket, white or cream blouse and, of course, a hat. I never saw her in a dress or any other colour. She wore long clothes and black stockings until the day she died in 1958 at about 86 years of age.

Granma was a widow for 26 years. During the war her widow's pension was ten shillings per week; her rent was seven shillings and sixpence. She never asked for assistance, people didn't in those days, they were too proud, and because of this she took in washing. I used to go round the town and help her collect the dirty washing from business people. Granma always looked upon these people as gentry.

The washing was hung out in the yard in all weathers. Sometimes it was bitterly cold and her hands were all crippled up with rheumatism, but she never complained. The ironing was done in the evening on a large kitchen table by oil lamp. Nobody else was allowed to touch the clothes. The kitchen range would be roaring away, the flat irons all at the ready. Granma would test them on a piece of blanket before commencing to iron. I can remember she had a tiny iron which was oval and like glass underneath, to polish the gentlemen's white starched collars. When completed everything was laid out in the best room in piles, then priced, parcelled up in brown paper and string, and delivered by Granma which entailed many trips. I used to help her sometimes, and at the end of the week she would give me one shilling and sixpence, a bottle of red sauce (a special treat) and a Mickey Mouse comic.

My grandmother fed me very well. The table was always laid with a white damask linen starched tablecloth and everything was just so; this came from Granma being in service as a girl in the big house facing the Bell Hotel. I often think of her with fond admiration; how did she ever manage? She had a hard side to her though. If I was naughty she would lock me in the larder in the dark, all the evening sometimes. I could see her ironing through a crack in the woodwork. I would call out, "Let me out, I will tell my parents." That really made her laugh but she wouldn't open the door. I believed as I got older that perhaps she only did it for devilment.'

GROWING UP IN RAMSGATE

'One of my earliest recollections is of being taken to the train and sitting in a big seat in the guard's van ready for the journey to Herne Bay from Ramsgate – a big adventure for a two and a half year old. The station at that time was on the sea front and I was allowed to travel in the care of the guard to be met by my grandmother.

We grew up in Ramsgate in the 1930s; although times were hard and there was little money, we had happy times. Playing in our street, we had the skipping season, hopscotch, whip and top, five stones, hide and seek and sardines, all in turn. After school we were not allowed to go out in school clothes; they were to be kept "nice". Although we had a Sunday set of clothes, which were for going to church and Sunday school, I don't recall that we had a lot.

My mother recounted a story of the apprentice boys who came to her home for meals. No doubt they slept in the Smack Boys' Home by the harbour. At Christmas I imagine they got a bit extra but everyone ate in the living room and, as my mother was one of 13, it must have been a tight squeeze.

In the summer, bedrooms were let to visitors, mostly from London. Some brought their own food which my mother cooked. For others she cooked breakfast and evening meals. It was my job to wait on the holidaymakers. We got quite friendly with some who came year after year and only the outbreak of war stopped the visits.

When I was old enough I had a job in the school holidays, helping in a fish shop where cooked meals were served and jellied and stewed eels. I could never face an eel!

As I was the eldest in our road I was delegated to take out the younger children. We would set off to walk out to Pegwell and enjoy the field of buttercups and beach. Other times we would walk to Dumpton Woods where we picked elderberries. The pram would be full and the children had to walk home. One of the neighbours made elderberry wine, which she made in a huge cask in her kitchen and sold for a shilling a bottle in the winter. Her husband fished for long-shore herrings which they smoked in the garden.

The highlight of the year was Christmas. We made paper chains which were hung up. We were allowed in the parlour and stuck cottonwool on the overmantel mirror to read "Happy Xmas". My mother baked and iced the cake, which was put in there. We also attended the Sunday school parties and the "Druids", my father being a member. At this time we had half an orange and half an egg – what a treat! When my father was out of work, my grandmother sent us a sixpenny postal order, which enabled them to get a meal, once a week.'

LIFE ON THE ROAD

'My brother, sister and I were born at Brenzett and lived along Ashford Road just past the church. My father drove a steam engine and went ploughing. I saw him once – another driver was one side of the field and my father the other and the plough went to and fro on a belt across the field. My mother used to work in the fields, walking almost to Appledore station across the fields near the railway line, thistle-spudding across the field from nine to four then walking home. She pushed her bicycle with my sister, who was the youngest, in the basket on the carrier, my brother on a piece of wood across the frame with a cushion on it and me on the saddle, though when old enough I had to walk. She also walked almost into Old Romney and cut turnip seed. We used to wait at the farm with several other children for the man who used the horse to hook on to the bodge (a large wooden box) which slid on runners. We had a very bumpy ride out to where the women were. When it was filled up we ran behind for another ride; we did this all day long. Then she walked over the road from our house to an orchard picking cherries, plums, damsons, apples and pears, up and down long ladders all day long.

Every Saturday morning my sister and I walked past the school just along the Brookland Road to a bungalow where we learned

92

dancing. Two sisters about 13 and 14 taught us while their elderly mother played the piano. I can't remember how much it cost. I learnt the Charleston, my sister started ballet. We also did ballroom dancing, and every now and again we would perform of a Friday evening at the hut. My mother would leave work early those days and call at the school with brush, comb and curling rags and we would have our hair done in the lobby. My sister and I had long hair which was rolled into curling rags every night – very uncomfortable to sleep on but we got used to it.

My father changed his work and drove a steam roller mending roads, always away. He would get up about 2.30 am on Monday mornings and have breakfast. My mother would pack him two large, long meat and potato pies and two large cakes, which she cooked Sundays. He also took a loaf, butter, cheese and home-made jam, tea and a little milk to last until Monday when he would buy fresh. He would leave about three and cycle to where he was working – Heathfield, Haywards Heath, Uckfield and Cuckfield, Sussex were some places. He had to get the steam engine fire lit and enough steam up to start work by seven. He would be home Saturday tea time.

Two months before my tenth birthday our parents decided they had had enough of living apart so some furniture was sold and the rest stored at a friend's. A tin trunk and three large wooden boxes, the feather beds, bed linen and pots and pans were packed to take with us. All was loaded up with just our dolls, books, wax crayons, slate and pencil, a ball each and my brother's motors etc. We waved our friends goodbye one Friday soon after tea, my brother and I in the back of the van on the bed linen, my mother and sister in the front; off we went to Hoo, near Rochester. What a surprise when we arrived. Our home was a dull red caravan, with no springs, four iron wheels and a corrugated rounded roof which echoed every time it hailed or rained.

We were in Kent, Sussex, Surrey, Hampshire and Berkshire. We were by roadsides, in farmyards, woods, Biddenden railway station and once in an airfield. We had to go to school everywhere we stayed in four years. We went to 51 schools, sometimes twice and three times. We never stayed away, only when travelling. We would arrive one day and the next we were off to school, our mother pushing her bicycle and timing us to arrive home at the end of the day. Woe betide us if we were late – no going out to play.

We were always taught not to talk to strangers. We were coming home from one school, a long walk one summer, when the "Stop me and buy one" Walls ice cream tricycle stopped. The man called us, we hesitated, then remembered we had had an iced lolly on a stick on the Saturday. He gave us a block of strawberry and vanilla that was melting so he couldn't sell it. We never ran so fast home!

Every winter morning we had porridge with brown sugar and butter, also bread and butter and marmalade before we left for school. We all had a spoonful of cod liver oil and malt, and never had a cold. When we arrived home there was always a basin of hot soup, meat and vegetables, and also a pudding, sometimes sponge, suet pudding and treacle, spotted dick or fruit pie and custard. We went to Sunday school every week and during summer had an early tea and went for long walks, stopping for lemonade and crisps before going home to bed.

I had a happy childhood but would never recommend it for school children unless they liked strangers – there was nothing worse than standing by a headmaster/mistress and seeing lots of strange children's eyes on us while our mother gave them our names, standards (not class or grade), address, last school and why we left. We were separated; my sister and I played together but the boys had a separate playground and we couldn't wait until the end of the day when we could walk home together.'

A SLEEPY LITTLE VILLAGE

'I was born in the early 1920s in Headcorn, a sleepy little village in the Weald of Kent, number three in a family of four children. Father was a poultry farmer in the days when the birds ran about free as the wind – no loathsome factory farms or battery cages then. As well as the flocks of chickens we kept turkeys, geese and bantams, also our much-loved pony, lots of cats and a dog and numerous pet rabbits. Our house stood in eight acres of land which included two orchards and two lawns – one large enough to play tennis or croquet, or even a slightly restricted game of cricket! Remembering my two sons' childhood in a small town garden with just two cats I often think how very lucky we were – but childlike we took it all for granted and often grumbled about the jobs we had to do to help out on the farm.

For a long time we had no gas, electricity or running water. Every morning Father would fetch our drinking water from the "big house" about half a mile away, but water for washing and all other purposes was brought up in buckets from one of our four ponds. Our privy (or toilet) was in the garden, a pretty little hut covered in honeysuckle and pink rambler roses, very picturesque in summer, but on dark winter nights with snow and ice and the wind whistling it was *hell*! We used to "bottle it" until the last moment and then put on coats and scarves and make a dash for it! Saturday was the worst day as

94

Innocent days of freedom and sunshine in the 1950s. A group of children playing by the river Stour at Wye stop to chat to the local carrier, John Coulter.

Mother always gave us a dose of syrup of figs on Friday nights – I need say no more.

We lived in a quiet lane which in those days was on the outskirts of Headcorn, quite a long way from the "village", which is what we called the main street where the shops, churches etc were. Nearly everything was delivered to the house by cheerful tradesmen who whistled, sang and joked with us children.

About once a month Mother would take us to the "village". I remember getting as excited about this as today's children would if taken to London! Our main object was to pay the monthly bills, but we would visit each shop in turn or if we were not actually going in, would peer into it, noses pressed against the glass. One of the sweet shops had its window full of little saucers, with a few unwrapped sweets on each – the fact that in the summer flies buzzed happily over the sweets did nothing to detract from its fascination for me. In the grocer's, we watched the jolly white-coated man patting the butter into shapes with butter-pats, and putting attractive pictures on them. If he was not too busy he would unlock the door of his China Department and show us a rich Aladdin's cave where tea pots, vases and plates, etc. were laid out carefully on the shelves. After Mother had made her selection, even if it was only a couple of items, it would be carefully wrapped and delivered the next day.

When I look at the enormous ploughed fields with very few hedges that are part of modern intensive farming, I think back to the fields and meadows that surrounded my home as a child – Horse-daisy Meadow that was one mass of tall white daisies right through the summer; Bluebell Wood, carpeted with blue every spring; Cowslip Copse; and the hedges where birds nested every year and ditches where yellow primroses and bluey-white milkmaids grew in profusion. At the bottom of our fields were four ponds where as children we spent many happy hours fishing for tiddlers, looking for tadpoles, frogs, newts and water-boatmen and watching the dragon-flies skim over the water. Moorhens nested in the reeds and if we kept very quiet we often saw the gorgeous blue-green flash of a kingfisher. Every spring pussy-willows bloomed round the edges of the ponds and by summer the ponds were covered with water lilies and golden kingcups.

As soon as I started school I was given one penny a week pocket money. Oh! What wealth! My sister used to bring the penny when she came to meet me on Friday afternoons and we went straight to the village sweet shop where I always purchased a pennyworth of Sharp's choc toffees. I soon learned that if the owner of the shop was serving he only weighed me four toffees for my penny, but if Kate, his jolly assistant, was there I would get five. If my sister was not meeting one of her many boyfriends I would persuade her to wait outside the shop until Kate was serving! That penny was very precious!'

REMEMBER THE FLOOD?

'I lay there in the big double bed, my rubber ring tucked under one arm, my favourite doll and swimming hat held tightly in the other. I was nine years old, not yet able to swim, absolutely terrified but ready for the worst! I have to smile and relate this story when the subject of the "big flood of the 1950s" comes up in conversation, because lying there in that big bed is one of the most vivid memories I have of that terrifying time.

Other memories are of my dear Aunty, who slept downstairs, being woken by the wall-plug by her bed going "pop". She swung her feet out of bed into water, ankle deep. Of my sister wading through the house with water up to her waist, rescuing cats and handing a bucket of coal and a kettle of water and the tea tray up to us on the stairs. Of one of the cats sailing by on a rug, so terrified and wet, to be plucked to safety. Of lighting the fire in my bedroom and boiling the kettle for "a nice cup of tea", and making toast. How grateful we were that my Aunty always stuck to her wartime routine of getting everything ready for the next day before going to bed.

When daylight finally came, the water was almost up to the ceilings downstairs. We had a verandah on the front of the house and I shall never forget the sight of Nurse Jones clambering out of a rowing boat and onto the verandah. My Aunty had to have two injections a day and our lovely nurse was not going to let her down.

Late that day the long boat came down our street and collected us all. I don't remember much of that trip except I was wearing pyjamas under three jumpers and two shirts, topped with a coat, hat and wellies. There wasn't room for suitcases!

It was a few days before the water went and my last memory brings the biggest smile – as we walked back into the devastation of our home I was told to tread carefully because of the inches of slimy mud covering everything. What did I do? One step inside, my toes came up and I landed on my bottom in all that horrid mud!'

RICH AND POOR

Childhood experiences could be so different, from the safety and security of a well to do upbringing, to the poverty of a farm labourer's family.

I WAS 'NANNY-BROUGHT-UP'

'I was born in 1910, the youngest of a family of nine – seven boys and two girls, my sister being the second eldest and 16 years older than me.

There was no car in my early years, but we all had bicycles from an early age, and my parents had a carriage and "pair" until the First World War, when the horses were commandeered for war service. I remember the lovely smell of horse and leather, and the flip-flap sound of the reins on the polished chestnut backs of the horses.

There was also no radio or television, of course, and we had to make our own amusements. We all loved games of every kind, and out of doors played hopscotch, touch wood, feet-off-the-ground, grandfather's footsteps, two-and-threes, etc. On our daily walks we invariably took either a hoop (with a wooden stick for me, but an envied iron one for the boys, with a hook at the end), a skipping rope, a scooter, or (in my case) a doll's pram. Balls were only allowed in the park, not on roadside pavements. In the 1920s the bouncing pogo stick was invented, and some of my school friends bounced to school on them, until someone broke a leg and they were banned. To my regret, I was never allowed one.

In 1916 a family Games Club was formed, and run with businesslike efficiency; a committee was chosen, and President, Vice-President, Captain, Secretary, Treasurer and Handicapper appointed, and regular committee and general meetings took place. A tie was worn, in the club colours of blue, green and grey, and a monthly magazine was produced and bound annually by different members (I have them still). We played tennis, badminton, ping-pong (table tennis), croquet, billiards, chess and draughts; cups were presented at annual tournaments, and winners' names painted on boards round the billiard room walls. A few close relations and friends were also allowed to join, and in the Christmas holidays we played hockey matches against the school attended in succession by my sister, three of my brothers and myself.

I was "Nanny-brought-up", and my early years were spent mostly in the nursery with my youngest brothers until they went to school. The rocking horse, given to my eldest brother in 1892, is now in our hall; there was a large dolls' house and a toy cupboard full of toy soldiers, Lott's and Tudor building bricks, plasticine, slates and chalks, paintboxes and jigsaw puzzles, and a fascinating kaleidoscope.

I loved drawing and painting, and wrote and illustrated a "magazine" called "Monthly Nursery Notes", for Nanny's benefit. Nanny came when my eldest brother was a month old, in 1892, and gave her unstinting care to all of us, and we loved her dearly and accepted her discipline happily. (When she came to my mother in 1892 her wages were £18 per annum, and she stayed until my mother's death 54 years later.)

My mother taught me to read by the age of six, and from then on I was accused of being a "bookworm". Like today's children, we had our comics; *Rainbow* and *Tiger Tim's Weekly*, later *Schoolgirls' Own*, *My Magazine* (edited by Arthur Mee, of the *Children's Encyclopaedia*), and *The Children's Newspaper*.

My father, who was a great linguist, tried to instil into us his own love of languages; each morning we visited him in his dressing room, and had to read a text for the day from a book which gave it in about seven or eight languages. On Sundays after breakfast he came to the nursery, and read aloud to us from Longfellow's *Hiawatha*, *The Psalm of Life*, etc and several of Shakespeare's plays. After Sunday lunch (at which we joined the adults for dessert), "Pater" (never Dad or Daddy) would get us to read in turn from *Gulliver's Travels* in French, and *A Thousand and One Nights* in Spanish, translating the passage (if we could!) as we went.

On weekday evenings we were taken down to spend an hour or two with Mother (again, never Mummy). Sometimes she would make lovely little villages of cardboard, with tiny thatched cottages and farms, and a village church, delicately painted in watercolours; alternatively we were shown how to make lavender bags, cross-stitch kettleholders, pincushions, and penwipers in the form of red-cloaked witches, made from the wishbones of chickens! When melons were in season, their pips were dried and we threaded them to make necklaces. All these could be sold at Mother's frequent charity bazaars and sales of work.

Sunday evenings, however, were dedicated to the family orchestra. We all learnt at least one musical instrument, and the orchestra consisted of piano (Mother), sometimes organ (there was a small chamber organ which my sister played), three violins, viola, and two cellos; until I started learning the violin at the age of seven I was allowed the triangle! My father made a very appreciative and not too critical audience.

Clothes have changed a lot since those days, thank goodness! How I hated those woollen combinations, black woollen stockings, liberty bodices, buttoned boots and gaiters; also the Saturday task of threading pink or blue ribbon through the holes of my broderie anglaise-edged drawers. Clothes for parties – and later on, dances – were much more fun then, whether lovely taffeta, crepe-de-chine or fine georgette creations (often made by Nanny), or exciting fancy-dresses which she also produced on her old chainstitch machine. Children's parties might be simple affairs of Blind Man's Buff, Hunt-the-slipper, Turn the Trencher, General Post, etc, or special entertainers might be hired, with marionettes, Punch and Judy, or a conjuror. Later there were proper dances, with small programmes with pencils attached by a silk cord, which one hoped to get filled with the initials of one's future partners – the supper dance, one hoped, with one's best boy friend.'

NO SHOES ON OUR FEET

'I was born at Broad Oak, Sturry, in 1918, the third daughter. My father was a farm labourer. Went to Sturry school with my sisters, when I was three years old.

My parents moved to Denstroude, Blean (I was four then). Moved on an old waggon. There was no gas or electric, no water laid on, it was pulled up from the well. Old open fireplace with the oven. The old copper was lit for washing days. Boil up the washing, rinse out and put through the mangle. Ironing with flat irons heated on the front of the fire, jolly hard work for mums.

We went to Dunkirk school. Had to walk. Old sand roads. Being poor, no shoes on our feet at times. We had to take our dinner. The master would tell us to bring cocoa and sugar so they could make us a drink at dinner time. In those days there were a lot of children in the village. Sometimes they had an old van to take us in the winter, didn't go very well. Get in and it would run back down the hill, so we had to push it back up. 'Course being kids, we loved that – made us late for school.

Our toys were a wooden hoop, whip and top, hopscotch and skipping ropes. Never had radio. Living on a farm we had pets, a few chickens so we got eggs, and tame rabbits. Dad used to snare the wild rabbits so we had them to eat. We used to like watching the steam ploughs. Two engines, one at each end of the field, pulling the plough across. We were taken to Canterbury fair sometimes, to go on the swings and have a go at the coconut shy. We would go by train from Canterbury to Whitstable for our Sunday school outing on the "Winkle Line". Boat-swings on the beach, donkey rides and had tea. Very hot summers we had then.

November 5th we made a guy. Walked for miles, a big gang of us, got a few coppers, we enjoyed it. Carol singing at Christmas, same old gang, tramped the roads up to Dunkirk, back up to Blean. I can remember when we hung our stocking up at Christmas. Lump of coal in the bottom, orange, apple and a few nuts, pencils and paper.

I know I was a bit of a dunce. My father could not read or write, so he never helped us a lot. My mum got clothes from secondhand shops as money was short (I had got a brother by now). In the school holidays we had to go hop picking. Out in the hopfields by 6.30 am. Jolly well had to work. I had the job also of walking up to Hernhill to fill the two billy cans, getting back and get them boiled. Men used to come in the fields calling "Doughnut" or "Bramley" and "Hot Fried Fish" – I know we never had any. Bread and dripping or bread and jam for us.

We also walked to Blean to Sunday school. One of the teachers who taught at the Sunday school gave me a bible, I've still got it. In June my mum went picking strawberries at 4.30 in the morning. All those jobs were done early for market. Blean school opened in 1929. All Denstroude children went. My brother was old enough to go. There were hot dinners at the school. Mother could not afford them, they were two shillings and eightpence for two, so we had to take our dinner. My brother wanted to take this in his little work basket tied round with string, but he would always swing it round and round. At dinner time the children who took dinners had to sit together. When my brother opened it, it was breadcrumbs and lumps of lard! It made me cry. We had free dinners for a while after that.

My mum had two more children, another girl and boy. I was ten years old when my brother was born. My grannie and grandad lived at Blean; in her day she had 24 children. One of my uncles mended our boots. Leave them on the way to school, call for them on the way home. I got a little better at school. Loved singing songs (was in the school concert at times) and netball and softball matches, played away sometimes.

My sister was in service at Whitstable. I remember she was ill, came home for a week. I was twelve years old, my mother sent me to do her job to keep it open for my sister. I was very afraid. Had to do housework and washing up. The housekeeper I didn't like. I had to work hard, peel veg's ready for meal. I didn't see much of it. I remember when she was making plum jam, gave me the stones to suck, also the rind of the bacon. I told her my mum was poor but she didn't do that to us.

Time went on and I left school at 14 years. Mother got me a job, I was sleeping out in service at 14½ years. Didn't like it, had to stay, never allowed to go home. I was there for three years, left and got this other job. Got on very well there because I had my training at the first job. Was Cook Housekeeper at 17½ years. Had one half day a week, every other Sunday afternoon. No cars then, rode a cycle everywhere, not much money – got 28 shillings a week.'

TREATS, SWEETS AND GAMES

Songs and rhymes bring back memories of happy times spent playing in the roads and lanes, when the only danger came from the occasional horse and cart or an early car. Some children also joined in organised activities, such as the Girl Guides, and later, of course, there were the delights of radio and early television to be savoured.

MUSICAL MEMORIES

'Our family were all musical – we had a wind-up HMV gramophone and many records, ranging from *Oh for the wings of a dove* to *Don't do that to the poor puss cat*. My brother and I were very fond of altering the speed on the gramophone and I am ashamed to say we fell about with laughter as we made Dame Clara Butt sing *Abide with me* very, very slowly basso profundo, then altered the speed to make her sound like Pinky and Perky – you can't do that with today's equipment! I was second to last in a family of seven and my grown-up brothers and sister would buy records of the latest hits – they came on the "Sunshine" label and cost sixpence in Woolworth's. We knew all the popular songs.

In the street we had many singing games. We played "Poor Mary sits a-weeping" and with a fine disregard for grammar chorused, "Oh Mary, what yer weeping for?" in the second verse. We knew many parodies of songs which went round like wildfire – for instance *Red Sails in the Sunset* became "Red stains on the carpet, Red stains on the knife. Oh Doctor Buck Ruxton, you murdered your wife" at the time of a famous murder – and of course parodies on carols, bawdy or scurrilous, including "Hark the herald angels sing, Mrs Simpson's pinched our King" at the time of the abdication.

Deal was woken each morning by a bugle sounding reveille from the Royal Marine School of Music. Marines played a large part in our musical life. On Sunday mornings I was taken to the barracks to watch Church Parade when the public were allowed inside the grounds. The band marched up and down making complicated marching manoeuvres whilst playing. They always played *Early one morning*, the regimental slow march, and finished with a rousing *A life on the ocean wave*. What a sight they were in their blue dress uniforms, white pith helmets and gleaming boots and instruments. The drummers sported real tiger skins and the drum major twirled his mace and threw it high into the air and caught it. At the end the Commanding Officer took the salute – how proud we were of "our" marines.

Sometimes beforehand I was taken to Matins at the Garrison Church where the sound of *Eternal father strong to save* sung by many young soldiers and accompanied by the Marines orchestra was very emotional. Once a year the public were invited to the dress rehearsal for the Royal Tournament and I can remember being moved to tears during the Sunset Ceremony when the flag was lowered and the Last Post played.

The first week in September was Regatta time – the Regattas now are but a poor shadow of the glories of my childhood. The lovely Victorian roundabout had a steam organ; it was very ornate and well endowed plaster ladies in tights banged drums and hit triangles in time to the music. I was fascinated by the perforated music roll, and the sound of the marches and waltzes, specially magical when it grew dark.

At seven years of age I went to a brand new school – South Deal Junior. The headmaster Mr Tucker took us for singing and he was not afraid to be adventurous in the choice of music. We sang songs from *Merrie England*, Shakespeare arrangements, *Nymphs and shepherds* etc and lovely songs from the *National Song Book* – I wonder if that wonderful anthology is ever used now. On Empire Day we sang *Land of our birth we pledge to thee*, *This Royal throne of Kings* and *There's a land, a dear land* and were glad to be British where *The honest poor man is as good as a King*! We always chanted our tables, starting with two-times and finishing with a triumphant "Twelve twelves are *one hundred and forty four*!" Once a week a mountainous lady called Miss Young, with her wind-up gramophone, came to teach us country dancing and the boys and girls all hummed the jolly tunes of *Gathering peascods* and *Newcastle* as we danced and clapped.

These were all the sounds which were part and parcel of my fortunate and happy childhood in Deal in the 1930s.'

GAMES WE PLAYED

'In 1917 I lived with my parents in River. All the village streets were rough flint and we children usually managed to have scabs on our knees where we had fallen over. At the bottom of our road was a ford through the river Dour and we liked to play in it. Unfortunately, after my father's demob he worked in the Co-op Stores which faced the ford and my little boyfriend's father worked in the adjoining bakehouse so we seldom had a chance to play in the river before one or other of our fathers would come and send us home. However, further along the road to Dover was a sort of ramp where the carters took their horses for a drink, so that is where we went to play. There was also an abandoned brickfield either side of Lewisham Road which was an ideal playground.

Our pocket money would be a penny a week, if we were lucky, and we would rub our noses all over the local sweetshop window before deciding which delicacy to buy. Such things as Cut Cavendish (pretend tobacco), sherbet suckers, aniseed balls at 20 a penny for large and 40 a penny for small ones, and, of course, gob stoppers. When still quite young I can remember the Marks and Spencers shop in Dover was an open-fronted place with a counter running round three sides and a roller shutter which was pulled down when the shop was closed. I think everything was one penny or less. I know we called it the Penny Bazaar. Woolworth's was always threepence or sixpence.

The games we played were very simple compared with today. We had hoops and sticks; the boys had iron hoops with a metal stick attached and the girls had wooden ones with a separate wooden stick. Of course, we girls always wanted an iron hoop as it made more noise! We also played with tops, usually peg tops, but if you were lucky you got a "window breaker". These were slightly dearer, but much more fun. I think they were about one penny and twopence each respectively.

Another game we enjoyed was Cowboys and Indians. We made our own bows and arrows, the bows being of ash, and we cut designs in the bark. The arrows were nice straight pieces of hazel.

Hopscotch was also popular, but it was a bit difficult to find a suitable place to draw our pitch, the roads and paths not being smooth surfaces. Another game was tip-cat, which involved hitting a bullet-shaped piece of wood with a stick. The shaped piece was about four inches long sharpened to points at each end, and you gave the pointed end a bang with the stick which sent it into the air and then tried to hit it with the stick. The object was to hit it further than anyone else. We also played marbles, though it was mostly the boys who played this, as they did "faggies", played with cigarette cards.

The usual types of ball games were played on the brickfield – rounders and pig in the middle being two of them, and we played skipping and jumping over the rope.

On Sundays you would find the whole family out for a country walk together, usually over the local minnis which is between River, Alkham and Temple Ewell. Sometimes for a change we would go on the tram to the western docks and walk out onto the Admiralty Pier. You would meet the same families from the villages each Sunday. Dad would have a glass of ale and the rest of the family lemonade or zolacone at a pub called The Newcastle on Ewell Minnis, if we went on a summer evening. On the way home in the dusk you could often see glow worms in the hedgerow.'

'At Northbourne in the 1930s we could play tennis in the road. There were so few cars and those there were travelled so slowly that they presented no danger.

We played diablo. We held two sticks, one in each hand, with string between to balance a large cotton reel-like contraption. The aim was to keep it moving and throw it in the air and catch it on the string again without it falling. Great skill was needed. It came in at about the same time as yo-yos but never caught on in the same way.

Amateur dramatics were the highlight of my childhood. Early on my mother took a hand and we rehearsed in our living room. We presented our efforts to local social events and fetes. Later we formed our own club using sheds as theatres, our favourite being a round chicken house with a centre "dropping" board for the stage. We wrote most of the plays we presented. A farm band was also formed, using tissue paper-covered combs for melody and all sorts of farm and house castoffs for other "noises" – drums from old oil drums, containers with stones for rattles etc.'

'My pocket money consisted of a penny for shopping for my grandmother, a penny for shopping for my neighbour, a penny from my grandfather and a halfpenny each day from my mother – giving me a grand total of sixpence ha'penny a week.

The games we played included leap-frog, hopscotch, whip and top, hoop and stick, diablo and skipping. I was very fortunate as I possessed a scooter, and later on a secondhand bicycle. One trick we used to play was to tie a piece of string to one front door knocker and the other end to the next door which we knocked, so that when the door opened it knocked the one next door. I don't remember getting caught.'

'Our old barn at Goldwell Farm, near Worten, was very useful. With an iron bar and a strong rope we managed to make a trapeze and fix it to a strong beam across the rafters in the roof. By standing on the wall we could jump onto the trapeze as it swung and do our circus acts, hanging by one leg, by two legs, by our ankles etc. When there were at least four of us we could play "keep the kettle boiling" – each time the trapeze swung one person jumped on, swung once and dropped off on the other side, then climbed up a plank onto the wall ready to jump out once again. This was a wonderful way of keeping warm in the winter. Lexicon was a favourite card game to play, sitting round a Tilley lamp in the evenings.'

'We children always played out in the street. There was no disturbance from cars, only the baker pushing his barrow up the road, the shrimp man with a basket of fresh pink shrimps from Sandwich Bay, or the miller with his horse and cart on a Saturday morning. Sometimes an Indian wearing a turban would come around with a case of house-cleaning things or clothes and he would open his case on the front doorstep and we would gather round, more interested in him and his dark skin than his wares as we never saw that many foreigners.

We had really organized play in our road (no adults!). Everyone knew the skills of the others and who to pick first when teams were needed. Games like French Cricket, Bad Eggs, Chase Me Over the Water and long rope skipping were all favourites.

French Cricket had no wickets, the person with the bat had to shield their legs, and anyone could throw the ball to them. The favourite way of getting someone out was to throw the ball to someone behind, who hit the back of the batsman's legs unless the batsman was very quick! The person who got the batsman out was the next to bat. The less skilful children, when they realised that they hadn't had a go at batting, would start complaining, "That's not fair, we want a turn, let's play something else".

Bad Eggs was where everyone ran in all directions and hid in gateways, but when the person who picked up the ball shouted "Stop!", everyone froze and didn't move a muscle. The one with the ball then had to try and hit one of the still children, who, if hit, was given a bad point; if the ball missed, the thrower had a bad point.

The person hit then took a turn at throwing the ball up – "Stop!" was shouted again. When ten bad points were collected, and everyone knew how many everyone had, the recipient went "through the mill". Everyone playing stood in a line with one hand against a fence and one hand free. The recipient dashed through the line as fast as possible to miss being spanked. This was not a vicious attack, sometimes someone hit a bit hard, but it was always surrounded by squeals of delight and loud laughter followed by a general gabble of how well they had hit or how fast they had got through!

Skipping with a rope stretched right across the road one pavement to the other, a typical song was –

> "Turn the rope, turn the rope,
> One, two, three –
> Jump in when it's your birthday –
> January, February, March . . ."

By "December" there could have been as many as six or seven children skipping simultaneously, boys and girls, six year olds mixing with older ones – an experience not to be forgotten and rarely seen today. There was never any fighting about who took the rope, the children in the street knew the rules and obeyed them.

Playing two ball or three ball in the junior school was very skilful, with all the tricks and different things that had to be done to follow on the game:

1) One, two, three up and let it bounce before you catch it (Bouncies).

2) One, two, three up and throw it under your legs (Leggsies).

3) One, two, three up and throw it around your back.

4) One, two, three and turn around once and still catch it when it comes down.

5) One, two, three and turn around twice before it comes down (this would usually signify the end of a person's turn!).

Each girl had a turn and the others patiently sat watching until the ball was dropped and the next in turn had a go. It was games such as these that taught us to play together and be patient.'

'When I was a schoolgirl in Sittingbourne in the 1930s and we were playing a game of "chase" and had to determine who was going to be "it" we used to say –

> "Eeny meeny miny mo
> Catch a nigger by his toe
> If he hollers let him go
> Eeny meeny miny mo"

giving the last person a dig in the chest. It was just a jingle to us and we had no thoughts about it giving any offence.

Another rhyme we used, with everyone making a fist to count on was –

> "One potato, two potato, three potato, four,
> Five potato, six potato, seven potato more."

My husband, living in Rainham, about five miles away, said

> "Alla, malla, mink monk,
> Ting, tong toozy,
> Oozy, woozy Wagtail,
> Ar var vat!"

A different version went as follows –

> "Alla, malla mink monk,
> Tink tonk toozy,
> Oozy voozy faggerty,
> Ar var vat!"

Another one used 50 years ago went –

> "Eeny meeny macker acker,
> Air I dominacker,
> Chicker popper, lollipopper,
> Om pom push!"'

HAPPY TIMES

'My mother kept a boarding house in Broadstairs when I was a child, as she was a widow. The season lasted from Easter to October and the house always seemed full. The winter was spent redecorating ready for the next season. Mother never had a holiday.

I loved to go on a picnic. This consisted of bread and jam sandwiches which I took down the road to the local park, up the drive and round the first flower bed to sit on the grass. My favourite sweet was Black Jack, a shiny slab which oozed black colouring everywhere but lasted for ages. We used to see how black we could get our mouths, and everything else for that matter.

In those days the shore-based fishermen took the local children for a free ride in their small boats on 1st May. The excited children were rowed round the bay before disembarking by the old jetty. My mother, who was afraid of the sea, recalled watching in anxiety as my brother sat in one of the overladen boats.

My brother was chief of a gang but had to take me along. In the event of flight from another gang, two of the boys were deputed to fetch me to safety and I was often dragged along behind with feet barely touching the ground. We had great freedom then and would wander miles along the shore without danger.

When we were taken to a performance of Uncle Mac's Minstrels at night on the end of the jetty, we received a lucky numbered ticket for a raffle prize. Also included in the small entrance fee was a free magazine, these being laid out on a table by the box office for the entrants to make their choice. After the show we would return home with our copy of *Tit Bits* or whatever we had chosen and perhaps a raffle prize.

The north wind did not seem so persistent and in summer there were what we termed "liner nights". Sometimes I was allowed to stay up late and on these beautiful still, balmy evenings we would go and sit on the front. As the great illuminated liners passed along the Channel, the music played on their decks wafted clearly across the water.'

WE LOVED EVERY MINUTE OF IT

'As Girl Guides the big event of the year was the summer camp, for which we saved sixpence a week until the grand sum of five shillings was reached. This was inclusive of transport, tent accommodation and food. When the great day arrived we clambered aboard a lorry with our kitbags and camp paraphernalia, bedecked in full uniform and wearing our umbrella-like navy hats.

On arrival our palliasse covers (sheets sewn into bags) were filled with straw for our beds. We slept on the ground, of course. A blanket, or two if we were lucky, were also sewn into bags to provide warmth. On a suitable night there was the joy of sleeping outside our bell tents under the stars, a never to be forgotten experience. Nor will the nights when it rained and the patrol leaders had to dress and then hammer in the tent pegs and adjust the guy ropes. All inside were under threat not to touch the canvas as it would leak. We fetched water, found wood for fires, made gadgets for our tents and convenience, and loved every minute of it, especially the singing of Guide songs around the camp fire before "turning in" with a cup of smoke-flavoured cocoa.'

'In 1920, there being no Brownie pack in the village, I joined the 1st Rainham Girl Guides, and a new life began. Camping, parading, country dancing, badge working, drilling, marching, church decorating etc etc, we enjoyed it all.

In July 1921 we stood for hours one day in the High Street as a Guard of Honour to welcome the Duke of York (later to be crowned

King George VI) when he stopped to give us a greeting, on his way through Rainham. His motorcade got lost and approached us from the opposite direction to that intended. His visit was brief indeed and I didn't see him. Later we were taken to the local cinema to see ourselves in the Pathé News. I had missed the Royal visit because in the brief moment when the great man appeared, saluted everyone and disappeared again – I was pulling up my socks.

Every year at Christmas time the Guides produced a Nativity play with carols and later a pantomime. We rehearsed for weeks beforehand, and enjoyed it all. My only accomplishment was dancing and I was usually cast as one of the fairies. On one occasion I remember I was to be a ghost wrapped in a sheet. Mother would not allow me to cut spyholes in the sheet and, blind, I missed direction and stood behind the piano. The ghost was never seen.

In 1925 the 1st Rainham Guide Company won all the trophies and competitions organised in Kent. One of my proudest days was the one on which I bore the King's Colour at the front of the Divisional Parade to Rochester Cathedral for the annual parade that year. My glory was reflected in the shop windows as we passed them – never to be forgotten.'

RADIO AND TELEVISION

'A Mr Leith had the first wireless in our road in Welling; it was a cat's whisker set, with earphones. All the children stood outside his house so excited, although we could not hear it. He let us go in, one at a time, very quietly, because if one made a noise the cat's whisker fell off the crystal, to put on those earphones and listen – it was magic.'

'I remember getting a new radio to replace the Rediffusion speaker. I suppose it must have been 1949, when I was five. It sat on a high shelf in the living room so that we couldn't fiddle with the knobs. *Children's Hour* was really good and when we were older there was *Journey into Space*. We would all settle ourselves and Mum and Dad would turn the radio on and we'd get really scared sometimes. If ever I was ill I would enjoy the grown up programmes that were on in the 1950s, like *Housewives Choice* and *Mrs Dale's Diary*.

My Nan and Grandad had a television, which was really exciting. We would go for Sunday tea and watch *The Railway Children*. When they came to live with us the television came too and we were envied by many of our friends. One of the first programmes I remember was *Muffin the Mule*. In 1953 Mum and Dad invited as many people as possible to see the Coronation on television. I think it was for the Coronation that a special magnifying screen was bought to go over the original screen.'

GROWING UP

Our first dance, our first proper hair-do, the embarrassments of meeting the opposite sex – nothing changes much in the agonies and delights of growing up. How innocent we were though, in those days when childhood lasted until we were into our teens.

MY FIRST DANCE

'At 16, in 1935, I went to my first real dance. My ankle length dress of yellow satin cost twelve shillings and sixpence and I felt like a queen. The tickets were one shilling and sixpence each, including refreshments. I was not allowed make up until I was 19, only Pond's Cream and powder on my face. Lipstick and blush were added after I got out and rubbed off before I went home!

I had my own cycle at 19. On this I went to many dances, with my long dress tied up around my waist and silver dance shoes in a bag. I enjoyed those days. We were free, we hadn't much money to spend, but we were happy. We did not expect great things from our parents, but we really appreciated birthdays and Christmas presents when they gave us the best they could afford.'

THAT SINKING FEELING

'When I started work in the GPO in 1943, my mother bought me two new dresses, some shoes and some underclothes, all marked with the Utility labels because of the war. There were a lot of shortages, one of the items in short supply being knicker elastic.

My first year at the GPO was spent as a probationer in the Telegraph Department, and our job was to collect the telegrams from the teleprinters and poke them into pigeonholes to be redirected. The telegram boys used to come into the room for the local deliveries and we probationers used to connive to be that end of the room to make eyes at them. One day I nearly died of shame as one of my new knicker legs minus the elastic had worked its way down below my dress and I was horrified that the boys had seen it. My mother spent that evening cutting the legs off my new knickers. It was some weeks before I had the courage to look in the boys' direction again.'

A NEW HAIR-DO

'My mother first had her hair permanently waved in 1936. It looked beautiful and we could hardly take our eyes off her – but oh, dear! She could not sleep or put a brush and comb near her head for about two weeks. Not knowing that the process was not supposed to burn her, she had sat and suffered for about four hours! The cost was ten shillings.

I had my first perm in May 1940 at the age of 14 years. It was a Eugene, which meant I was strung up to an electric machine but now there were rubber pads threaded through the hair to rest on the skull to prevent the heated curlers touching or burning! Then came the Calanan or machineless process and during the war the 'Home' perm, where the set was effected by combs and pincurls.

We did not have our hair set regularly but when we washed our hair, usually with green soap and rainwater, we towelled it dry and wound it with metal Dinkie curlers, and Kirby grips. I remember my mother rubbing bay rum into the scalp on a Friday evening, before bathing and washing our hair on Saturday.

As small children my sister and I begged my mother to curl our hair (our teenage aunts had beautiful ringlets) so she tore linen into strips and wound our hair up and tied it into knots. We thought it was fantastic – but often could not get our hats on to go to church on Sunday. We really must have looked a sight!

During the war I served with the Women's Auxiliary Air Force, where our hair had to be above our collars. It meant plaiting or rolling up long hair or having it cut short. As I worked shifts of eight hours on and eight hours off it became a bit of a bind, so I beseeched the camp hairdresser to give me an Eton crop. Then my cap fell down over my ears.'

POST-WAR TEENAGER

'As a teenager in the post-war period, life was far more restricted than it is today. We had to be in by 9.30 pm, or perhaps 10.30 pm as a special treat. There was no TV so the radio was our only source of information and *Saturday Night Theatre* was the highlight of the week. Sometimes if we could afford it we went to the cinema and usually

112

had to queue as this was a popular pastime. We were fortunate to have a local theatre at Ramsgate with a repertory company and I often went there with my aunt; they changed their programme every week, alternating between drama, mystery and comedy plays – the cost of the best seats was two shillings and sixpence.

On Sundays we were expected to go to church; the church had a youth club once a week, where we were able to play table tennis etc. Once a month the church had a social evening and here we played party games – quite happily, there were no discos or dancing in those days. At this time I had an American penfriend and we exchanged letters. Because sweets were still rationed over here, she would also send parcels of sweets and hidden amongst the sweets on one occasion was my very first pair of nylon stockings – a treasured possession. On reflection, I wonder how I kept those stockings up – presumably with suspenders attached by buttons to my liberty bodice.

Things sexual were taboo and never mentioned – in fact, my best friend noticed my mother was pregnant. I hadn't been told, although I was in my teens. "Expecting" was the word used (but not in front of the children), not "pregnant", that was too improper!'

THE HAPPIEST DAYS OF OUR LIVES?

Small village schools, coal fires in the classrooms and the smell of wet clothing, slates to write on, outside toilets and long walks to school – memories which will be familiar to anyone whose schooldays fell within the first half of the 20th century.

SCHOOLS BEFORE THE FIRST WORLD WAR

'We had ten weeks holiday in the year: one week each at Easter and Whitsun, six weeks in the summer, and two weeks at Christmas. If hop picking was late starting, we had an extra week in summer, and then we had only one week at Christmas. We had the odd half day such as Empire Day, when we went to school in the morning and ended up singing patriotic songs, and Ascension Day, when we went to church in the morning.'

'When I started school at River, there were only two classrooms in the infants school and one large and two small rooms in the "big" school where you went when you were about seven years old.

In the infants there were two classes in each room. Teacher Nelly had the "babies" and Teacher May the next class. After that we had to call the teachers Miss Edwards and Miss Hynes.

I can remember having two strips of leather about six inches long by three inches wide and metal eyelet holes in them which we had to learn to lace up with bootlaces, as we all wore lace-up boots in those days. The girls also wore white starched pinafores with a lace frill over the armholes. My poor mother had at least two a day to wash and starch as I always managed to get mine mucky.

We had slates and slate pencils for our written work – can you imagine the noise we could make with these? You could really make an ear splitting shriek with the pencil. Another thing we had to learn was "pothooks and hangers" so that we got the correct thin upward stroke and thick downward stroke required for copperplate writing.

When I was about eight years old I started to go to school in Dover. There were no school dinners then and we always went home for our midday meal. There were three of us girls from River who went to Barton Road school. This was about half an hour's walk from home and we were given money for our tram fare (a penny ha'penny return) to go home at dinnertime. This we seldom used unless it was raining really hard. We would run and walk and try to race the tram, which we usually did. Then on Friday when we left school we would spend the money saved at a baker's shop we passed on the way and sit on a seat in the lychgate of Buckland church and have a feast. My mother didn't find this out until after I left school, when she admitted she wondered why I was never hungry for my tea on Fridays.'

'At Northbourne we were sent to school at three years old and in those days it was hobnail boots, no wellingtons or mackintoshes as there are today, and sometimes we arrived at school very wet. We were allowed to take our stockings off and dry them before the fire. Our dinner consisted of sandwiches brought from home but the senior girls made cocoa, for which we were charged a penny for three cups, one cup per day.

I remember the building known as the Domestic Economy Room being built in the schoolmaster's garden, where we were taught washing, ironing, cooking etc. Amongst our other lessons we were also taught beekeeping. Mr Green, our schoolmaster, had several hives of bees in that piece of ground in front of the school. He had one glass hive where we could watch the activity of the bees without opening the hive – a lesson which in later life was a great asset to many.

There were long blackboards which reached from the ceiling to the panelling. On the boards were the names of girls who had won the prize for needlework and the boys for the best kept garden. Lady Edith Northbourne would present the girl with a work basket and the boy with a spade. Their name was printed on these boards with the year it was won. There was a small board by the side of the long board with these words for the girls: "A virtuous woman is a pride to her husband, her price is far above rubies". The boys' board said: "The Lord God took a man and put him in the Garden of Eden to dress it and to keep it".'

'I went to Rodmersham school, which consisted of two big rooms, the front one divided by a partition of wood and glass, which was pushed back for special occasions, and the back one divided by a thick, heavy curtain. We had four very good teachers including the headmaster, a Yorkshire man. The heating was open coal fires

A windy day for Alkham's schoolchildren as they walk to the church for a special service on 22nd June 1911 to celebrate George V's coronation.

115

surrounded by heavy iron guards for safety, and the latter came in useful for drying children's coats who had to walk a long distance and for drying gloves after a snowball session. We didn't have uniform but wore black button or lace-up boots, black stockings, and white embroidered pinafores. Hair was mostly plaited. Before marching into school we had hands and shoe inspection. When school closed at four o'clock, the master would stand at the classroom door and say, "Goodnight children" and we would pass him in single file and the girls would curtsey and the boys salute, and say, "Goodnight Sir".

My three brothers played cricket for the village team, and only boys who had been to Rodmersham school were allowed to play. We left school at 14 years of age and my sisters and I went into service.'

'In September 1915, spruce in a handed-down green dress, I started school and sat silent on a wooden form, looking through the window at the familiar conker trees beside the church. The long desks had sloping tops and the sand in my tray spilled over. My slate pencil squeaked as I drew my first A and my fingers got sore unravelling my first scrap of material to make stuffing for soldiers' pillows. Sewing lesson began with a brisk foot exercise, intended to de-rust needles by friction against the wooden floor. Blackboards, frames and coloured chalks were passed round to the boys for drawing instead of sewing. Looking through the glass partition I could see my sister's head and waved to her. She did not respond, she was standing on the form, in disgrace for talking.

School continued. Every morning classroom doors were opened, dividing curtains drawn back and governess said a prayer and we sang a hymn. At twelve o'clock we all stood up and recited either multiplication tables or the dates and lines of the Kings and Queens of England and sang grace, before filing out and home for dinner. At 1.40 pm we were back again with lessons until four o'clock.

The winter that I started school was a hard one, with snow and ice and a cold north wind. Wrapped up warmly however I was again lifted on to my father's shoulder, and during the whole of my first year did not miss an attendance. I was awarded a silver medal, which Father, with a chuckle, said should have been given to him. I have the medal still.

After school many of us fetched jugs or cans and went "down the milk". We had great fun playing steps-and-strides, statues and Red Robin, using the farm's iron fence as a base, waiting for milking to finish. Then at the farmhouse door we received our pint or quart measure of milk for twopence ha'penny or fivepence.'

'I went to Herne school when I was four years old in 1926. Heating was just a stove surrounded by a guard, which the teacher sat on thus keeping much of the heat to herself. There were no school dinners and many of the children walked three miles or more to school. All we had to drink was water from the one tap in the porch where we kept our coats, and the toilets were at the bottom of the playground, which was just stones and mud.

Our school was the nearest one to Blean workhouse so the children who were unlucky enough to live there came to our school. The girls wore red flannel dresses, the boys Eton suits with celluloid collars and boots. Oh, how well I remember those boots! I had quite a few kicks under the table from them.

When school was over we would go to the local park or playing field (mothers did not meet their children in those days) where we played our favourite games and visited our secret haunts. If you were lucky you had an old bike, if not you walked, but when we got home Mum would be there with perhaps a piece of cake or bread and jam to keep you going until teatime.

One thing I am grateful for is that our teachers taught us to knit and sew properly. I still get much pleasure from these skills and remember the ruler across the knuckles if it went wrong. We had to make a calico chemise with featherstitch trim and knit a child's vest – all at ten years old.'

'Ruckinge school had only 26 children in 1924. There were only two rooms; one small one for the babies who had their own pupil-teacher, and a large room where the rest of us worked under our teacher.

The chief stay of our educational life was the arithmetic book. We all worked with this, and the standard which we reached in arithmetic governed our place in school. We also wrote compositions, in my case long, long screeds which were practically indecipherable. I feel sure that the rudiments of history, geography and other subjects were taught us, but I certainly don't remember them. Some winter afternoons we were gathered round the fire and Mrs Baker would read to us. One book I remember was *Old Saint Paul's* by Harrison Ainsworth. We loved it.

Then I won a scholarship to the county secondary school in Ashford. This was a fee paying school for girls and every year twelve free places were offered to girls in Ashford and the surrounding area. On a certain day in May, girls of ten years old went into Ashford and we all sat a written examination. After a week or two I was told that I had been chosen to go into Ashford again for a viva voce examination. This news created quite a stir, and nearly everyone in the village told my mother that I was not to be downhearted if I did not win the scholarship. Lots of girls had been called up for the viva, but no one had ever won it. It was a very hard examination and it was most unlikely that I should win.

Fortunately my Mum disregarded this advice completely and I went into Ashford again quite happily. First of all I was given a poem to read, *The Lake Isle of Innisfree* by W.B. Yeats. I read and re-read this and soon knew it by heart. Then I went into another room and talked to two ladies. They were very nice and we had a most pleasant chat, and that was it. I went home and thought no more about it. But two weeks later I turned up at school one morning a bit late and Mrs Baker was all smiles and said, "Well?" She had a letter in her hand and when I answered, "Well what?" she said, "You have won the scholarship!"

Well, I had to go straight home again to see my Mum, and the rector came, because Ruckinge was a Church of England school, and he took us out to Folkestone for the afternoon. He had a Ford car which he had christened "Pansy", and we had a lovely time and a very good tea, with cream buns and iced cakes. I started attending the Ashford county school the following term. It was a large school and the work was hard but I made many friends there.'

'Lyminge was our nearest school and had four classrooms with about 120 pupils in the early 1920s. We had four teachers and each room was heated with an open coal fire with a guard in front. One winter one of our teachers was off sick and the female relief, who was quite portly, used to wash out her directoire knickers and hang them over the guard to dry. The remarks were far from flattering.'

'Before my fifth birthday in the early 1930s, I started school. It was a fairly new council school, with seven classrooms and a head's office built round the hall. Each morning we assembled here for prayers and hymns, which were conducted by the headmistress. During the afternoons it was used for the youngest pupils to have a nap on rush mats.

Physical education was called "drill", and taken outside. Girls wore vests and navy knickers and boys wore short trousers (never long trousers before the age of 14) and vests. We could wear a jersey if it was cold. We exercised in lines facing the teacher – very regimental! At playtime we had milk (twopence ha'penny a week) and played he, hopscotch, skipping and whip and top in the playground. On wet days we were allowed to play in the hall, which was superintended by the headmistress, who sipped a glass of hot water as she paraded up and down.

At the end of the Christmas term, every child was given a slab of Sharp's Creme Toffee, donated by the manufacturers. Another time we were all given an Oxo book to colour and enter for a competition. Each page bore the picture of a famous person and his invention, with the appropriate Oxo slogan. I enjoyed painting my way through this book, and consequently became the proud owner of a fountain pen with a 14 ct gold nib.'

'My early memories are of wearing Chilprufe vests with short sleeves, scalloped flannel petticoats, liberty bodices and fleecy lined bloomers (with a pocket to hold a purse when I was older; we schoolgirls invariably had one knicker leg hanging down with the weight of it!). We rarely went hatless. In summer we wore pretty straw ones and in winter a "pudding basin" velour. School uniform at my Folkestone school demanded white panama and navy felt hats with a heavy silver and enamel badge pinned in front. Our summer dresses were green and white striped piqué, with matching knickers (still with purse pocket), and a green blazer. In winter we wore a square-necked blouse of white piqué or cotton, navy blue gym tunic and girdle correctly tied with the knot dead centre. If cold, a green hand knitted sweater went over the top. In early days we wore black stockings, but later changed to beige lisle, the original Norah Batty models!

When I first went to school in 1926 I was armed against any deadly germs by a camphor block in a bag hung round my neck. This was not uncommon and I wonder now what the atmosphere was like around us. It was also quite usual to dose children weekly with senna pod tea, syrup of figs or similar aperient – how I loathed it.'

'The first school I attended was near London in a tiny cottage at the end of a row. It was run by two elderly ladies who still wore ankle-length black dresses, coats almost as long, and antique hats redolent of Edwardian England. Class lessons were held in the back kitchen of the cottage, complete with soapstone sink and range. There was a row of pegs behind the back door for our coats and about half a dozen or so pupils sat on a backless form behind one long desk. A blackboard stood in the opposite corner and completed the classroom equipment.

Sums and examples of handwriting were carefully ruled and written on the blackboard for us to copy and grapple with on our slates. The old ladies were always kind but firm. We learned our tables in unison. At break we ran about the tiny yard in the rear

119

which held the only toilet. Singing lessons were held in the front parlour, which was crammed full of furniture and an upright piano. The shorter of the two ladies played while we stood in a semi circle conducted by the taller with her baton.'

'My father, his brother and my three brothers were all educated at the boys grammar school in Folkestone, and my two sisters and I attended the girls grammar school. I started there when I was eight years old, previously having been at a small private school, Downs College, where normally girls whose parents had shops which displayed the family name over the front were not admitted. I think an exception was made in my case because of my father's membership of the town council.

At the grammar school our headmistress was an august personage. Her favourite dictum was, "If you can't be clever you can be courteous", and we were constantly reminded of our school motto, "Love and Serve". We were not allowed to fraternise with the grammar school boys if we were in uniform, though by about 1934 there were tennis matches between the schools.

Our sixth form at school had always just had two sections – Science and Art – but my father felt that girls needed to be trained for the commercial world and after talks with the headmistress a third section – the Secretarial Sixth – was formed. This was the forerunner of the Junior Commercial School which became part of the Technical Institute in about 1935, and was attended by boys and girls who had not gained entrance to grammar schools. They spent two years at the JCS taking Royal Society of Arts examination.'

THE 1940s AND 1950s

'I lived at Stone Street on the Canterbury/Hythe road and went to school at Petham. I remember going to school one day in the winter of 1947 with my two nieces and a nephew who lived next door, and walking the mile to school. The road to the school was down a steep hill and the snow was thick. There was just enough room to walk single file and the snow seemed to be above our heads in some places where it had drifted. I think the reason this particular day stands out in my memory is because when we arrived at school we were told off by our teacher for coming and bringing my youngest niece, who was just five, with us. We were the only children from Stone Street that day at school and there were only four from Petham!'

'During the Second World War I attended a little church school in the village of Bearsted. It only had three classrooms. In each was a

120

tall black, coke burning stove. This was fine for the children sitting in the front of the class, but the ceiling and windows were high, and the back of the room was cold. There was an ink well in each desk, and when it was very cold the ink used to freeze. Each child was allowed a small bottle of milk a day, the cost being one halfpenny. I enjoyed it in the summer, but it was warmed by the stove in the winter, which was horrid.

We walked to school. I lived about three miles away and we always went, whatever the weather. Sometimes we skipped, if skipping was in, or maybe played hopscotch, or two ball. When marbles were the rage we were often late. School started at 9 am and finished at 4 pm.

There wasn't room at the school to cook or eat school dinners. It had no kitchen or staff room. The cloakrooms had hand basins with only cold water, which we used for drinking, washing, mixing paint, and whatever water was needed for. The toilets were in the school yard. But we did have school dinners, and how good they were. They were cooked by the ladies of the Women's Institute. The WI hall was a few yards away from the school. Their stew, and jam tart and custard, were out of this world. It always impressed me to think the president of the WI had cooked my dinner.

One of the dinner ladies used to rush around the village on her bike, making sure that we all attended Sunday school. This wasn't easy as the venue often changed due to air raids. On one of her trips a chicken ran in front of her bike. I am glad to say she wasn't hurt, but we all enjoyed the chicken casserole the next day.

At the beginning of the war many evacuees from London came to our village. The school was much too small to house them and us all together, so a plan was devised. We all had to have a timetable. This was written on the blackboard. Those capable copied it, plus an extra one for the children that couldn't manage it. Woe betide the children that lost their timetables, they lost house points.

It worked out that on some days we only attended for half a day. On another day our class would meet at the "mission room". This was just a large wooden hut in a field. It stood a little higher than the main village street. It was fitted out with desks, the idea being that we achieved some written work, but the windows were low and there was so much to see. The milk lady came by with her churns and ladles, which she swished in the milk to make sure the cream was well distributed for the housewife waiting with her jug. The baker's boy would ride by, with the bread piled in a basket on the front of his bike. None of it was wrapped, but if it rained he had a mackintosh cover to put over it. Sometimes we would see a horse being led to the forge so that the blacksmith could make a shoe. One

Bethersden infants class in 1945. Schools had changed very little from the days of their grandparents.

day an army convoy came one way, as the farmer drove his cows the other way. Only the really dedicated finished their work that day.

Once a week our class went to the oast house. This was a round building with a rough brick wall. No desks here, just a circle of chairs. There we would learn our spellings or maybe have a general knowledge quiz. We would spend another half day in the chapel rooms. This was a dreary place, with no outlook, no reason to daydream, and only the noise of the steam train to disturb us.

My favourite half day was taken when we went to the King George Memorial Hall. It was large, bright, and the newest building that we used, with shiny red oilcloth curtains and a polished floor. Here we had singing, play reading or PT (Physical Training). The girls wore navy blue knickers with a vest or blouse, the boys just took off their shirts, as they all wore short trousers, winter and summer, until they left school at 14.

What fun it was when an unexpected thunderstorm caught many of us without a coat, and teacher lent us a red curtain to go home under, one between two of us.

We never minded walking to school as there were many routes

that we could take, with lots to see and do. In the spring and summer we looked for wild flowers. Each week our teacher would list six for us and we gained a house point for each one we found. We nibbled the new leaves of the "Bread and Cheese" tree (hawthorn), we sucked the nectar from the dead nettle flower, and chewed the stem of the fresh tall grass. In the autumn conkers kept us busy for hours. We collected chestnuts, hazelnuts, cobnuts and walnuts. We would roast the chestnuts in the ashes of our open fire and enjoy them while we listened to the wireless in the evening.

In the winter we couldn't wait for the village pond to freeze over. It wasn't very big, but large enough to make a grand slide and deep enough to fill your wellingtons when the ice gave way.

There were certain places that we had to pass, where it was imperative that we held our breath until well by. Any house where the occupant had TB was a great fear, and we didn't dare breath any air nearby. The same applied to another very large house for unmarried mothers!

We also passed the village laundry, which had an air raid siren on its roof. We would rush by and hope it would not go off. The noise at close quarters was more frightening than the raid.'

'I well remember that typical Victorian classroom in 1951 with its cavernous, raftered roof, ecclesiastical-style windows too high to see out of and rows of two-seater desks with clattering iron-hinged seats and *splinters*. The smell too is unforgettable – chalk, damp clothes and plimsolls, plus the occasional unwashed child or coke fumes.

The room was dominated by the huge black tortoise stove, the bane of my life. On a good, windy drawing day it needed replenishing at lunch time. This entailed dragging away the iron-barred guard, gingerly prising open the furnace door and feeding it with coke from a heavy metal hod.

Remember the days of school milk? Those neat little third of a pint bottles and cardboard lids with a hole for the straw? On cold winter days we were faced with whole cratefuls, frozen, with the cardboard hats perched aloft on columns of "ice cream". Custom dictated that one extracted bottles for those children who hated warm milk, then sat the crate on the stove to thaw out by playtime.

One memorable (and expensive) day, teacher stood *inside* the guard by the stove to give a homily on the stupidity and danger of such behaviour, when there wafted upwards an acrid smell of singeing. A large charred area on teacher's skirt aptly proved the point about stupidity!'

PUNISHMENT

'I lived in a small hamlet called Court-at-Street, which is between Aldington and Lympne. The school I went to during the First World War was a good two miles away and I had to walk there. Winter, summer, rain, snow and fog, whatever the weather I had to make that journey twice a day. There were no meals provided by the school, so we had to take our own lunch and drink with us. In fact, food was not allowed to be eaten on the premises, and I can remember clearly the time I was caught chewing a damson stone in class. When the master questioned me, I told him what it was and he did not believe me, he thought I was eating a sweet. He reached for the cane, and asked me to put my hand out for the punishment I would receive. I refused to obey him and spat out the stone and ran all of the journey home. I burst in through the back door and found my mother blackleading the grate. I blurted out the incident, and with that she took hold of my hand and marched me back to school. Angrily, she faced the master and told him that her children did not tell lies, and that was the end of the matter. I received no punishment that time.'

'In 1921 when I was 13 I was at boarding school at Broadstairs and loved every minute of it, until one day we were walking in crocodile along the esplanade, because the weather wasn't too good and we were not allowed to bathe. Vera Howard and I were the last couple in the crocodile and we saw our rival school, Bartrum Gables, bathing and I said to Vera: "Look at those lucky little devils!"

Unfortunately, Matron was in charge that day and heard what I said, so I was reported to the Head and, as my language was so bad, I was banished for a week to the sanatorium. The school assembly hall was large, and had the usual platform with a small balcony above, with a door leading into the sanatorium. So, every morning at assembly, I had to emerge and stand facing the school and then retire into the san. My lessons were brought to me and my meals and, in the afternoon, I mended towels and also had to write out many times something about the voice being golden, but I cannot remember it properly.

At the end of the week I was allowed to go back to my class, but during walks I had to walk with the mistress in charge and this time it was Miss Hattersly, the games mistress. Nothing could have been better – I had a crush on her and to be able to walk next to her for a whole week was worth all the bad language of "lucky little devils". But, may I add, I have never said it again unless relating the story, so perhaps severe punishments do help sometimes.'

THE NIT NURSE

'The Nit Nurse visited the school at Coldred regularly to inspect hair. She prodded the head with two knitting needles so that she did not actually have to touch the hair. A "Dickey comb" was used at home as well to search for fleas. The child knelt with their head over their mother's knee, across which was spread a white towel. The comb was systematically drawn through the hair and any foreign body was soon spotted on the towel and dealt with.'

SCHOOL DINNERS

'How I loathed school dinners; to this day I can see, smell and taste them in my imagination. Every week the menus were the same. Monday was stew day and the huge lumps of gristle would be pushed round and round the plate until, when the supervising teacher turned her back, I, and probably everyone else too, took the gristle off the plate and into a waiting handkerchief. The cabbage served with the meat was a ghastly khaki colour and frequently had additional protein in the form of creepy-crawlies. Tuesday was mince – slimy grey mince, also served with creepy-crawly cabbage. Wednesday was roast day and probably the best of the week, but no other roast meat I've had has ever tasted as that did. Thursday was mince again, probably with pastry on top. I can't remember Friday's lunch. Salad was substituted occasionally in the summer, only this time the creepy-crawlies hadn't been killed with boiling water, they were very much alive and crawled around the plate leering at me!

The only good thing we had were the puddings, my favourite being gipsy tart, a lovely gooey mixture of brown sugar and condensed milk baked in a pastry case. The jam tart and custard was called "hammer and chisel tart" because the pastry was so hard we couldn't cut it with a spoon. We were always very suspicious about what the black things were in Spotted Dog, but I loved the semolina and rice puddings if they had the dollop of orange preserve in the centre. I'm not really sure quite what it was but years later I was to give my children concentrated orange juice obtainable from the clinic and that tasted the same. We were made to eat these dinners and instead of enjoying my food I began to hate and dread lunchtimes. Fortunately my wise mother realised when it was becoming a serious matter and arranged for me to have lunch with her at her employer's house. She never forced any of us to eat vegetables but would give us the vitamins in soups or fruit dishes. Now, of course, I love vegetables.'

SCHOOL TREATS

'The winter gloom of our schooldays in Deal in the 1920s was lifted by a Christmas party paid for by our Conservative MP, Major J.J. Astor. We weren't worried if it was a form of bribery as we tucked into lots of hufkins and cakes supplied by John Tapping.

The Parochial, Deal, is a Church of England school. Once a year we had an inspection by the Rev Jackman, who came from Adisham. In 1927, on the day of inspection, there was an eclipse of the sun. Rev Jackman had the bright idea of marching us up to Victoria Park, where he produced a box of smoked glass so that we could watch the heavenly marvel.'

'In 1935, when I was ten years old, Kent Education Committee, along with Southern Railway, organised a great outing by train to Southampton. Schools all along the line from Dover to Maidstone, I believe, were included, and pupils boarded the train at their local stations. At the appropriate time we were given large paper bags containing sandwiches, rolls and a doughnut, which kept us occupied for a while.

On reaching Southampton we left the train at the docks – I had never seen anything like it! We split into groups and were escorted to a great liner, *The Majestic*, which was in the dock before going to be broken up. We were very impressed with the ornate state rooms, cabins and swimming pool. It seemed a shame that so fine a vessel was about to be pulled to pieces.

We spent our money in the shop on board, on tie pins, brooches and other souvenirs. On our return journey, once again a supply of food in a large white paper bag was waiting on all the seats as we got into the carriages. We got home that evening tired but happy after a wonderful day out.'

THE WORLD OF WORK

MAVIS STEWART

ON THE FARM

How things have changed on the land since the days when horses provided the power and men, women and children the labour. The work was hard and the days long, whether you were working your own mixed farm, a looker on the marshes or a cherry picker, but there was a great satisfaction and comradeship to be found – as the support shown within the farming community during the tithe revolt of the 1930s proved.

MIXED FARMING

'Farming as I remember my father doing it in Newington and Lower Halstow in the 1930s and 1940s was quite different from today. I can't remember his exact acreage, but it must have been something below 150 acres and it was a busy, bustling place. He employed a foreman, a waggoner, a stockman, a shepherd and about six general labourers, with gangs of women as required. He described himself as "the boy", as he did all the little odd jobs. His favourite saying was "The master's footsteps are the best manure", meaning that it was important to keep a watchful eye open all the time. He could turn his hand to anything from mending a fence to operating on a sheep with a prolapse.

It was a very mixed farm; the soil varying from a light loam to a heavy clay. There were several orchards, growing apples, pears, plums and cherries all in together, with damsons round the edges to provide a crop and act as a wind-break.

The men would usually gather by the farm buildings at 7 am when the foreman would give instructions for the day's work. Caring for the animals had to come first, and the men then "knocked off" for their own breakfast at 8.30 am. Dinner was at midday, either brought to eat at work or at home if they were near enough or had their bikes with them. There was very little in the way of protective clothing and people wore an assortment of old clothes. There were always empty sacks available, and both men and women would use them to keep themselves dry – one over the head, one in front of them and one at the back, all tied on with string. Men usually wore leather boots and tied their trouser legs up. Father himself was very particular about scrubbing and polishing his boots and the leather leggings he wore over his breeches. I remember that in my hearing Father was

128

referred to as the guv'nor or Mr 'Arlow, though I believe among themselves the men called him "The Bloke". The women on the farm were always called Mrs Smith, Brown or Jones, but the men had nicknames. There was a Kruger, a Chinger, a Knobby, a Tubby, a Tich, a Musher, a Smudger and an Ike.

The agricultural worker's wage in the 1930s was little over £2 for a 48 hour week, and many of them had large families to support, so money was always short. With animals to feed on Sundays and Saturday morning work the norm, they had very little spare time either. They had their gardens or allotments to look after to help with the food, and a lot of them enjoyed rabbiting to add to the diet. They very seldom left their village, and most never went as far as London. It was a treat on a Sunday evening to go up to the "top road" (meaning the A2) to watch the traffic go by. They were countrymen with a great understanding of their surroundings, and when I was a small girl they showed me many things which stayed in my memory, like the kingfisher's nest in the bank along the stream, and the skylark's nests which they always marked with a stick and carefully avoided when working in the fields.'

'My home was a farmhouse on Romney Marsh, built astride the boundary of two parishes, Newchurch and Ruckinge. I slept in Ruckinge, my parents and sister in Newchurch.

Ours was a mixed farm; cereals, sheep, cattle and pigs. At lambing time in April, lambs on the hearth were nursed back to fitness in front of the fire and rubbed with a sack which got their circulation going. Father was out in all weathers as the sheep were his responsibility, stock around the farm being my uncle's charges to care for. Father and his brother were partners. In later years I came to realise what a hard life it all was, being very dependent upon the weather for profit or loss, good crops or poor.

The 1st April was the beginning of lambing always, for us, and always outdoors. Shelter was provided for some by thatched hurdles or wattle gates thatched with wheat straw during cold winter days, put up in threes to make a pen for a ewe that had too little milk for her lamb or needed persuading that her baby was her responsibility. Some lambs had to be partly fed with cow's milk when mum had too little. When a ewe had a dead lamb then, when possible, she was given another, maybe an orphan or one of twins from another ewe. This foster child would have a new coat, that of the dead lamb's skin which Father would remove and put on the new lamb in order that it smelt like the ewe's own.

After lambing and lambtailing (castration of male lambs and tail docking of all lambs), June/July brought shearing. That was weary work. The fleece came off best in warm weather but of course the hotter the weather the more the shearers sweat. Our machine was powered by a small petrol engine and had two shearing arms and heads. The knives had to be frequently sharpened and oiled to get a good finish and cleanly shorn sheep. Wool was rolled and tied up fleece by fleece and packed in great hessian bags and eventually taken to the "wool store" in Ashford. Most of our lambs were sold at Ashford Market lamb sale; these were every Friday but ours always went the last Friday in August every year. There was great satisfaction in the whole family if our best pen of lambs made top price of the day.'

'We came to live in Sellindge in the late 1920s, but my father still had the farm at Hamstreet and in spring and autumn the cattle were moved to the marsh for the summer grass and back to the yards for the winter. In spring, on a suitable Saturday for the maximum labour available, we would set out for the long walk – about 14 miles. Of course there wasn't so much traffic, but the journey could still be very exciting, herding 30 to 40 cows and calves of assorted sizes along the A20 to Church Lane (Oxenleas Lane in those days) through Aldington, Bilsington and Ruckinge. The children were sent ahead to shut gates, to keep the cattle out of people's gardens and fields. I remember one calf diving up an alleyway and finishing in a kitchen in Aldington! I don't remember that the owner was particularly irate – all part of living in the country in those days.

The journey was always easier if some of the animals had made the journey before. They seemed to remember the way and would lead the others. Cows are not silent travellers so our coming was well advertised. People were used to seeing us pass and were generous with sweets and biscuits to help us on our way.

Father drove the pony trap, so having got the cattle to their summer home we would climb into the cart thankful that we didn't have to walk home as well. I'd be sent to the post office once a year to get the cart licence; for the last ten years we had consecutive numbers, then the licence was discontinued.'

'On Romney Marsh in the early 1930s only horses were seen doing the general agricultural work. Then later on many farms had a Fordson or International tractor for ploughing and heavy work, such as binding the corn and making it into sheaves. This was heavy pulling on wet land, or if it was a heavy and laid crop. It then had to be stooked in the fields before it could be stacked, as it was cut before it was dry and only dry corn sheaves could be stacked or it would go musty.

Often broad beans would be cut with hooks or pulled by women and laid into loads in carts, as each woman worked her own quarter of an acre or such allotted to them by the farmer. The beans were bundled up in the evening or early morning when wet with dew, as the pods would split open if too dry and the beans would be lost. Often the husbands would help with this, though it only paid a small amount per cart.

Potato picking was a real sight to see. Many fields on Romney Marsh grew these back-aching vegetables. Sometimes they were ploughed out by horses and had to be scratched for, or were spun out by a tractor, and that meant them being spread over six to eight feet around. Men, women and children did this picking by the hundredweight bagful at twopence or threepence per bag. They came from the nearby villages and towns and it was one of the last jobs for casual workers before the winter came. Sugar beet was a winter crop but only a few farmers grew this, for it had to be sent by rail to the sugar beet factories and this needed a permit.

Hay in 1940 was either cut using two horses or tractors trailing mowers; there was no going back with these tools, only forward, so we often had to run over the cut grass at the corners of the field. With seed hay, therefore, it all had to be turned by hand and very carefully pitched onto waggons by men with pitchforks and rakes, so as not to knock the seed out. It was put into a stack and next spring threshed by a huller to get the seed out. This machine normally belonged to a threshing contractor who also had corn threshing machines, and some men of his own to operate them.

Mangel-wurzels were grown for sheep feed. These were pulled by hand and clamped for springtime.

The cleaning of waterways on the Marsh was done manually. Petty and main sewers were brushed and cleaned by men with knives, scythes and rakes every year; the different lengths were put out to tender and men quickly selected which one they wanted. All the reed and weeds were put on top of the banks so they didn't fall back in and stop the flow of water. This was done in September and October before the water level was up.'

'In my early years on the land there were many skills which have since disappeared: stacking, thatching, laying a hedge and mowing with a scythe, broadcasting by hand. I learned all these things and had to use my skills when I began farming. In those days I had no drill, and all my fields were sown by hand, not just corn but grass and clover seeds and fertilizers. The man who taught me to broadcast was in his sixties; he left school at twelve years old, and to some was "just an agricultural labourer", but he gave me a skill that served me well.

Many people think there is not much to be done on a farm in winter, but February is a busy month for the shepherd; if he has lambs in the fold they need some dry food and hay in the trough, and the in-lamb ewes need careful feeding as lambing time draws near. One always likes to get plenty of twins. An old shepherd whose flock was most prolific, near the end of his life passed on his secret of how this was achieved to his son. It was this: "In the spring you kill a male stoat, put it in a bottle and cork it up, then bury it while it is still warm in a dung heap where it will stay warm through the summer. In the autumn there will be some liquid in the bottle; squeeze out what's left of the stoat and mix the liquid with some soft bread and make a mash and feed that to the ram before he goes in with the ewes and he'll get an awful lot of lambs"! I wonder what the scientific explanation of that is?'

THE FARMERS' TITHE REVOLT

'1930–32 was the period when all the farmers joined together and refused to continue to pay the tithe collected by the Church Commissioners. The chief organiser of the revolt was Mrs Rash, a farmer's wife from Norfolk who wrote under the name Doreen Wallace. In those hard times, farmers' stock and machinery was having to be sold to pay the tax and auctions were held on the farms. Many got together in protest and "reclaimed" their animals.

One midnight I set forth with three students in my Austin Seven to Shepherdswell, where they collected the stock sold that morning in lieu of payment and returned it to its original owner. I also sat in the road with others at a farm near Ashwell to prevent a lorry taking away a load of oats. I came home to find my parents' farmhouse barricaded to keep the bailiffs out – one was pushed into the slurry and my father was fined and could no longer remain a JP!'

WORKING WITH HORSES

'My Dad was born on 8th October 1900, the seventh child in a family of 14. He was christened Henry John, but was always known as Harry. When he was eleven his father was killed at his job of woodman at one of the estates near Dover. There were no pensions for widows in those days, so his mother had to go to work, one of the older girls staying at home to look after the small children. The youngest one was three weeks old when the accident happened.

When he finally left school at 13, he got a job as gardener's boy and boot boy, doing all the mucky heavy jobs the maids couldn't do at the big house. At 18 he moved on to a job as a general farm labourer, working on thatching, hedging, and ditching, and anything else that needed doing. By the time he was 21, he was an all-round farm labourer, and had at his finger tips many skills he never forgot.

At 21 he really found his life's vocation: Horses! To start with he took a job as a waggoner's mate, living in a room at the waggoner's house, being looked after by the waggoner's wife. For five years he lived in this way, never hungry but on a very meagre diet. How many people in these days would go to work on a breakfast of bread and milk with a lump of boiled fat pork in it? He did, every day for five years including Sundays. When Dad was 30, the waggoner left and Dad was offered the job.

A typical day for Dad was to get up at 5.30 am to light the kitchen fire and put the kettle on to boil (no electricity). Then out to the stable (electricity from a generator out there), to get the horses up and feed them, then back indoors to have a cup of tea and breakfast, take Mum a cup of tea, then out to the stable again to groom the horses, throw out the bedding and get the corn and water etc ready for their meal when the morning's work was done.

Harvesting in the Alkham valley in the 1920s, when the horse was still an integral part of farming life.

133

In those days men working with horses kept peculiar hours. They went out to the fields at about 7.30 am, at nine o'clock they'd stop for 15 minutes for a hunk of bread and cheese (dry bread), and a drink of cold, milkless, sugarless tea from a lemonade bottle in the summer or a bottle of cocoa in the winter, the bottle snuggled up in about three or four legs of old socks. There were no Thermos flasks for the likes of farm workers in those days. This break was called "progger time". I've no idea why!

After this break, off they would go to work again until 2 pm. They then went back to the stable, put the horses inside, gave them the food prepared in the morning, then went off to their own home for a meal, returning at 3.30 pm until 5.00 pm. During this time the horses had to be groomed, the harness cleaned, and the evening meal prepared, corn measured out, fodder and hay chopped, and water put into the reserve trough. The stable was swept out and all the bits brought in from the fields got rid of. These jobs and the way the hours were worked, were called a "one yoke".

After going home to tea at five o'clock, Dad's time was his own until 7.30 pm in the winter and eight o'clock in the summer (if he wasn't working late) when the horses had to be bedded down and their last feed given; this was called "serving up".

That was a typical day, whatever the job, whether it was ploughing, harrowing, rolling or carrying manure in a small boxy cart, called obviously a dung cart, or driving one of the long harvest waggons loaded with the sheaves.

Until the end of the war, when the farm workers began to be appreciated, there was no overtime pay. They had to work as many hours as they were asked for no extra money. For years my Dad's wages were £1 7s 6d and out of this he had to pay three shillings and sixpence for rent. We also got a two pint can of skimmed milk every day; one of the children (usually me) had to go to the back door of the big house either before or after school. My Dad got sixpence more than the other men because he had the horses to look after.

After the war, the wages did get progressively better. This life went on until the 1950s, when the farm horses began to disappear. Poor Dad, it broke his heart, when first one then two then three tractors appeared. His employer let him keep one old horse to do odd jobs on the farm, taking food to the sheep in winter etc. But came the day when the axe finally fell. There was just nothing for a horse to do, so he had to go. Someone a few miles away gave him a home, and he spent his final years in a nice wooded meadow with a couple of donkeys, and he was happy. Dad took us to see where he was one Sunday. He stood along the wall around the field, and called his name. The horse looked up and just took off galloping across the field; he made such a fuss I just stood and cried.

After losing his beloved horses, Dad was asked if he would like to learn to drive a tractor. The polite translation of his answer was. "No, thank you. You can't talk to a tractor, and they don't stop if you say whoa."

As almost everything on the farm was by now mechanised, there wasn't a lot of work Dad could be given, so the next question he was asked was, "How would you like to look after the garden, clean the shoes, bring in the coal etc?"

For Henry John, known as Harry, born in 1900, by 1960 his life had come a full circle. He died in 1972 having worked for 48 years on the same farm. This was my Dad, the waggoner.'

THE LOOKERS

'Ask anyone "Who looks after the sheep?" and they will say a shepherd. That may be right for most of the country, but in the Romney Marsh area they are called "lookers". In the past the land was a lot wetter than it is today and only fit for grazing. The parishes of Newchurch, St Mary's, Ivychurch and Old Romney had several mixed arable, sheep and cattle farms. The rest was split up into holdings of 20–100 acres owned by town dwellers or farmers that had hill farms, who sent their cattle down to the marsh for summer grazing and had them back to fatten and make dung for their hops during the winter in their yards.

Some of the grass fields were kept for ewes and their lambs. These were known as breeding land and a better pasture was kept as fattening land. These blocks of land were looked after by what we would now call self employed men who *overlooked* the land. They were paid so much an acre per year and were in complete charge of the stock while on the land. Every animal had to be accounted for and the money received for the skin of any that died.

On many of these holdings, brick and tile sheep houses were sited where medicines, sheep mark, tar, tools etc would be stored. There would be a fireplace where milk could be warmed for sickly lambs if a breeding flock was kept and, of course, shelter for the looker.

Extra money would be earned by lookers for cutting ant hills and carting them to low places in the field. Sometimes a ditch had to be mudded out. These were piecework jobs. Sixpence an acre is quoted for lookering and one shilling and sixpence for cast cutting (anthills) an acre.'

CHERRY PICKING

Mr Leslie Hadlow has a very clear memory of his life as a boy at Dargate, a pretty village between Whitstable and Faversham, well known for its orchards and roses, where he was born in 1904.

In addition to having his own orchards – cherry, apple and pear – Mr Hadlow's father used to attend the auction sales held in mid June each year, when crops were sold for picking. They visited the orchards first to assess how many half-sieves (baskets each holding 24 lbs of cherries) there were, so that they could choose the most promising orchards and make their bid. His father bought one particular orchard at Kingston for 13 years running. Once the crop had been bought the fruit had to be protected from the birds for six weeks or so, until harvest. They used a number of means to do this – carbide guns which fired at intervals automatically (after 7.30 am as these were not popular with the neighbours); stones in a tin hanging from the trees; a man walking round with a rattle or gun, a mock hawk hanging in the trees; but mainly by netting the trees.

When harvest time came they employed local labour, mostly women, who often brought their children and prams with them. Sometimes Mr Hadlow would have to collect them and take them home, in the early days by horse and van and later by motor vehicles. There was always a ladder mover in the orchards to help the women. As a young man of 18 or so he would have the job of looking after one orchard and moving the ladders for 16 or 17 women pickers. In those days the trees were left to grow to their natural height and were very tall. The ladders were a special kind, narrow at the top to get between the branches and wide at the base for stability. Sometimes the ladders had as many as 56 stales and had to be tied at the top for safety. The women wore their normal longish skirts (no trousers in those days for women) and black stockings. How they climbed these ladders is a bit of a mystery, but manage it they did. The cherries were picked into kibseys, special baskets which hooked onto the ladders, and could be moved up as one picked. They worked from about 8 am to 5 pm, depending on the amount of fruit to be picked, and brought their own lunches. Each woman's fruit was kept separate and her pay calculated at the end of the day. Piece workers were paid a shilling a half-sieve in about 1920 and a good picker could pick eight or nine half-sieves a day.

There was a knack to picking the fruit. Cherries had to be picked complete with stricks (stalks). Mr Hadlow remembers one man who came to the house asking for work. He assured them that he was experienced in picking cherries and ladder work, so they showed him a tree, gave him a ladder and left him for the rest of the day.

When they went back for the fruit they found he had picked it, but it was all "plumbed" (ie without stalks), was quite useless and had to be thrown away!'

HOP PICKING

A seasonal task, remembered mostly with great affection by Londoners and locals alike, hop picking was an essential part of many people's budgeting in times past. Only if the whole family, young children included, worked long and hard for the three or four weeks of the harvest, could clothes and other essentials be paid for in the coming winter.

WORK TO BE DONE

'The longest day had passed and summer holidays stretched ahead. No school for two months. However, Dad came home from work carrying several old hessian sacks. My twin and I knew what that meant. He would spend the next few evenings fashioning three aprons, one large and two smaller ones for Mother and us for hop picking. The stain from the hops was so strong and penetrating that it could not be removed from clothes, which when washed would come out covered in small brown marks all over. Washing machines and stain removers were things of the future.

Next, Dad arrived home with a few small pieces of wood with which he made a wooden "mat" for our mother to stand on to prevent her feet from sinking into the mud, if the season was wet. The old billy can was retrieved from its winter resting place in the shed, tested to discover any leaks, cleaned and put to join the aprons and foot mat.

The first day arrived; 5 am we were out of bed, cold and shivering, dressing in all our oldest clothes. A quick breakfast, and we were ready to start our journey. It was necessary to wear our thickest coats and hats as we stepped out into the foggy, damp morning. It took about 15 minutes to walk, carrying all our gear to the picking up point. When we heard the sound of the horse's hooves, "hopping" had really begun. We all piled into the farm waggon, filling it to capacity, and with a steady gait the faithful old farm horse took us through the lanes to the hop garden.

Our farm was a small, privately owned farm, where no Londoners were allowed; we were all "respectable" local families!

The farmer and his men were waiting for us, to set each family to a hill where the empty bin was waiting. As I gazed up the hill the hanging vines reminded me of a cool dark cathedral and from an early age I was overcome with the beauty, but we were not there to enjoy the scenery; there was work to be done. The tally was set; if the hops were good, big and ripe, we had to pick eight bushels for one shilling; if smaller, not so many bushels. I never remember anyone querying the tally, though sometimes I heard the older people complaining among themselves about the rate.

The smell of the hops was really overpowering and a few people, my mother and myself among them, were quite badly affected, feeling sick and faint for the first few days, after which we became immune to the smell.

There were pole pullers who carried a long pole with a sickle-like tool or hook attached to the top. With this he cut the vine at the root and, with the hook, shot the vine up the pole, cut the string and deftly placed the vine by the bin for the pickers to start picking. Our mother would pick off a few branches and toss them to my sister and me who would spend the whole day picking into an old umbrella or a box.

Halfway through the morning the farmer, measurer and book-keeper came round to collect the hops from the bin and put them into the bushel basket, tipping them into a sack, counting one, two, three as he emptied the basket. The book-keeper wrote the number in her big book and onto a small card, which was presented to our mother for the duration.

When the poles were all denuded of their vines it was time to move the bin up the hill and start again.

The empty vines could be bunched together and with a sack or coat over the top made a comfortable bed on which to rest, particularly if one was poorly.

The pole puller was kept busy until midday when the cry went up "Pull no more bines". It was dinner time and we were all relieved. My mother was a hard worker, but she could not manage without a hot cup of tea midday. We had been dispatched to collect a faggot – a bundle of twigs – and Mum quickly had a fire going with the billy can strung over the fire to boil the water for the tea. Loose tea was spooned into the boiling water and we were soon enjoying the hot, sweet brew. The group of pickers nearby came along with their cups; my mother never refused anyone a drink until it was all

Grandma Steadman hop picking in the 1930s at East Farleigh. The money she made clothed her growing family for the coming winter months.

gone. Our meagre lunch, which usually consisted of several hunks of bread with a small piece of cheese, was washed down with the tea. The worst thing was the taste from the brown stain with which our hands were covered, which smothered the food we were eating.

The one o'clock call "Back to work" came all too soon, and the morning's work was repeated until the four o'clock call, "Pull no more bines". Dirty, tired and hot, for the morning mist had turned into a hot, sunny day, we began our homeward trek; *no ride home.*

The four mile walk was the worst part of hopping for our heavy coats had to be worn home ready for the next cold morning. However, we were luckier than most; our Dad was on shift work arriving home about 2 pm and he had a hot meal ready for us by the time we had scrubbed up. The stain was difficult to remove but we were not allowed to the table until we had pumiced it all away at the kitchen sink.

My sister and I were given no respite after our meal to relax a little with a book or game. After washing up it was straight to bed and sleep, so we were ready for the next morning.

After about five or six weeks the longed-for last day arrived and we were able to sing:

"Hopping is all over, Money is all spent.
Don't I wish I never went hopping down in Kent."

This was the Londoner's refrain, but we all knew it.

It was all over, but the best was yet to come. Our mother gave her card to Dad, who reckoned up the earnings and about a week later, we all dressed up in our best clothes to walk to the farmer's house to be paid. Usually our sums matched that of the farmer, so everyone was happy.

One year we twins got new winter coats and the next year the winter's coal was bought with the proceeds.

This happened at the beginning of the 20th century. My mother went hop picking when we were babies until we were in our early teens.'

'During the 1930s Les and his brothers and sisters went off with their mother to the hop fields. Dad had his work to do so he stayed at home and looked after himself for six weeks and visited at weekends if he had time.

There were five families in the street at River where they lived and they all went together on the back of a lorry with their bedding, cooking equipment, clothes and some food to last while they settled in. The hop fields were at Littlebourne. The one where they worked was called Lower Garrington at the top of the field, and the other was called Upper Garrington which was at the bottom – most odd!

They had the same two huts each year which were about ten feet by ten feet. The only window was an opening with a wooden shutter at the side of the door. One hut was for sleeping all the family in and the other was for general purposes. The cooking was done on an open fire made of faggots outside in front of the huts. The water was collected from the nearby stream and there was no lighting except by candle or oil lamp, so everyone went to bed as soon as it got dark.

140

The toilets were the bucket type at the end of the field for everyone to use.'

FROM STRINGING UP TO BAKING

'The farm on which my father worked at Wingham was a fruit and hop farm with a few animals. A great deal of time was spent in the hop gardens. About Easter time when the gardens were bare it was time to prepare the string for training the bines up. This was done in a big shed in our garden. A home-made gadget of a large wheel, similar to a small water-wheel with a handle in the centre stood at one end, the circumference of which was the necessary length of the strings to reach from the top wire to the bottom wire. We placed a large skein of coconut string on a smaller wheel at the other end. When the wheel had been turned 100 times, the string on the large wheel was tied in two places about a foot apart then cut between the two ties. The new "run out" skein was then tied to my father's waist. Using a ladder he would strap himself into his stilts. The strings would now hang down. From his waist he would take one at a time and tie it to the top wire. My mother walked behind with a pole about six ft in length, a small hook in the end. She would catch the strings and tie three at a time loosely on the breast wire. When the weather was windy the strings blew all over the place which made it very difficult for "catching". We all helped to tie the strings to the breast wire and finally to the bottom one. Stringing took about three weeks; my sister and I spent most of our school holidays helping but our skin became very sore as the string drawing through our hands was very coarse and rough. Dry soap was the only way to build up a barrier. Gloves only lasted a short while – they were soon in shreds.'

'Special men were employed to pull the hops from the poles, called a pole puller. Hops had to be picked up from around the bins. When the bins were full the measurer came round with a bushel basket and the number of bushels were entered into a book; one book for the pickers and the other one for the farmer. Hops had to be prepared for measure with no leaves or stalks. A special person called the booker made sure the correct number of bushels were entered into the books according to the size of the hop. The pickers were paid per bushel. It could be four to six bushels for one shilling. Bags of hops were then taken to the oast house to be dried. This was a specialized job, so a hop dryer came each year for this long, trying job of 24 hours. Hops were put in the oast kiln and baked for a certain length of time, by the use of anthracite coal and some sulphur and charcoal. The hops were then pressed into pockets, which were large bags with the farmer's name and address written on them. They would then be sent to the brewery to be made into beer.

If the weather was cold the children would light a fire in the hop field to keep warm. In the wet weather people would make a tent of waterproof material to put over their heads and continue picking. If the weather persisted everyone abandoned picking until the next day. Lunch times were a special occasion when everybody sat on the picked hop branches and exchanged all the local gossip.'

THE KENT MINERS

The beginning of the 20th century saw 'coal mania' in East Kent, with the development of some nine collieries proposed. Out of those nine, four were actually successful – Chislet, Betteshanger, Snowdown and Tilmanstone. Today, the closure, one by one, of East Kent's collieries is 'leading us towards a generation for whom Kent coal is something "that used to be, years ago".'

TILMANSTONE COLLIERY

'Sinking at Tilmanstone began in 1906, despite difficulties of access for all the building materials and heavy engineering equipment needed. The nearest railhead then was the South Eastern & Chatham Railway's station at Shepherdswell, some two and a half miles away. To complete delivery to the colliery site, since motor lorries did not then exist and the sheer weight and quantity was beyond horse and cart transport, the only answer was the steam-powered road traction engine. Continuous journeys wrought havoc on the unmetalled country lanes and it is said that an apparently pointless kink in the present Shepherdswell-Eythorne road is due to someone my husband knew in later years swinging further and further out to avoid an area he had already churned up to mud as he drove his traction engine from Shepherdswell station to the colliery. These problems were solved after five years – and still before the colliery became operational – when the East Kent Light Railway's first line, from Shepherdswell to Tilmanstone Colliery, was opened for freight traffic.

To the 1930s generation, the collieries were, and are, and evermore shall be – though we ought to have known better, for even by then some of the main workings at Tilmanstone were over a mile and a half from the pit bottom. This must be one early sign of a colliery beginning to become uneconomic – too much underground travelling and too little actual working time in an eight hour shift. But there was no public thought of that at the time.

Tilmanstone had been further developed in 1929/30 by the construction of a cross-country aerial ropeway, carrying buckets each holding about three quarters of a ton of coal from the colliery to a 5,000 ton capacity bunker at the seaward end of the eastern arm of Dover harbour, whence the coal could readily be gravity loaded into ships.

Gases (causing explosions and fires), subsidence and water can all beset mining undertakings. There was, of course, constant vigilance for gas at Tilmanstone, but we do not think any was ever detected. Subsidence, too, has never happened and does not seem likely when the main workings were over 1,500 ft down. Indeed, when all four collieries were operational they were spoken of as among the deepest in the country.

Water, however, was a constant problem at Tilmanstone, from the very outset and throughout the colliery's working life. The cost of keeping pace with it by unceasing pumping was considerable, and when it was brought to the surface there was another problem – what to do with it. The solution adopted was an extensive network of waterways, where the theory was that it should soak away or evaporate. Unfortunately some of these waterways, adjoining the colliery site itself, were alongside the public road, and, as the water came up just slightly warm, it needed only the right combination of wind direction and atmospheric humidity for clouds of mist from the waterways to drift across the road, like a local fog.

The outbreak of war in 1939 brought Governmental pressure for increased domestic coal production. The industry became a "reserved occupation" – those engaged in it were not called up for service in the armed forces; indeed, later on some young men who were called up under wartime legislation were directed into coal mining rather than into the armed forces, and became known as "Bevin Boys" after Ernest Bevin, Minister of Labour in the then coalition government.

Tilmanstone's biggest problem in trying to increase output above its average of about 5,000 tons a week was absenteeism – coal face workers failing to attend for a full five (afternoons) or six (mornings) shift week. To some extent this may have been genuinely for health reasons – men feeling the need for a break from arduous work in unpleasant conditions without being ill enough to need more than

143

one day or to obtain a doctor's certificate. To try to discourage absenteeism, an attendance bonus was introduced – one shilling per shift provided the full week was worked. Five shillings extra for completing a five-shift week may seem derisory now, but in those days the five shillings put, for example, into a slot machine would have produced 100 Players cigarettes, in five packets of 20, each with a halfpenny change within its cellophane wrapping.

The attendance bonus, however, did little to encourage a small bolshie minority, who said "This is a capitalist war – why should we do anything to help?" It took Hitler's attack on the USSR, so that the USSR and Britain automatically became allies, to change that!

For Tilmanstone, wartime black-out produced an unusual problem, as well as just dousing lights as everyone else had to. In the mid 1930s, an EK Railway engine crew, on shunting work in the colliery sidings, cleaned out their fire box and simply threw the red-hot clinker out by the track side. Unfortunately, the whole area was the levelled top of an enormous colliery spoil heap, probably started with the original excavated material from sinking the shafts and built on continuously over the next 25–30 years with shale, etc which was of no use but had to be mined to get at the coal seams. In the nature of things, this waste material had some coal mixed with it – not enough to be worth the cost of trying to sort it out, but enough to take smouldering fire from the railway engine's red-hot clinker. Presumably it was well alight before it was realised that it would not go out of its own accord; and then, despite all attempts to extinguish it, the whole area went on smouldering for years, giving off evil-smelling fumes and with flickering flames appearing here and there on the surface. Even the diversion of some of the waste water pumped up from underground to flow over it failed to put it out, and merely added to the foul smells, such as result from spraying water on red-hot cinders. Presumably some way was eventually found to end it when it became essential to meet the black-out regulations.

The post-war years brought nationalisation, ever-increasing carriage of coal by road, and ultimately closure one by one of the four Kent collieries, leading us towards a generation to which Kent coal is something "that used to be, years ago". Will they, we wonder, regret the passing of the industry – or will they be glad that in Kent at least the 21st century does not ask men to put in eight hours a day deep underground in such demeaning conditions?'

THE MINERS OF TILMANSTONE

'Dad came to Dover looking for work during the 1920s recession, and found work at Tilmanstone Colliery. He used to cycle there and back every day from his lodgings in Dover. After he married and we were born my uncle also came to work there. In later years a bus was laid on and every day when Dad and my uncle came home from work they went straight to the bathroom and stripped to the waist, and my brother and I used to scrub their backs before they had their bath. We always kept plenty of vaseline as this was rubbed around the eyes to soften the hardened coal dust before it could be washed off. My brother and I got quite used to seeing the blue scars on their backs where the coal dust had got into the cuts and not been cleaned out properly.

It was nice for us when the pits had the baths built and the men could come home nice and clean. When they were working down the pits they wore hardly any clothes, but heavy boots, knee pads and, of course, the miner's helmet were essentials. It sometimes took nearly half an hour to get to the coal face, walking or crawling after getting off the underground train.

We used to look forward to them coming home on Friday afternoons when we would run and meet them and they would open their snap tins (which were used for their food) and we were given a penny each. We couldn't wait to get to the shop to buy a gobstopper or some aniseed balls.'

'Before the mining village of Elvington was built, miners had to live in Dover, travelling on a little train nicknamed the Paddy to the colliery. The miners were not popular in the town and sometimes found difficulty getting lodgings. Some landladies with rooms to let added to the vacancy notice in their windows "No Miners or Dogs", which greatly incensed the miners.

Many men, like my father, suffered from respiratory troubles from breathing the fine coal dust, and found the steep climb home after an eight hour shift very exhausting. At first all the men came home black, but in 1930 some fine pit head baths were built.

Water was always a hazard in the mine. For every ton of coal mined, 17 tons of water had to be pumped out. My father often told us how the men who wore only briefs and boots perspired in the terrific heat. One day out walking with him we passed one of the outlets from the mine with water gushing out and I innocently asked if it was the miners' sweat.'

'Elvington was a cosmopolitan community. Men and their families had travelled from Wales, Somerset, the Midlands and the North, even Scotland.

The community spirit was very high. Mr R Tildon Smith, who owned the colliery, had turned the barn over to the miners for their recreation and it was made into a leisure centre run by the miners themselves. Weekly dances were held, the Dramatic Society made use of it and also the boxing tournaments, to name but a few.

There were some amusing characters in the village, including Mr Crane who played a one string fiddle and other musical instruments. He and his wife had had 21 children. He was also a local comedian and often performed at the Working Men's Club. His wife Louisa always smoked a clay pipe and played the organ.'

BETTESHANGER COLLIERY

'Friday, 25th August 1989 is a date that will be remembered by not only the 630 men employed at Betteshanger Colliery, but also by those who had been employed there over the previous 60 years. The closure of the colliery also ended the existence of the Kent coalfield.

In the 1930s men travelled from all over the United Kingdom to this new colliery which was owned by Messrs Pearson and Dorman Long Ltd. Many men did not have the fare to travel by bus or train and so walked to Deal and the surrounding district to find work. On arrival at Deal they were not made too welcome by the local inhabitants, who were rather concerned about the mass influx of "foreigners" into this seaside town and farming area.

After the housing estates had been built at Betteshanger Colliery village and Mill Hill in Deal it was said that there was an invisible barrier at the bottom of Mill Hill, above which was not looked upon as part of the town of Deal. It must be said that whilst some of the newcomers were rather rough and ready, the majority with their families wanted to settle in their new environment and mix with the locals. Some grocer's shops displayed the sign "Miners Bacon", which were the cheap cuts, but as time went on the traders realised that the workers at Betteshanger Colliery had a considerable bearing on the increase in their takings.

The number of employees increased to nearly 3,000 and the colliery had a very good customer in the Southern Railway as the coal produced was excellent steam raising coal. It also supplied the domestic market locally.

As the colliery was the one closest to France it was bombed a number of times during the war. Although there was an anti-aircraft gun site at the end of the colliery tip, the German fighter bombers used to fly very low across the English Channel, undetected by radar, drop their bombs and quickly return to their bases in France. On one occasion part of the colliery boiler house and fan house were destroyed and several men lost their lives. This caused a problem for the men working underground as they could not be brought to the surface as the winding engines were steam driven. The men had to wait underground for several hours before an emergency winder could be erected which brought the men to the surface a few at a time, a very lengthy process. One bomb dropped just outside the lamproom, making a big cloud of black dust and a very large hole, but luckily it never exploded. On examination later it was found to be full of nuts and bolts, thanks to some foreign worker in a German factory.

After the war working conditions at the colliery were poor. Coal was produced by pick and shovel and the ventilation was very bad. Men emptied their boots when they became full of sweat. Wages were on piecework and men were paid on results. If geological conditions were poor then wages were low and men had to make their money when conditions were good. At this time many coal faces were affected by water and at times men were working in water up to their knees and sometimes above.

In 1947 the coal industry was nationalised and after some time conditions of work did begin to improve and much money was spent on dust suppression underground as many men suffered from silicosis or pneumoconiosis, the scourge of all miners.

Later the first miner to be elected as a Councillor on the Deal Borough Council was Billy Marshall, a real character, who could be seen every Sunday on Deal seafront speaking on his "soapbox". The miners were being recognised as inhabitants of the town of Deal at last.

As time progressed mechanisation was slowly introduced underground and the pick and shovel method of working gradually began to disappear, although some types of work could not be mechanised. Men had to be trained in this new method of working and the younger element found it easier than the older ones.

Over the years the colliery had its "ups and downs" and geological conditions in Kent were not as good as some other coalfields in Great Britain. In 1969 Chislet Colliery was the first to be closed. Tilmanstone Colliery was the next to go in 1986 and Snowdown Colliery followed in 1987. A large number of miners took either voluntary retirement or voluntary redundancy or were transferred to other collieries. In 20 years the Kent coalfield had gone from four collieries to none.'

IN SERVICE

For most young girls in the first decades of the 20th century, going into service was the only employment available. In the days when even modest middle class families had at least one servant, there was always a job for the hard working maid.

THE SCULLERY MAID

'At the beginning of the 20th century there was only one thing that girls from a working family could do; that was to become a servant in the home of a wealthier family. My mother was the middle child in a family of seven and as soon as she left school she was found "a place" as a scullery maid, the lowest of the low. She was never allowed in the "upstairs" rooms or to meet any of "the family" but was responsible to the cook, the parlourmaid, the kitchenmaid and all other uniformed staff.

Her first job at 6 am each morning was to clean the kitchen grate and bring in the sticks for the fire, which had to be burning well before any others came down. Next, to make tea and take it up to Cook in bed, and woe betide if it was not exactly to Cook's liking; she would be scolded and made to throw it away and make another. Next, winter and summer, she would have to scrub the outside steps on her hands and knees.

The vegetables were then brought in for the day and Mum had to scrub them clean under the cold water tap in the scullery, where she sat to eat her meagre breakfast of what was left after Cook and the others had finished. She worked at the beck and call of Cook throughout the day until the family had eaten their evening meal, when the piles of dirty saucepans and dishes were brought out for her to wash up. By then Cook was ready for her evening cocoa, which had to be exactly right. She would then crawl up the back stairs, which were bare boards, to her miserable attic bedroom – no fire, a tiny window through which the sun never shone, bare floorboards, a narrow, hard bed with one threadbare blanket, one broken chair and a stand with a cracked jug and basin containing cold water for washing.

Mother was given a half day off per week and one Sunday per month. Needless to say she was very unhappy. One morning she woke to find her nightgown muddy and wet and, on arrival downstairs, she found the wood laid on the hearth to dry. She must have walked in her sleep to perform this task, so worried was she. Her mother allowed her to leave and find another place when she realised how unhappy she was.

This was a smaller establishment with fewer restrictions, so she could enjoy the "comforts" of the kitchen. However, when her mother visited her unexpectedly in her kitchen and found her eating her tea, which consisted of crusts and scraps from her mistress's table and the watered-down tea from upstairs, she was horrified. At that moment her mistress came down and when she saw my grandmother, she chastised my mother, saying, "Had I known your mother was coming, I would have found a tablecloth and supplied decent toast and butter, etc." However Grandma retorted, "What is good enough for Emily is good enough for me. She gets better food at home. Emily, pack your bags, I am taking you home with me." That was the end of Mother's days in service.'

THE 'TWEENY

'When I left school in the 1920s I trained in needlework with a local dressmaker for a short while, before working in the basement of a departmental store which made loose covers, for one shilling a week. I didn't do much needlework, only cleaned up bits of material and threads from other people's work. Dissatisfied with this, I decided to go into service. At the age of 15 I began as a between maid, or in other words a skivvy to everyone else.

A Scottish lady owned a large house in Hythe where the staff included a parlour maid, a cook, a between maid and a house boy, all of whom lived in. It was my job to do all the scrubbing and cleaning in the house, and I can remember seeing carpets for the first time – we only had lino at home. I had to buy my own uniform, which was a blue dress with apron, black shoes and stockings and a frilled cap which I wore for visitors.

I had one Sunday off in three, but I didn't leave until about half past two. I had to clean all the pots and pans first. Also I had a half day on Tuesday but by the time I had walked three miles home it was tea time. I was paid six shillings and fourpence a week, and was very happy at this house. I slept in the attic, and each morning had to take a cup of tea up to the cook before she came down to cook the breakfast.'

'On leaving school at Nonington at 14 I went straight into service in a big house. There was no choice for me as it meant one less mouth to feed at home. I started as a between maid doing the scrubbing and all the kitchen washing up, which meant a lot of pots and pans and sieves, which were hard to clean. When the parlourmaid left to get married I was promoted to housemaid, which entailed a lot of polishing through long passages and down the stairs, which were uncarpeted. We had to make our own polish, which consisted of beeswax, castile soap and turps. These were cut up and mixed in a stone jar and placed in a pan of boiling water until dissolved. Sometimes it turned out lumpy, which made it hard to rub in.

I had to rise at six o'clock to get the kitchen range lit to boil the water for the master's shave. After that I had to clean the dining room and lay breakfast. When the family were down, all the staff went into the dining room for prayers; then it was all systems go to get the beds made and room and bathrooms cleaned, before cleaning the silver which was kept locked away, the parlourmaid being responsible for the key. We had two hours off on alternate afternoons and two hours every other Sunday. There were no electrical appliances so the polishing and carpet sweeping was done on hands and knees. I slept in the attic, which was freezing cold in winter – even the water in the jug used to freeze. I stayed in service for four years until I was 18 and then decided to join the ATS, which was a different life altogether.'

UPSTAIRS, DOWNSTAIRS

'Seventy years ago, I lived at the Golden Bell cottage in School Lane, Tilmanstone with my granny. She died when I was 16 and I went to live at North Court, the home of the village squire, Mr Henry Rice, and his wife Kathleen. I suppose you would say I was a lady's maid. I had my own bedroom, and in the cold weather Mr Bill Luck, one of the staff, used to bring up some coal and sticks for me to light a little fire in my room. The other girls did not have fires in their rooms, so I was very lucky.

When Mr and Mrs Rice went away, I used to have Billy the mastiff in my room. The village policeman, Mr Webb, was asked to "keep an eye on things" and given £5 for his trouble. Sometimes at night, on his round, he would come into the kitchen for a cup of tea.

One of my regular jobs was to brush the hair of the lady of the house, and fasten around her hair a black velvet band which she always wore. I also washed out some of her delicate clothes and sometimes ironed these after lunch, and pressed any items she needed for the evening.

When the family went down to Berkshire I very often travelled with them. The family chauffeur, Mr Ernest Neale, took us to the station in the car and I sat with them in the train. My wages were paid at the end of each month and it was good money in those days.

There was a little dairy building near North Court and sometimes Mr Rice would tell me to "take one of those small jugs over there, and skim some of the cream off for me, and have some yourself". The dairymaid usually knew I had been in there for some cream.

In the evenings I enjoyed playing my sixpenny Woolworth's records on a small gramophone, which the master of the house referred to as "that infernal machine". The staff went to bed at half past ten after a milk drink or cocoa, and we all had to call "Goodnight ma'am" and "Goodnight, Sir" when we passed by their rooms; they knew when any of us was late and asked where we were!'

'I worked in service as a housemaid at Chilham Castle before the last war. Sir Edmund Davis owned the castle then and he used to come down at weekends.

I used to visit home at Ramsgate on the train and, once, arriving back at Chilham station at ten o'clock at night, I was approached by a man and pulled into a car. I managed to escape and get help from a nearby house and was walked home to Chilham Castle. After that Sir Edmund arranged for a policeman to meet girls coming home on a late train. Once I had to get out of the train and shelter in a ditch as the train was near Manston airbase and it was being bombed.

I stayed at the Castle for seven years. We used to wear white pinnies tied at the back with a big bow. Once I was stuck under a bed for an hour with my dustpan and brush, as my bow had become entangled with the underside of the bed and I could not get free. Nobody heard my shouts for help!

I went on two train trips to London from the Castle. Eight or nine of the maids went and we were met by the butler, who took us to Harrods for lunch and to a Lyon's Cornerhouse for tea. Once we saw Royalty. The third kitchenmaid was wearing a new hat, made and embroidered by her mother, and in the excitement this hat got knocked off and trampled on by a horse. She was very upset and did not know how she was going to tell her mother about it.

The staff took it in turns to go to the South of France with the family each year, but Sir Edmund died the year it was my turn, so I never went.

It was during my time there that the Castle had a big robbery and Sir Edmund's Rembrandts were stolen. Two were found abandoned and another was retrieved from an aeroplane.

They were happy days, but it was hard work.'

FISHERMEN AND BOAT BUILDERS

From oysters to herrings, harvesting the seas provided a living for many men over the years, as did building the boats, big and small, which enabled them to do the job. Each in their way was a craftsman.

FAMILIES OF FISHERMEN

'All the family were fishermen and my great great grandfather owned several fishing trawlers. He used to purchase them in Mevagissey and sail them home round the coast to Folkestone.

The house where my great grandfather was born had a scullery which went under the footpath and in the cellar there was a well. My grandmother and mother both told of passageways leading off from this well which formed part of the intricate system by which the smugglers used to avoid the excise men in days gone by. My mother said she did see this, although it was covered over many years before she lived in the house. The secret ways led from the cliffs in Folkestone to Hockly Sole, then called Hockeys Hole, several miles from the shore. These old buildings are now all demolished, but my great great grandfather's house has become famous and is depicted in many postcards of the area.

The rooms above the house were used to store and dry their nets and the Tanlade next door was used to preserve the nets by dipping them in "cutch" which turned the nets a tan colour when dry. These buildings date from the 17th century.'

'My uncle Robin Tart lived at Lade, just along from Dungeness, and shared a boat, FE106, with a relative, "Fiddle" Tart. Uncle Bob was a handsome man very like the sailor in the advertisement for Player's Navy Cut cigarettes, and he always wore a "tan frock" (a fisherman's linen tanned smock). He married my mother's sister and they lived in a little black tarred house, a stone's throw from the sea, all their long married lives – a kind, quietly spoken and much loved couple known to everyone in the area as Uncle Bob and Aunt Flo.

Life must have been very hard for them. Uncle would go out fishing in the boat all night and half into the next day, sometimes with no catch at all. In the herring season he would be luckier. He had a herring hang, a tall narrow brick building with a single chimney in which he could smoke over 1,000 fish. They were smoked for two days using *oak* sawdust, and never have bloaters tasted so delicious!

Shrimps were another of his catches; they were boiled and then taken to Lydd railway station (long since vanished!) and sent further afield. Uncle Bob and Aunt Flo had no family and never strayed much further than Lydd (where they would have to have walked over the shingle) but they were two of the most contented and kindly people I ever met.'

Mending the fishing nets on Folkestone beach.

'"Come on, son, the boats are ashore." It was my mother. I tumbled from my bed, looked at the clock and saw it was six o'clock.

Between mouthfuls of steaming hot porridge I asked, "How many they got then?" "About a last a boat and don't hang about, your father will be waiting for this jug of tea." It was bitterly cold and I slipped a couple of times on the sheets of ice in the road as I hurried down to the beach, stopping on the corner of the rough road for a sip from the big enamel jug.

A last a boat – that's 10,000 herrings each for the two boats that were herring drifting, all of which had to be shaken from the mile and a half of drift nets and counted out into boxes, a "warp" at a time (a warp being four herrings). It would take until midday, and with luck my father would ignore the ringing of the school bell and I would have a whole morning fetching, carrying and counting the seemingly never ending pile of herrings that were shaken from the nets. But not this morning. As the school bell began to ring I climbed aboard the boat and hid in the cabin, hoping that I wouldn't be missed. It wasn't to be. "Come on, cut along now, you've had enough this morning. Get home and get washed before going to school and get a note from your mother to say why you are late."

As I climbed out of the boat a thought struck me, and instead of going home I went straight on into school, already an hour late. I took my place by the large open fire. Mr Bigg laid down his chalk and made his way over to me, opened his mouth to deliver the usual remarks, stopped, sniffed twice and said, "Boy, you stink. Go home and wash yourself."

The rest of the morning was happily spent on the golf links catching newts from the pond, which would sell at four for a halfpenny.'

CRAFTSMEN IN WOOD

'Collar Brothers shipyard in Whitstable was founded by my great grandfather and the family were boat builders for many years. The shipyard was sold in 1910 but before that it had been a thriving yard, building fishing smacks and dinghies and repairing colliers.

On the seaward side of Island Wall was the yard's sawpit, six feet or more deep and many feet long. The timbers for the boats were hand cut, the seasoned timber being pushed over the pit on rollers. The logs for the keels etc were cut end to end by a hand saw some five feet long, with a handle at each end, with an up and down sawing action. The man at the top needed very strong muscles to continually bend up and down and the man at the bottom had a very hard and dirty job, with all the sawdust falling on him.

154

Mr Wallace Harvey, the historian, tells me that the yard had two slipways, reaching from the top of the beach, across the shingle and foreshore to the muddy flats, probably a distance of 80 yards or so. There were many shipways at Whitstable, some 28 I am told, at the height of the shipbuilding industry. When I was a child very few remained, but I had some adventurous times clambering on a very high, long and slippery one at West Beach – when my mother wasn't looking.

During very severe winters, especially 1895, when Whitstable Bay was icebound and the fishing boats were unable to put to sea, great distress was caused in the town, and Collar Bros opened a feeding centre at the shipyard to give a hot breakfast to those in need.

The yard specialised in oyster smacks and built some 250 boats over the years. One of their boats, *The Gamecock*, built in 1907, was the last working oyster smack. It has been sailed and lovingly maintained by Mr Bill Coleman, and until recently was used for the ceremonial landing of oysters to open Whitstable's annual Oyster Week celebrations. Other boats have been spotted as far afield as Ayrshire and Spain. My grandfather was a quiet, unassuming and modest man, and pride would have been quite foreign to him, but I think he would have felt a glow of satisfaction that the yard's workmanship still survives.

The site of Collar's Yard can still be seen at Island Wall, beside Collars Alley. Its timber yard was on the other side of the road and formed part of the site of what is now a building called The Saltings.'

THE WHITSTABLE OYSTER FISHERY CO.

'My great grandfather, Mr William Camburn, was a director of the Whitstable Oyster Fishery Company.

The oyster fishery has an unbroken history of 200 years. The Royal Whitstable Natives had beds of several thousand acres, all as carefully maintained as flower beds, over about six square miles stretching out into the Swale Estuary off Whitstable. This included breeding grounds and the larger fattening grounds. When the sea froze over in 1895, 1929, 1940, 1947 and 1963, millions of oysters were killed.

Sea algae, the oyster's favourite food, was grown at Seasalter in a mixture of fresh and salt water which made the Whitstable oysters thrive above all others.

A Native takes seven years to become adult and it starts the size of a speck of sugar. The spat, as it is called, floats in the water for a few days before it falls to the bottom to anchor itself by a sticky substance to a shell or the side of some other hard substance to which the general term "cultch" is applied. It settles deeper, left shell uppermost, the flat or right shell being next to the ground to enable the oyster to eject sand or grit.

The Whitstable Oyster Fishery Co extended the close season for Natives until Partridge Day, 1st September to protect the spawning period. The oysters were dredged up from the flats by fleets of fishing smacks under full sail or open rowing boats, working up or down with the tide with a crew of four men. A Whitstable yawl, clinker built, was the most common boat. The "dredge" was special to the oyster trade, each boat working five or six dredges at different levels to bring up the catch. The catch was brought ashore in baskets for sorting and selling.

Once ashore the oysters were stored, suspended in bags, in large sea water tanks called "pits" in the storehouses. From here they were sorted, measured and sold in quantities with names such as a "wash", a "peck" (half a wash), a "nipperkin" (a sixteenth of a tub), a "bucket" (a twelfth of a tub), or a "pottle", which was two quarts. The oysters were then packed into tubs and sent to Billingsgate Market in London on waggons. In 1912 over 19 million oysters were sold. The Oyster Fishery Co was ruined by the introduction of the diesel engine and the oil seeping onto the oyster beds.

The boys used to make grottoes of the oyster shells and little pieces of candles, and I can remember my brothers with their piles of oyster shells and their cries of, "Please remember the Grotter". My brother Sid died after a pile of tubs in which the oysters were packed fell on top of him.

My aunt remembers, "The outstanding pleasure was the pie Mother made on "Court Day", full of various fruits probably supplied by Grandpa Camburn, for he had an orchard as well as a long garden". Court Day (its proper name was "Water Court") was the day every July when the officials of the company were elected and when the apprentices, after serving their seven years, became Free Dredgers.'

OTHER WAYS WE MADE A LIVING

There were, of course, hundreds of other ways in which people made a living, from watercress growing to nursing to making bricks. Here are just a few memories of working life in the past.

IN THE BRICKFIELDS

'The exact date when bricks were first made in Stanford is not precisely known, but it would have been in the late 1800s. The brickyard is known to have formed part of the Sandling Park Estate and to have been working, in a small way, in 1898, when my grandfather, Mr Beeching Down, came from Westwell to take over and run the yard, under contract to Mr J Egerton Quested of Cheriton, Folkestone. At about this time Mr Quested leased the yard and some years later bought the property and the right to dig "brick earth", from which his bricks were made.

A new kiln for "burning" the bricks etc was erected and was a vast improvement on its predecessor. The quality of the hand-made bricks and tiles soon became well known in the area, often being specially demanded by architects for important buildings, including the House of Commons and the Duke of York's School, Dover.

Clay for the bricks was dug from the field behind the brickyard, and that for tiles was obtained from a pit adjacent to St David's, just north of The Drum Inn. In both cases about three ft of top soil had to be removed before the clay was exposed. This was then dug out by spades in thin slices and built into a large pile for future use – this work was usually done in the winter when bricks and tiles could not be made, as they would have been damaged by frost.

The burning or firing of the products in the kiln was the culmination of a great deal of hard work and called for a high degree of skill in placing items in the kiln in order that they were correctly fired and did not suffer damage. The furnaces were lit by wood and then stoked by special coal, using some 40 tons during the process. The cycle took approximately one week to load the kiln, one week to fire it and another week to cool down, before it was emptied. During the burning period the furnaces had to be stoked every three hours, and towards the end of the week, every hour. It was possible to walk round the top of the kiln and look in on the products being burnt. Flames could be seen over the top of this area, which was

Re-roofing the brick kiln at Stanford in 1934. The quality of the hand made bricks and tiles made here became well known.

white hot, and at the end of the week sand was shovelled on the top to retain the heat as the kiln cooled down.

Whilst the kiln was being emptied the items were carefully checked and those in good condition were stacked for future sale. Any damaged or sub-standard items were placed on special heaps, and it was well known that one local builder, responsible for erecting a number of houses in Stanford, would arrive with a very large hand barrow and ask for "a shilling's worth of bats". He would spend ages sorting through the reject heaps of bricks, which went into the building of his houses.

In its many years of operation the brickyard relied on horses for its power – electricity was not connected until long after the Second World War, although it was close at hand.

After the war Major Quested, who had taken over from his father, decided to sell the brickyard, and it was bought by Messrs Lamb and Sons, a large firm of brick and tile manufacturers in Surrey. Some changes were made, but in a competitive market hand-made bricks and tiles were much more expensive than those made by machine and, eventually, Herbert and Walter Down decided that as they were long over retiring age they had had enough, and the brickyard eventually closed in October 1953.'

'My father was company secretary and accountant of a small brickmaking firm at the time of the First World War, and spent hours writing minutes and writing out cheques in the most beautiful copperplate handwriting.

Many of the bricks made where Father worked were transported up the Thames and Medway to builders in London or other of the towns near the rivers. Each barge had a two-man crew. We had a telephone extension from the office, switched to us in the evenings, so that barge captains could contact Father if they were in trouble in the evenings – and they frequently were! The captains rang up to say a man had not turned up or was not sufficiently sober on arrival to be of use. They needed a mate soon or they would miss the tide. Father would get on his bicycle, or walk if it was dark and hurry to Milton to try to find the missing man or another bargee willing to go. Sometimes the call came after the barge had reached its destination. The mate had gone ashore and not returned or no one was there to receive the bricks. Should the captain put them ashore? This was a great problem. If unloaded someone might claim salvage for moving them. The barges usually returned to base full of "rough stuff". This was household waste, consisting mainly of cinders and ashes from coal fires. In the brickyard, this was sifted. The cinders were used to help burn the bricks and the dust was mixed with the clay to make more bricks.

The time came when road transport took the place of river transport and the barges were sold.'

'My father and his six brothers all worked on the mud barges. Our village of Murston consisted of brickmaking and cement works, and they used to have to work with the tides. They cycled or walked from Murston to Elmley Ferry, about two and a half miles, then got in a small rowing boat and rowed across the Swale to Elmley Island (known to us as Turkey Island). I remember him having to get up and go off at 2 am sometimes, or whenever the tide allowed them to dig mud and load the barges, which when loaded would sail up the Milton Creek to Murston Brickworks. The tool they used to dig the mud was called a fly tool and was similar in shape to a boat oar.

I have also known my father to put a stop net down across a reelway at low tide and then go back at the next low tide and pick up fish by hand. He would come home with a large zinc bath full of flat fish, and my mother would string them in fives and sell them to folks in the village (five massive plaice for a shilling).

Our next door neighbour worked in the brickfields and it was almost certain that when the boys left school at 14 years old they too would work in the brickfields. I recall having to go there with the girl next door when we came home from school at lunchtime to take her father's dinner to him on an enamel plate tied in a red patterned handkerchief.'

WATERCRESS GROWING

'Within living memory, watercress growing was a thriving industry in Newington, near Sittingbourne. As all the work had to be done by hand, it employed quite a number of people. Originally, watercress was grown in a natural stream in the low-lying, boggy part of the village. As time went on, artesian wells were sunk to supply more water, which came up at a constant temperature of 52 degrees. Beds were dug with concrete walls alongside and concrete blocks across at intervals into which boards were slotted, enabling the depth of water to be regulated. At first, the bottom of the beds was just mud, making it difficult for the men working there, for before wellington boots became available they wore leather thigh-boots, and had wooden duck-boards on which to stand. In the 1940s it was decided to cover the bottom with brick-dust from the local brickfields. This made it easier to keep the beds level as an even flow of water was essential for the successful growing of watercress.

The beds had to be completely cleared and replanted each autumn. Once they were clean and weed-free, they were drained almost dry and cuttings saved from the previous crop were dropped all over. Too much water would wash them away, so they were allowed a few days to take root before the water was dammed and allowed to reach the required depth of about four inches. In winter, it was necessary to protect the cress from frost, by making sure it was under water. The water level would be raised and the cress either rolled with a roller made of slatted wood, or knocked down with a long-handled broom made of willow twigs.

Two sorts of cress were grown. Brown cress with slightly bronze looking leaves was grown for cutting from February onwards and green cress for summer cutting. Brown cress was popular in the London markets, and was considered by the growers to be superior in flavour. Cutting was always done by hand, using a long, thin, steel knife. Cress was cut in "hands", the cutter first filling the space between his thumb and first finger, then between the other fingers until he had as much as he could hold. The hands were packed in "pads", rectangular baskets with flat lids, made locally from the willows, or osiers, growing alongside the watercress beds. These were taken by cart to Newington station and thence by passenger train either to London or the coastal towns of Margate and Dover.

As time went on the water table lowered and water had to be pumped into the cress beds. Finally, it became uneconomic and, sadly, the watercress industry declined.

At my home we enjoyed watercress for our tea. Father would cut a hand, tie it up with a willow twig, and Mother would "pick" it, removing any yellow leaves. Then she would wash it and stand it in her watercress dish. This was a bowl with holes in the bottom which stood on a matching plate. She would have been amazed at the tiny bunches one sees in the shops today. We usually just dipped it in salt and ate it with bread and butter. Delicious.'

ON THE RAILWAY

'The beginning of this century was the heyday of railways. Our town was the site of a large railway junction, and it seemed that the majority of the working men worked on "The Line". One of our uncles was a train driver. We really respected him; he seemed quite rich to us. Another was a guard, which seemed almost as grand to us, for our father worked in the goods department, as did his father before him.

I remember when he came near us the smell of lead pencil, because he kept all his pencils in his peaked cap on his head. The most exciting thing was his lamp which he regularly brought home to clean; it was magic, as with a little twist the light became green, next twist yellow, the next red. We were not allowed to touch, just watch as Dad adjusted the colours. The lamp was a very important item, as it was used as the trucks were shunted into and out of the sheds. One day live cattle were packed into an animal truck and Dad was most distressed, as he opened the door, to find the noise was coming from a bellowing cow who had given birth in transit and whose calf had been trampled to death in the crush. Dad reported the incident but we never heard what happened to the thoughtless farmer.

The uniform consisted of a rough navy blue jacket, waistcoat, trousers, a peaked cap and a pair of heavy boots. My father always had to shorten the trousers. I can see him now with a great carpet needle and yards of thread, sewing up the trouser bottom after cutting off a great chunk of material. He also "clumped" his boots, ie nailing on a thick leather sole before he could wear them comfortably. His feet were covered in corns and he could not bear to feel anything through his shoes. It was not until he had retired through ill health, aged 63 and he was dying, that I could persuade him to let a chiropodist come and attend to his feet. Like many of his age group he was afraid of hospitals and "the knife".

Dad was on shift work, sometimes late, sometimes early. If he was on early turn he would walk home about the time we were returning to school for the afternoon. We would try to meet him and, perhaps, get a halfpenny or a farthing from him for some sweets if he was in a good mood. The railway workers were very poorly paid, so not many pennies came our way.

Though the railway workers were so poorly paid, everyone was proud to work on the line and the families could hold up their heads because their man was in full time employment, with one week's paid holiday per year. One railway pass was allowed annually, enabling the family to travel anywhere on the Southern Railway free. This covered the south of England and our family enjoyed a week by the sea each year.

Pay days were each Thursday afternoon and it was quite a sight to see the workers lining up at the passengers' ticket office for their week's earnings.

One of the worst periods of our young lives was during the General Strike when it seemed the whole world stopped working except our father, who did not believe in unions or in the idea that the workers told the employers what to do. He was reared in the tradition that workers "doffed their caps" to employers and did as they were told. Our whole family was shamed in public, called

162

names and verbally abused. At our tender age we did not understand what was happening, so we felt guilty and ashamed. Today I would be proud of my father for having the courage to stand by his own convictions.'

'On a Saturday morning in May 1925 my father, who ran the successful forge in Saltwood, had to visit Mr Deeds from Saltwood Castle, well known in the village as "Squire" Deeds. When they had talked about the job he wanted Father to do, he walked a way with Father and I heard him say, "Are you going to put your son into the business?" Father replied, "No, I don't think so."

So Mr Deeds said, "Why not try the railway? I'm a shareholder of the newly formed Southern Railway." He told Father he would write to head office to get an application form sent to me. This came within a week and I had to go to Waterloo station for a medical and a written examination, and I started as a probationer at Folkestone Junction station, a large goods station. That was the start of a railway career that lasted 48 years.

In November 1925 all the probationers were stood off until the spring, then I was sent back to Folkestone for a few months before going to Shorncliffe, now Folkestone West, during the General Strike. It caused chaos on the railways, but was not an authorised strike, so some of the railway chaps when they came back to work were stood off as a punishment. The better off ones helped the men with families out. I still have in my possession a printed document which was issued to all those who remained loyal to the railway when the strike was on. It was from the then general manager, later to be Sir Herbert Walker, and we received two days' pay as a reward.

One day at Folkestone junction when I took the mail up, there was quite a lot of excitement on the platform and I saw a marvellous shining new locomotive pulling the train. It was either *King Arthur* or one of the first of that class bringing the boat train down. There were a mass of bowler hatted and top hatted gentlemen there and it was all very exciting. Later on we had wonderful engines like the *Britannia* class and they were a marvellous sight coming through the railway arches at Ashford shining so brightly, with the French and British flags on the front of the locomotive and a golden arrow on the side.

In those early days the Hythe branch had a double track and went through to Sandgate for the summer. With the good sea fishing available, there would be as many as 400 fishermen on the platform at Sandling waiting to be taken to Hythe or Sandgate. There were steps leading down from the station and they just had to cross the road to be on the beach.

The early train at Sandling was called the paper train and Saltwood papers were wrapped and thrown out by the guard at Castle crossing. Someone from the Castle would pick them up and then smooth the papers out so that they were fit to read.'

CHARCOAL BURNING

'A charcoal pit was a round dirt patch about 12 to 15 ft across. Any wood – stumps of trees, spiles etc – was arranged in a pile until it got to the form of a wigwam with a hole in the middle. Straw or any litter that would burn was put down the hole and when it was built up straw was put all around it to cover it in. It was lit from the top of the hole and then covered and when it was burning inside, water was doused around it to stop it flaring up. To test when the charcoal was ready to use, it would have a ringing sound when tapped. Pieces of charcoal about three ft long were then built into a square and this charcoal was used in the oast house, instead of coal, for the drying of hops.'

'An uncle of mine would retreat into the woods for months to burn wood slowly into charcoal. He built the stoves with corrugated iron and lit the fires with smokeless fuel; the stoves were packed with wood then the lid put on and the warmth of the fire smouldered to take out the pitch and sap. When his cart was loaded with charcoal he would take it to sell in London. Some of his earnings were spent in the pub and, so the family say, he would stagger out, fall in the cart, and the horse would bring him home.'

COAL AND WOOD MERCHANT

'My father was a local tradesman serving the community of Hamstreet and Ruckinge as a coal, coke and wood merchant.

The coal and wood yard was my playground and a happy time was had climbing up piles of timber, balancing on poles and playing in the sawdust. The timber was purchased in lots of 50 and 100 poles at the local underwood auctions which were held at The Duke's Head Inn in Hamstreet, but sometimes Dad would buy a cant or two of wood to cut himself. Most of the timber came from the Orlestone woods and was felled with no other aid but the axe and saw, and drawn out by the horse and tug, a type of open-sided waggon. Sometimes our timber was delivered. What a thrill it was to hear the sound of the horse's hooves clip clop along the road, and the creaks and groans of the heavy waggon as it was manoeuvred into our gateway. The old horse's pace quickened as he headed towards the well and all work stopped to pump up a bucket of fresh water, because we knew he'd go no further until he'd quenched his thirst.

The timber was thrown into large piles to season and was used in rotation. It was always a pleasant sound when the logs were being cut. The saw bench was out of bounds while running, but I loved the whine of the blade as it zipped through the wood and the screech of protest when the blade hit a knot. The sawdust cascaded out in a fountain of yellow speckles, letting off a heady aroma of cut wood which lingered in the air for days. The oak logs were usually split with an axe to manageable size and put to one side for special customers who had a discerning taste, oak being considered of better quality for burning on the open fire. Beech, birch, ash and hornbeam were also used on the open fire but chestnut was not considered suitable as it sparked.

The coal trade, in the early days, did not have the same fascination for me, which was probably because a great deal of the work was carried out at the Ruckinge siding. It was there that the goods train stopped at ten past five, to leave a truck of coal. Dad, by that time, was having tea so he would send me out to our gate to watch for the train. If it stopped Dad had got some extra work to do digging out ten to twelve tons of coal by hand, which had to be done within three working days. If he overran his time, Southern Railway charged a demurrage on trucks not emptied.

The small yard at home housed the gas coke that was delivered from the Ashford gas works. There was best kitchen nuts for the ranges and silkstone for the inglenooks. These sometimes came in extremely large lumps which could weigh half a hundredweight or more. These lumps generally ended up as walls to keep the coal in. The coal was sold by the hundredweight and was weighed by hand, and even in those days the scales and weights were stringently checked. Dad always believed in keeping a good fire and on a winter's night he would select a special lump for himself to sit by. He said that was his privilege.

After the war the wood trade fell into decline and by the mid 1950s Dad was purchasing ready cut logs for the few customers who used them. By the early 1960s the coal trade, which had come into its own, was also under threat. There was talk of "cutting" the railways and Dad thought that his livelihood was threatened. Coal, now, is transported by road.'

THE CARRIER

'The Coulters had been carriers in Wye for over 400 years. The ancient business only ceased at John Coulter's death in 1963.

I recall my first sight of him in 1946, a great man of huge strength driving his cart down the middle of Wye village street accompanied by his beautiful red-headed eldest daughter Marjory, who helped to heave the hefty packages as well as any man.

The business expanded in his care. Many and devious were the journeys; meeting trains and conveying passengers to their destinations; taking pigs and sheep to Ashford market; carrying household goods from one end of the village to the other; conveying building materials for Leppers the builders; and long trips to Warehorne, Bonnington and Hamstreet. His horses pulled the fire engine, also the hearse. He conveyed the local doctor and parson to outlying villages to make calls. He had in use a brougham, waggonette, landau, governess cart trap, four-wheeled dog cart, two trolleys, eight horses and two ponies. Most of the vehicles are now on show in The Old Mill, Horley, Surrey.

There were ten domestic staff at Olanghigh House and he was hired to take them in the landau to and fro on their afternoon off. He had five daughters, who all had to play their part in the business. I am greatly indebted to Dorothy, who supplied me with a vivid description of their life.

Other children had time to play, but all John's daughters had jobs to do. As children they used to lead the horses two miles to Boughton Lees for shoeing, and were delighted if they were allowed to blow the furnace. The harnesses were cleaned by being brought into the kitchen and sponged down with warm rain water, which was heated on the range. They were hung out to dry, and the next day the buckles and leather were polished.

When coal was being delivered to the hilltop village of Hastingleigh, a trace horse was required for extra strength to pull up the hill. At eight years old, Dorothy used to meet the coal load at Cold Harbour farm, then walk the horse (three times in a morning) up the lonely wooded road to the village.

When there was a fire one of the daughters would ride behind the fire engine with spare traces, lest any was needed in an emergency. One horse called Dunster loved a fire and would never tire in his efforts to pull the fire engine.

One dark evening the carrier called into his home for a moment at a time when the horse was habitually taken to the station to meet a passenger from the train. The horse amazed everyone by meeting the train on his own. The passenger got in and was taken home, none the wiser that he was in a driverless carriage.

Despite the busy life, on summer Sunday afternoons the family used to take a leisurely ride in the varnished governess cart, which was upholstered in mole-coloured corduroy made by Brown of Slough. They rode around the country lanes, often stopping at Crundale church where sisters Mary and Marjory played the organ while father pumped the blower.

As time went by life became more mechanised. There was less work for the carrier, but he was in great demand to take folks to church at weddings and christenings. Many people enjoyed a delightful ride in one of his carriages moving at a steady pace as they surveyed the country scene.

When he finally died in 1963, his coffin was taken to church in his old carrier's cart, pulled by two of his horses.'

NURSING AT THE KENT & CANTERBURY

'For some time I had felt drawn towards making a career of nursing and I ended up by applying to the Kent & Canterbury Hospital. After a number of preliminaries I had an interview with Matron, Miss Annie Purchas. She was very tall, rather forbidding, and I was so nervous – she looked about ten feet tall! But I was accepted, and started as a "junior pro" – the lowest form of hospital life. The hospital was in Longport Street, in part of the grounds of the ruins of St Augustine's Abbey, and the cellars looked like it and were supposed to be haunted! In 1937 the old hospital was closed, then used by the Canterbury Technical College, and demolished in the late 1970s.

In those days there were no preliminary classes, no probationer training school, and I did not even know how to put my uniform on. The dress was very thick tough cotton, with tucks in the skirt making it even more bulky, buttoned to the waist and then across to the side. (Later on one nurse got into real trouble for having put an extra pleat in her skirt to smarten it up!) Then we had the collar, cuffs and wide belt, starched and polished, and the collar was guaranteed to make one's neck sore. We used to rub soap along the edge to make it wearable. These were fastened with studs – which always went missing. Over all this was the apron, large, white and again heavy cotton – serviceable being the operative word. Black stockings, and shoes, rubber-soled for quietness. (Only the office staff were allowed to wear "click-y heels".) Then the cap. This was another mystery – it came flat, with tapes run through a casing, and we had to dampen it with our toothbrush to soften the starch so that we could pull the tapes up to fit across the back of our heads. And it was no use hurrying – the tapes would break or come adrift. No jewellery, except

167

a wedding ring (and only one nurse was married). No loose hair, all had to be tucked away under one's cap or secured at the back (germs could be harboured there!).

Apart from going to and from the nurses home we were not allowed to go out in any of our uniform – once more in case we brought "infection" back to the wards, and it is amazing how an unseen ward sister could spot black stockings and/or one's striped dress, however voluminous the top coat. Also uniform was not to be added to in any way whatsoever, for instance no cardigan. Our regulation nurse's cape was supposed to be adequate.

I am not sure what our salary really came to, but by the time they had done the deductions for food, living accommodation and laundry we were left with less than £5 per month. My mother helped me out with the occasional ten shilling note, but she had her problems too.

During my years of training the new hospital was being built at South Canterbury. As time went on the number of patients was gradually reduced and when the day came for the move I was delighted to have the chance to travel with the first patient to the new hospital – women's surgical, Whigham Ward. It was so nice leaving the old worn out building, and starting again in a lovely new one.'

THE POST OFFICE

'My father was the first Post Office messenger boy at Lydd to have a uniform. He became a postman and walked miles over Romney Marsh delivering letters. One family used to post a letter to themselves, which meant his having to cover a vast distance all for a halfpenny stamp delivery!

He went to Folkestone in 1900 and worked there in the GPO for 46 years, finishing as Inspector and earning his Imperial Service Medal. In the early days there were five deliveries of letters daily, beginning at 5 am and up to about 7 pm. All the men wore navy blue uniforms piped with red braid, white stiff collars with a black tie, and I can remember Father wearing a shako type hat. Discipline was strict and woe betide any man caught smoking on duty!'

'In 1936 I took a part time job at Ramsgate post office as a telegram delivery boy. When I first arrived I found the messengers' rest room occupied by two large, self-confident, lads in full uniform; blue serge tunic, trousers, cap and belt with leather pouch. They greeted me – a callow, slightly built schoolboy – with amused tolerance and thinly veiled derision, but condescended to tell me what to do.

I was given a metal disc with a number stamped on it, a belt, and a leather pouch containing a telegram message pad. I was introduced to my bicycle, which was a bit of a shock. I had, of course, seen telegram boys before, but never knew that their bright red bicycles were so massive, rugged and heavy, so much different to my own which by then I had modified in the interests of lightness, speed and convenience! In place of my three-speed gear there was a single gear, very low and incapable of fast travel except when free-wheeling downhill. Mudguards were twice the width with double stays, the saddle springs were big enough to support a rider 20 times my weight, and the whole machine was obviously designed for long, heavy duty! No doubt a wise decision by the GPO, but not my idea of carefree, speedy travel.

The terms "telegraph office", "telegram boys" and "telegram forms" seem unfamiliar in these days of widespread use of the telephone in so many homes, but in the period described the telegram was the only means of speedy communication for the large majority of people and in the circumstances was very efficient. A simple form was completed and paid for at the post office, the message was transmitted to the nearest office to the destination and rewritten onto a form which was then handed to my contemporaries, and off we sped, ensuring that messages were delivered to any part of the country within a few hours.'

'In 1937 Mr Lewis Lemon came to Newington as postmaster and it was at this time that I trained as a Post Office telephone operator at the Newington Exchange. The area covered all of Newington, Hartlip, Lower Halstow and parts of Upchurch, Bobbing, Borden and Stockbury.

At the time there were about 150 lines, which doesn't sound very many but it did really keep us quite busy, as it was then still a manual exchange. All calls were put through by the operator; our only dialling at the time was to Chatham Exchange for London and long distance calls. Every call was noted and timed, and the dockets (slips of paper with your telephone number, destination and time on) were sent through to Canterbury Head Office every week. At busy times we wore headsets but when work slowed down at certain times of the day we used handsets. For any night calls, covered then by the postmaster, a bell was switched on, which could be heard right through the building.

There was only one operator on at a time, as this was shift work. In the larger exchanges, such as Sittingbourne, there would have been two or three girls working at any one time, but they would have a supervisor in attendance to see that they carried out their work correctly and to answer any queries. At the Newington Exchange the postmaster was responsible for this, but we also had a travelling supervisor from Canterbury every so often to check on us. This must sound all rather lonely but it was not so. Mr Lemon and his wife worked very hard there and we were a happy little group; they could also take over the switchboard if any of us girls were ill. Our work on the switchboard was all very confidential; we could not talk about it.

The telephone at that time had very little to do with the social side of the village. The phone was used mainly for people in business – the butcher, grocer, the garage proprietor, the doctor, the railway station, the local brickfields and most of the farmers. This being a fruit-growing area, the farmers would be in touch with Covent Garden early in the morning to know how much their fruit had made, so they could also decide whether it was worth picking for that day.

When war was declared many big houses around the area were taken over by the armed services and once their telephone was connected they were given priority status, which meant that there could be calls for 24 hours a day, so extra staff was then taken on to cover the night calls.

I think that the Newington Exchange went fully automatic in the latter part of the 1950s.'

BASKET MAKING

'My grandfather had a basket making business in the village of Newington in the early years of the century. This ended with his death in 1926, but during the 1939–45 war my father, who was farming in the district, could see that there would probably be a shortage of baskets in which to send fruit to market. He got in touch with the surviving basket maker in the village and put him to work in an outbuilding behind our house. Mr Barrett was already into his eighties, but he set to with great enthusiasm, practising his old skill. He sat on a sloping board with his basket between his legs, his only tools being a bodkin, a knife and a piece of metal he occasionally used for "knocking down" the cane between the stakes. Most of the time he did this with his bare hands, which became hard and horny. He was by this time bent almost double, but still very sprightly. We never saw him without his clay pipe – it seemed he never took it out of his mouth except to drink the cup of cocoa we always made him at midday.

Quite a lot of the osiers, or willows, were grown on the farm. These he used unstripped or "brown", often using a mixture of

170

Bill Barrett (left) with the load of fruit baskets he made in the 1940s. Mr Barrett worked at his craft in Newington until his death at the age of 93.

brown and stripped willow. The willows had to be soaked in a big galvanised tank and I shall never forget the acrid smell. He made huge hop baskets, bean-picking baskets, bushels, half-bushels and pecks for packing fruit for market, and kibseys. These were flat on one side, had a handle over the top, and were strapped on the fruit-pickers' backs when picking. The handles were made from hazel, cut from the hedges, but they were bound with cane which had to be imported. Mr Barrett would make an occasional trip on the "workman's train" to go to the supplier in the East End of London to place his order.

After the baskets were made, they had to be "picked". This meant trimming off the loose ends with a sharp knife and very often my father did this himself as a form of relaxation. Many of the fruit baskets were bought by wholesalers in the London markets, and Father would paint their initials on the side. They were, of course, returnable and were used over and over again.

In 1947 Mr Barrett made me a clothes basket as a wedding present, and which I still treasure. He continued to work until a few weeks before his death at the age of 93. At about the same time, it became the practice to pack fruit in wooden boxes, so we were sad to see both the passing of a great character and the end of a village craft.'

HAIRDRESSING

'On leaving school my father paid the then princely sum of £25 for me to be apprenticed at a hairdresser's in Folkestone. We learned to make shampoo from soft soap, sewed little muslin bags into which we put dried camomile flowers to use as a rinse for fair hair, learned to shampoo, cut and set hair and also to Marcel wave with tongs. We also singed hair if requested and a permanent wave was a mammoth task with the customer strung up to a machine and the whole business, to me, fraught with danger! We were taught to manicure and give facial massages and other beauty treatments, and as the firm made their own hair tonics and beauty preparations we were surrounded by all kinds of creams and lotions. Just as I was coming to the end of my apprenticeship the war began, so I am afraid my knowledge was never really put into practice!'

THE POLICE FORCE

'My father in law was a police officer in Canterbury between the wars. He told us that at weekends two officers would go on the beat in the poorer parts of the city as when the pubs turned out there used to be quite a few fights, and according to my father in law, there were lots of pubs in the city in those days! They did point duty in the main street of the city, two hours at a time.

On the lighter side, whilst on night duty he was pounding the beat when he had quite a shock as walking towards him was a person all in white. But it was only a man walking in his sleep, dressed only in his nightshirt.'

'On leaving the RAF after the war in 1947, my husband joined the Kent Police Force. Life carried on much as it had been and the men were used to discipline and service life. No matter what shift they were working, everyone had to attend pay parade at two o'clock on Mondays to collect his wages. Uniform was thick and heavy and the local doctors referred to the closed neck tunics as "pneumonia jackets". Capes when wet weighed a ton, and if a man was on traffic duty he could not manage wearing a cape so got wet! There was a boot allowance of a shilling a week and sixpence a day cycle allowance if using one's own cycle. Talking to members of the public was strictly forbidden and was referred to as "idling and gossiping". There were no personal radios so a system of points was used and each PC went to a phone box on his beat at specified times. At elections each polling station had a PC on duty all day and I remember having to push my daughter in her pram some distance in Dover to take my husband's meals on such occasions.

Fish and chip shops were beginning to open up again in war-torn Dover and sometimes the hungry young PCs would buy some and pop them into their helmets before finding a quiet corner where they could be consumed!

In later years we had a country station and I worked nearly as hard as my husband answering the telephone and coping with people at the office door. Rest days were often non-existent if someone arrived in trouble. I remember several Christmas Days being ruined, but that was how it was in those days.'

FARRIER AND BLACKSMITH

'My father was a master farrier and blacksmith and he had his own forge at Dungate, Rodmersham, from 1922 to 1950. His day started at 6.30 am, with him occasionally working through until 9 or 10 pm. Farmers from the surrounding villages sent their horses to him to be shod. He similarly looked after the horses from the local hunt (Tickham). He also made and repaired farm implements, ploughshares, hoes, forks, thistle dodgers, mattocks etc, and sharpened axes, saws, knives and scissors.

He was also a wheelwright and renewed the iron tyres on wheels for waggons and carts. He had to heat the iron tyre and fit it over the wooden wheel very quickly, tapping it into place and dousing it with water. If I happened to be helping he would yell at me to throw the water quickly over the iron tyre because there was a danger of it catching fire; the cooling by the cold water would ensure a tight fit.

I liked to watch him at work and can still remember the pungent smell as the heated shoe was fitted to the hoof. If I was lucky I would get a ride on a beautiful shire horse as it waited to be shod. On the wall where the horses were shod were the swots; these had wooden handles and were made with a horse's tail for keeping the bothersome flies off the horses whilst my father was shoeing them.

The forge was a meeting place where local farmers exchanged any news or gossip. The local policeman would call in for a chat and a crafty cigarette. The tramps also called in to boil their billy cans to make tea. People could buy paraffin and carbide for their bicycle lamps from my father at the forge.

He obtained his first car in the mid 1930s, a black Wolseley Hornet. This enabled him to visit farms and do work on the spot. During the war soldiers camped locally used to come and help him.

Father competed in shoeing competitions at agricultural shows all over southern England, gaining many certificates, but he never achieved that elusive "First".'

WAR & PEACE

THE BOER WAR 1899–1902

The war fought far away in South Africa was closely followed by ordinary folk in Kent, and aroused strong feelings, as the account of the Margate Riots of 1900 shows. When good news was received 'back home', such as the Relief of Mafeking later that year, it was enthusiastically celebrated.

THE MARGATE RIOTS 1900

'On 17th March 1900 my aunt Clara Smith began a long letter to my mother, her sister, about the events that had electrified the whole of Margate. The letter is decorated with a Union Jack flag and "God Save The Queen".

"I am sending you a paper for you to read about the pro-Boer demonstration. We have had some fun here lately. The paper does not give you any idea what the affair was like, so I will proceed to describe it. It began on Tuesday by Mr Powell hanging out a Dutch flag and very soon a lot of boys got round, then Mr Powell began to rant on about the war and the Royal Family. The boys laughed and jeered which made old Powell wild, then he stuck a portrait of the Queen in his window upside down. As soon as he came to the door one of the boys (who was eating a pennyworth of pease pudding) took all the pudding he had got left and slapped it clean in Mr P's mouth. Mr P caught hold of the boy and was going to thrash him but all the boys set on to him so he came up to the police station for protection.

While he was gone some of them climbed up and got the flag and tore it into shreds. After the police got down there the boys came up to Mr Knighton and bought all the pease pudding he had got and then went down and covered the front of Mr P's shop with it.

The next morning the sight of the shop made the people ask what was the matter and of course the boys made the most of it, and a lot of the gas works men and men who are working on the electric railway vowed he should pay for insulting the Queen, and as soon as it got dark some men from the gas works brought up three pails of tar. During the day the boys went to all the fruiterers in the town and got several bushels of speckled oranges, rotten apples and bad potatoes. The men dabbed on the tar and the boys threw the fruit, stones, bricks and anything they could get. The shop windows soon went smash. The police kept blowing their whistles for assistance and very soon you could not move in King Street from Musareds corner to the gas works. Thousands of people were there. Mr Austen [my aunt's employer, a draper I believe] would not let us go out, but we could hear them singing and cheering and making a rush every now and again. All the police and fire brigade were there on duty until half past two in the morning. During the evening four men were locked up and the hooting and hissing was awful. The paper says two were locked up, but that was not true.

About 1.50 am the Mayor made a speech and asked the crowd to quietly disperse, then the crowd gave three cheers for the Mayor but never attempted to go away. Then several of the Councillors made a speech but still they would not go. Then the Chief Constable got up and said that some of the police had been on duty all day and some of them had been considerably knocked about, and he thought that they – the crowd – had quite wrecked Mr Powell's premises (when he said that the crowd cheered like anything) and would they please go quietly away. Then some of them shouted that if the Chief would let the prisoners out they would go away. But the Chief wanted his way and said that if the crowd would go away, when all was quiet he would let the prisoners out. Oh no, not good enough shouted the crowd, you must let them out now unconditionally, meaning that they were not to appear in the morning. The Chief said he could not do that so the people said that they would stay there all night and sing songs to keep them awake and as soon as it got light they would smash up old Powell's house, so that the Chief had to let the prisoners out. I will leave you to imagine what the cheering was like out here at two o'clock in the morning. Then they gave three cheers for the police, sang *God Save The Queen*, three more cheers for the Queen, and about ten minutes after there was not a soul out there.

All day Thursday there were six policemen outside Powell's, and at about six o'clock in the evening there were about 20 policemen, all the fire brigade and about a dozen Specials. Then the crowd began to collect. Mr Austen went out to a dinner and we shut the shop up early and Eddie and I went down to see the fun. It was nearly ten o'clock when we got there. Men and women, boys and girls all together. We got near where Strattie was standing. The people were all singing *Soldiers of the Queen* when we arrived. Then Strattie said that Lord Roberts [commander of the British forces] had sent word that this position *must* be taken tonight, that we must storm those Kops (meaning the police), then someone shouted out "Charge" and all the crowd pressed forward on the police, who were linked together from one side of the road to the other and stood about three deep. Then there was a mighty shout of "Hooray" as about a dozen or so managed to break through, then an awful smash of glass and crockery, but there were a lot of Special Constables round the shop who soon pushed them out. The other lot of police were across the road from Price's corner to that fruiterer's.

There was more singing and cheering, then someone at the back would shout, "Come on lads, rally round, that position must be taken at all costs, there must be no turning back this time, push on my lads, push, hooray, push, hooray" and so they kept on but they did not always get through. Someone would shout out "What's this, Spion Kop?" and someone else said, "I do not know if it's Spion Kop, but I just copped someone on my toe and they weighed about 14 stone." There was a soldier standing near us, he was a great big fellow, and when the crowd pushed forward he pushed with all his mighty weight, and my goodness he could push. He would not go up near the front because he might get himself in disgrace but the people behind clapped him and told him that he deserved the Victoria Cross for distinguished bravery in front of the enemy.

At last Eddie and I came home because it was just on eleven o'clock. After the pubs were shut the half drunken men and all the rest determined to get through and get through they did and it was during the last struggle that PC Clark got hurt. There were no more windows to smash so they pulled out the window sashes and frames and if they had only had some tools they would have knocked the very house down but the police managed to get them outside again and after about an hour's singing they all went home. The next morning the police had the place boarded up and bills were posted all over the town and in every shop warning the people not to have any more such scenes.

I shall never get this epistle finished if I go on like this. We are busy cleaning up and feel too tired to write when all else is done . . " '

THE RELIEF OF MAFEKING

'One of my father's earliest memories was at the age of five. He was born and brought up in Teynham and remembered that when news of the Relief of Mafeking was received the village held a celebration bonfire and burned an effigy of President Kruger, the leader of the Boers in South Africa.'

THE GREAT WAR 1914–18

Kent has always been in England's front line against invasion, but the conflict which began in 1914 brought the horrors of war to the streets of Kentish towns and villages for the first time. Added to the food shortages, and the poignant sight of soldiers marching to the ships which would take them back to the trenches in France, was the threat of sudden death from the skies. Thankfully, few attacks were as terrible as the bombing of Tontine Street, Folkestone in 1917. And even when it was all over, families had to face the problems caused by long separation and the scars of war.

GROWING UP IN WARTIME

'When the First World War was declared we were in Barrow-in-Furness; I was seven years old and my brother Dick was nine. We were a Naval family and my father, an Engineer Officer, was supervising the building of HMS *Penelope*. He was immediately sent with the ship to Chatham which was to be his home port, and as soon as my mother had packed up and put everything not likely to be used in a war into storage, we travelled down to Kent to stay with my grandmother over Christmas.

Her house was on the front at Sheerness and on Christmas Day while we were eating our dinner there was a great commotion outside. My grandmother was not a person to miss any excitement and we all rushed outside to see the first German plane of the war flying over the town. It circled round and then flew back over the Channel without trying to cause damage, and nor was there any firing from Sheerness. It was the first plane I had ever seen!

In the meantime my mother had been house-hunting in Rochester and had been successful in renting No 6 Watts Avenue. She was lucky as the owner was a foreigner and the spy scare was at its height in Rochester. Lights had been seen showing from the attic and he had found it wise to leave. We lived there for the first two years of the war.

At first the war went on over our heads. "Not in front of the children" was a firm rule in our family, and with no TV or radio, the news came mostly by word of mouth or the newspapers we were not allowed to read.

The first air raid warnings started with the Zeppelin raids. From

Dover was a restricted area during the First World War and Mrs Hall had to show her Permit Book every time she entered and left the town.

our attic window we could see the Medway and the Zeppelins followed the river up to London. As soon as the warning went we would rush up to the attic to watch. It was quite exciting and we saw one shot down in flames. I never thought, or realized that people were being killed. After a warning or two we were not woken up and I don't remember that the Zeppelins came for very long.

Wounded men came over from France, and there were quite a

number in Rochester. We saw them in their blue convalescent uniforms wandering around the town. New war work was now being organised – first to entertain the soldiers and then to arrange money-making affairs to buy comforts for them. I joined in both these efforts. I remember big parties being held in what seemed to me to be a huge hall. I used to hand cigarettes and sweets round to the men, while my friend Robin – seven years old and also not at school – would recite quite happily poems his elder sisters had taught him.

As the war came nearer the soldiers were moved inland and the entertainments for them gradually ceased. When Christmas time came families tried to make things as normal as possible. We still had parties and of course went to the pantomime. This was our great treat because we went out in the dark in a cab which we shared with friends, and were really late home to bed.

The second year of the war now started and everything became increasingly difficult. There was no rationing as in the Second World War and food was gradually becoming scarcer. Sugar, butter and later meat were the first to go. Sweets and iced cakes began to disappear. My grandmother came to stay with us and developed a sense for finding short supplies. Something called "honey sugar" in seven lb jars was on sale in Maidstone and she organised an expedition by train to see what we could find. We all went, including Dandy the bulldog. We were lucky, the jar was bought, and Granny took us to the café for tea. Iced cakes were only served to customers sitting at the tables. Granny ordered bread, butter and cakes; she tested the bread and butter on Dandy – he always spat out margarine – and he duly spat it out. She complained about this, then when we each had a cake she went to the counter, asked for some bags and coming back to the table filled them with the cakes we had left and the sugar from the bowl and, giving them to Dick to carry, called for the bill and we left the shop. She couldn't understand why Mother felt embarrassed – she had paid for everything!

During this time we seldom saw my father – he was at sea, in what I think was called the Harwich Flotilla of light cruisers; he had a few days off when the ship went to Chatham dockyard. He wanted to be with my mother as much as possible in the limited time he was on shore but sometimes brought the younger officers who lived too far away to go home back to tea or an evening meal. We enjoyed this very much – but had to be sure not to be a nuisance!

The war then came very near to us for my father's ship was torpedoed; he brought it back safely and he was unhurt. I never thought my father would be wounded or killed and so it was exciting news, we felt very proud and boasted to the other children. Then suddenly, more news – my father was to have a shore job and we were to go to Glasgow.

What happened next is another story but after nine months we travelled south again this time to Gillingham and a small house in Barnsole Road quite close to Darland Banks and the Fort. The house had belonged to my grandfather, who died while we were in Scotland. We did not know where my father was, only that his home port again was Chatham and he was on a "hush-hush" job.

The war was very near to us there. Night after night soldiers from the Fort marched past the house on their way to the Front. We used to lean out of the bedroom window and call good luck and goodbye. They always marched to the tune of *Colonel Bogey* and it was many years before I could hear that music without a shiver. We learned our father was to go in the parent ship to back up the famous First World War Zeebrugge raid. Again he came safely back and was greeted as a Zeebrugge hero by a stranger who wished to shake his hand! He was then sent to Africa.

Meanwhile at home I went to the grammar school, but it was a long awkward journey. By now air raids became frequent. As there were no air raid shelters the schools shut and sent the pupils home. For the first time I felt rather frightened as I ran all on my own to catch the bus home; after all I was only eleven years old! My mother kept us home as much as she could.

By then some food was on ration and scarce unrationed food became very dear. My mother lived mostly on porridge so that we could have most of the rations. It was a very cold winter with lots of snow and the flu that killed almost as many people as the war ran like wildfire through the soldiers in the Fort. Their cemetery was in the road behind us and there were army funerals every day.

But it wasn't all gloom: we had blackberry picking picnics on Darland Banks, we went to the "pictures" and saw Charlie Chaplin and Jackie Coogan, and even had a party or two at Christmas.

Then, suddenly it seemed, the war was over, my father's trip to Africa was cancelled halfway there and he came home. It seemed strange to have peace, but our lives went on. As usual we were on the move – next stop Plymouth!'

'I was born at my grandmother's house in Dover, my parents having arrived back in England from Canada just before war was declared. I stayed on with Grandma after my parents got a small cottage at River, which was then just outside Dover, but is now part of it. I can remember Grandma taking me in a pushchair out to River and we had to pass through a military guard post. All adults had to show a permit to enter and leave Dover, which was a front line town. At that time we had trams in Dover which ran as far as River and the guard would stop the tram and examine the permit books.'

'In 1917 I started school in Margate. One of the first things I learned was dug-out drill. The tiny playground at Holy Trinity school had an entrance cut in it and quite a roomy shelter was cut in the chalk underneath. In my time it was never used seriously, but there was an occasion at Northdown when a Zeppelin was heard and seen overhead and we took cover in the shelter on Captain Friend's estate, where my family worked. A later occasion was when a German gunboat was shelling all along the coast from Deal to Thanet. They were aiming for Richborough, which was used to send munitions to France. They didn't succeed there but one shell landed at Northdown, just outside the estate.'

'At school in West Wickham I had to learn, when a whistle blew, to dive under the desk in the infants class when there was a warning of an air raid. Fortunately one never came our way. But one night my mother got me out of bed to see a German Zeppelin over London, quite a sight with the searchlight playing on it. Later it was shot down over Essex.

My father was working in London for the Swiss chocolate firm of Nestlé, and when rationing came they provided their employees with butter. We were all right for sugar too, as people were allowed so much for each of their fruit trees and we had several big trees in our garden. Mother was able to make lots of jam and sold some in the shop. In fact, the shelf was so loaded it collapsed, the earthenware pots broke and left the jam standing up like jellies on the floor. At one time during the war we had about six soldiers billeted on us. They loved jam and called it "possie". *Give I lots of possie* was a wartime song. They were very friendly and made a fuss of me, their "Little Pudding" Iris, and each put an entry in my autograph book.

1918 – Armistice Day, 11th November, and we rushed to Norwood for flags to put up. At 11 o'clock we heard cheering which, they said, came from the troops at Crystal Palace, which was then being used as a transit camp.'

'My earliest memory is of sitting on the kitchen table being washed by my mother before bedtime. I was three years old and we lived then in a village on the edge of the river Medway. When the gas light went down my mother put a blanket round me, called my two sisters and took us quite a long walk over rough ground to a big chalk cliff which had a tunnel through it. There we met a lot of people from the next village, candles alight in the niches of the cliff and all singing. I can't recall how we knew it was all clear, but the same thing happened night after night.'

'The war began when I was only four. What do I remember? First, my much loved second brother, then 19, coming up to the nursery to say goodbye, in his London Scottish kilt, before going to the Front, from which he never returned. He was killed that October. Then I can remember the ration books, and the lentil-based "meatless joint" with a paper frill to make it look like a ham. We were told the pips in raspberry jam were really tiny bits of wood; instead we had a new spread called "honey sugar" though I can't find any of my contemporaries who remember that, nor the little booklets, like stamp books, from which Mother would tear a saccharine-loaded "stamp" to put in her tea, afterwards removing the paper!

I can also remember the air raid warnings, when the warden would walk down the road calling "Take cover", and when the raid was over, "All clear!". During the raid we would all descend to the basement, where Mother, Nanny and I would knit for the "boys at the Front", balaclava helmets, or in my case cuffs, with a different number of stitches in almost every laboriously worked row. I only hope they kept some poor chap's wrists warm. Mother helped the war effort by turning the croquet lawn into "allotments", ie a vegetable patch which she dug with great enthusiasm. But she caused us acute embarrassment by rushing out to the road every time one of the horse-drawn tradesmen's vans went by, armed with bucket and shovel and hoping for some free manure for the cabbages! She also made use of nasturtium seeds instead of capers, and when on holiday in the country gathered nettles to replace spinach.'

TRAGEDIES OF WAR

'After the outbreak of war in 1914, my father, having volunteered for active service and been rejected, became a Special Constable and Volunteer Auxiliary Postman. After his early postal round on 26th November 1914 he came home in great distress and said, "*The Bulwark* has gone down." Looking across the river towards Sheerness 14 miles away he had seen the ship, when suddenly she was hidden by a blinding flash. Then followed thick smoke and a thunderous boom. Later, pieces of charred paper floated like black snowflakes into our garden. Seven hundred and forty two men lost their lives and only twelve survived.

Just six months later from Sheerness came the sad news that mother's cousin Nat, while working as a shipwright on the *Princess Irene*, had perished in a similar explosion.'

'One evening when I was about seven years of age, a warden came round warning all householders to open their windows. This was the night HMS *Glatton* was blown up in Dover harbour.

I was standing on the sea front watching great billows of smoke issuing from the stricken ship when my mother came hurrying up and took me home to St James's Street, near the sea front. From there we went to my grandmother's house opposite, where we waited in a lower room. That evening there was a huge explosion and I remember my grandfather saying, "Poor devils, they never stood a chance." '

'My father worked in the Gun Cotton at Oare, Faversham. It was in the spring of 1916 that the explosion occurred, on a Sunday around noon. There was much confusion, with many men killed or injured. The cottage hospital, Salvation Army church hall and the Methodist church hall were all used as emergency first aid posts. I was twelve years old at the time and I recall my mother taking me to the long railway bridge where we could watch the burial at the cemetery. The dead were interred in a communal grave. I think between 60 and 70 men died; fortunately my father was not among them, but most Faversham families were hit by the tragedy.'

BOMBING RAIDS ON FOLKESTONE

'On the Friday before Whitsun in 1917 the first daylight bombing raid took place. We lived in Folkestone, in Tontine Street, above a shop. In those days it was a busy shopping centre and on that particular Friday, not long after tea, when a great number of people were doing their shopping, the raid took place. The German bombers had tried to get to London and been turned back. They were being chased and had to jettison their bombs, which fell on our crowded streets. Sixty seven people were killed and many, many injured. Two shops were completely demolished and a gas main fractured and caught fire. Much later that night a Silver Queen airship flew very low down the street to tell us it was all clear.

My parents used to dread opening the daily papers and reading the names of the hundreds of casualties of the war. We children used to watch the soldiers marching down the slope from the Leas to the harbour to board the troop ships to take them to France. At first, they all came down singing as they marched, songs like *Pack up your troubles*, *Take me home to Blighty*, *Keep the home fires burning* etc. Later, as the war went on, there was only the sound of their marching feet. This road is now called The Road of Remembrance.'

185

'We lived in Grove Road, which backs onto the railway line in Folkestone. I liked to play on the embankment but on this particular day in 1917 I wasn't allowed to go there after tea as I'd misbehaved.

About a quarter past six, we heard planes. We dashed outside and there they were – about half a dozen planes with swept back wings coming towards us from the direction of the viaduct. We ran back into the house. Suddenly everything rattled. A bomb had been dropped, and pretty close at that.

Some time later my brother, who was on leave from the Navy, came in covered in blood. He went to the sink and began scrubbing his arms. He told us he and his mates had been in The Clarendon in Tontine Street enjoying a pint when they heard planes, and then a tremendous explosion. They rushed out into the street and were stunned. All the people around Stokes, the greengrocer's, were lying around, some of them screaming. There was nothing left of the pony and trap, or the farmer, from Hawkinge. There were no ambulances, but tradesmen brought their carts along and my brother and his mates set about loading them with bodies. The horses carted them all, alive and dead, off to the Victoria hospital.

I was glad I hadn't gone out on the railway bank. The donkey that lived there had been killed by that bomb that shook our house.

A year later I was playing in the park when the air raid warning sounded, and all the ships' hooters, and all the steam train whistles. Then the soldiers and sailors at the bottom of the town started throwing fireworks about. It was Armistice Day, and the fighting had finished. That dreadful war was over, at last.'

"WHERE'S DADDY GOING TO SLEEP?"

'I was two years old at the beginning of the First World War, when my father was sent to Flanders with his regiment, The Buffs, to fight for his country. I couldn't remember him, but I have an album of pretty cards to "My Darling Girlie" which he sent whenever away from the front line.

One winter's evening, my brother and I were playing on the mat in front of the coal fire when there was a loud banging on the front door. Mother opened it and I heard shouts of joy. I looked up and saw what I thought to be a tramp. Dad had come home straight from the front line, filthy and caked in mud. I was horrified at the look of this strange man!

After he had cleaned up, neighbours were called in to celebrate, and all went well until it was time for me to go to bed, a bed which I had always shared with my mother in Dad's absence.

186

Innocently I looked up and said, "Where is Daddy going to sleep?" The shout of laughter was incomprehensible to me!

Father told us stories of the awful conditions in the trenches, of the freezing cold and standing knee-deep in mud. It was so cold at night that he made a friend of a water rat and they huddled together for warmth.

Another memory is of having to go to the soup kitchen for food as Dad was only a private and soldier's pay was poor. My brother and I had to go to the local school with a big basin covered with a white cloth. Somehow I sensed it was belittling to get free food, and hated going. The soup was always split pea or lentil, and the pungent smell assailed your nostrils as soon as you opened the school door. To this day that smell brings back memories and makes my stomach heave.'

'I can just remember when my father had to return to the Front after leave. He went outside and brought in his khaki uniform to my mother and whilst one held the garment, the other held a candle to the seams to kill the tenant lice. The uniform was then put around the fire to dry out. Later Dad was mustard gassed and burned. He was brought home to hospital in Portsmouth where he was put into

The Victory celebrations at Deal in 1919. 'That dreadful war was over at last.'

187

a "bath" of cotton wool. In later years he could never bear to pull off a piece of cotton wool if any of us needed it for a cut, and was a semi-invalid for the rest of his life.'

'Father was wounded in the war, so was often ill and unable to work. If there was no money coming in from wages he applied for Parish Relief, which came in the form of vouchers to purchase groceries as listed – these were the very bare necessities. At Christmas some of the wealthier people in the village would bring a hamper or parcel of "goodies". The weekly wage for a farmworker was £1 13s 3d; we paid five shillings and threepence rent for the cottage, the remainder fed and clothed a family of six. During the school holidays we went hop picking for six weeks to earn money to buy clothes for the winter. It was a long day, starting at 7 am and working till 5 pm, going home tired and dirty.'

THE SECOND WORLD WAR 1939–45

'Hellfire Corner', 'Doodlebug Alley' – just two of the names earned by this hard-hit county that was both on the bombing run to London and a target in its own right. While British and German pilots fought in the skies overhead, those on the ground watched and prayed and survived the seemingly endless air raids as best they could. In 1944 a new menace flew over their heads – the sinister V1 flying bombs and later the V2 rockets.

SURVIVING THE AIR RAIDS

'How young the lads were who first flew with the RAF at the beginning of the war. They were all very well spoken, public school, university and college boys, sons of the well to do. They were stationed at Hawkinge aerodrome and used to visit Dover in their MG cars. Some had as little as 20 minutes in the air before they "caught a packet". These were not the brave young lads of novels but boys who needed their mother's shoulder to cry on.

The most frightening time was at the beginning of the war, when Germany was attacking. When the Allies began to push the Germans back times became happier. People also became accustomed to living with danger. The sirens were not the main warning for the people of Dover. We soon learned the procedure of 1) a flash in the sky, followed by 2) the thump of the missile being fired from France, and then 3) the wail of the siren. This must have been unique, the sound of the siren being the main warning in the rest of the British Isles.'

'The whole of the south eastern area was declared a War Zone and permission had to be obtained to travel to some areas. The coastline was very bleak and full of barbed wire fencing. As we lived in the area we were allowed to move around as normal. We regularly made up a coach party from the RAOC Depot to go to the dance at Leas Cliff Hall, Folkestone and while we were dancing the German shells were noisily landing around us from across the Channel. A frightening experience was when, in the daytime, dive bombers used to come out of the clouds and drop their bombs without warning, and machine gun the streets. One night at Ashford on the way home from work at teatime I just kept ahead of one, and got through my front door seconds before he shot up our lane. One of my friends was unlucky and was killed. Another time I was lying in bed when I saw the bombs leave the plane. I have been teased ever since for the record speed I got out of bed and down the stairs before the bombs hit the ground!'

'My husband was called up two weeks after we were married and was away for six years while I tried to run our mushroom farm. Being a town girl, this was not easy. We were on the "line" of the bombers and fighters on their way to London. You could hear the uneven beat of the German planes from miles away as they crossed the Channel. Our dog always heard them first and used to hide under the bed or table. The worst time, though, was when the bombers were racing back to France, as it was then they would drop their loads of bombs to get away more quickly. There were hundreds of "dog fights" every day, usually, it seemed, at mealtimes. Food was short, so to have it ruined while one was hiding in the shelter was an added burden. We could see the planes fighting – first the racing and attacking Spitfires and Hurricanes circling the huge bombers and then often the horror of a plane twisting and falling out of the sky. We used to wave and yell at them "parachute, parachute", but it was rarely possible.

One day I could hear a dog fight going on very high in the clouds, and suddenly a plane appeared over the farm and there was a parachute drifting down towards the woods and someone was shouting – it was the parachutist. I started to run to see if I could note where he was going to land. We had soldiers in a camp nearby and two of them joined me running into the woods. We could hear the airman shouting in German and found him tangled in a tree and badly wounded. We got him down and onto a frame. He said, "Spitfire, two Messerschmitts, still no good." He died in hospital.'

'On a warm summer's day during the war, a friend of mine was called out to a farm which was situated rather off the beaten track, and unfortunately nearer a vast munitions dump and ordnance depot than she liked.

When she and her passengers arrived at the farm, just in time for the afternoon milking, they had hardly stopped before the hum of heavy bombers could be heard and the wailing of the siren. To their horror they heard the distinct sound of machine-gunning overhead.

What on earth did she do, I wondered. "Oh, we just got back into the car and closed the sunshine roof."'

'Our saddest day was when our house was bombed in Whitstable in August 1940. Father's dairy was demolished as well. I was buried under the collapsed house and when rescued was taken to hospital. Because my nightdress was blown off I was concerned about my naked appearance, so a workman who was helping with the rescue kindly put his jacket around me. Upon reaching the hospital, because of the jacket and the grey hair from the dust of the plaster in the house, I was taken to the men's ward as they thought I was an elderly gentleman! At the age of 18 and being bewildered with shock at the time, I did not find it very funny – but we have laughed at it since.'

'Living in Thanet at the beginning of the war, we used to "run for the tunnel" when the air raid warning sounded. This was a disused railway tunnel which ran between Dumpton Park and the Ramsgate sea front, where we were comparatively safe from bombs.

At night, roused from sleep, we hastily threw on warm top clothing left ready by our beds, and usually entered the tunnel as the last wail of the siren faded away. This unusual activity in pitch darkness during the blackout used to wake the birds, who, normally silent at that time, would serenade us with whistling and twittering like a dawn chorus. As children this was exciting, an adventure meeting and playing in a forbidden area when we should have been in bed.

One evening I had been sent to bed in disgrace for some misdemeanour just after tea, when the siren sounded. Imagine the loss of dignity and face in meeting my friends in pyjamas when they were still in school clothes. It was more of a catastrophe than any bombs. I never lived it down.

My grandmother had a curtained cubicle within the tunnel with a bed, a fold-up chair, a small primus stove and tea-making equipment, where she slept nightly for two years during the worst of the bombing. By then, of course, most of the children had been evacuated to safer areas.'

'We lived in a top floor flat and had to go downstairs and along a passageway at the side of the house to get to the clothes line and coalshed. One day, as I opened the shed door an enemy plane came very low, shedding its bullets which rattled along the fence. I flung myself onto the heap of coal, absolutely terrified. When all was quiet, the couple who lived below came out to find me and had to force my hands from the lumps of coal I was clutching; they took me indoors and gave me brandy.'

'My father and his brother Tom who lived with us, were both miners and so exempt from the forces during the war. They had digging in their blood. Several men in Temple Ewell decided it was time for a communal shelter, and my dad and uncle went along to help with the digging of trenches in the local playing field. When it came to putting a top on they were stuck for suitable materials so the trenches were never finished and we children had a lovely time just playing in them.

About then the powers that be decided it was time we had official shelters and three were dug in different parts of the village. My mother thought that as they had gone to so much trouble we should use them, but I never saw anyone else in them during a raid and so the idea soon fizzled out, as they were rather cold and creepy, especially at night.

Dad also had some bright ideas at home. First it was the chicken shed, which he reinforced with sandbags, and my brother and I spent a few exciting nights cooped up with the hens and one cockerel. Then Dad dug a deep hole in the front lawn and shored it up with wood planks and put the spare earth on top; it felt very secure. But the first night we used it, as I ran from the front door to the shelter a piece of shrapnel hit the porch roof and landed beside me. When we found it the next day it was a nasty jagged piece about four inches long. I don't know to this day whether we would have been safer indoors, but we certainly had a variety of shelters and took a few risks getting to them.'

'I lived at the Forge House, Hamstreet, with my parents, my grandfather and my Aunt Connie, Dad's sister. When the siren sounded for an air raid, we had to rush to a shelter in Lacy Collard's

191

cherry orchard. My mum and I slept there every night, as did many other villagers. The air raid shelter was a long dark room, with bunk beds on either side and a small area at the end where we could make a cup of tea. The youths of the village kept us kids quiet by raiding the orchard for cherries, plums and apples. I won't mention any names but if your grandad's in his sixties, why not ask him?

My grandfather, George Sage, had been kicked by a horse in his younger days and walked, badly, with the aid of two sticks and couldn't get to the air raid shelter, so he stayed at the Forge House, sleeping downstairs. My dad stayed at home too, so Grandad wasn't alone. There was a big walk-in cupboard beside the fireplace, and when the air raid warning came, they would both go inside the cupboard. Grandad said that it was a good place, as chimney stacks were always still standing after a house was bombed. One day a neighbour was at our house when the siren went. "Where are you going?" she asked. "I'm going in the cupboard," said Grandad. "Well I'm coming in too." After the All Clear, my mum went to make a pot of tea, and Grandad and the neighbour emerged. They were decidedly unsteady, having sampled most of the bottles of wine and cider he kept there. "I'm coming round here next time," she said, "It's much more enjoyable inside that cupboard than in the air raid shelter."

One day my father was having a shave, when bombs began falling in the Carters Wood area. The blast lifted him and threw him back against the wall, where he sat quite dazed for some time. He was all right, but great holes in the plaster remained where his elbows had gone through.

Living as we did, on the main road, we could feel the tanks coming from right up the school hill. My mum would shout, "The Churchills are coming". The noise, and the tremble of the ground under our feet got steadily worse, as we ran round the house collecting up glassware, clocks and mirrors, anything which we could hold until they had passed by. Clutching our breakables, we watched as they rolled by, a long line of them, nose to tail. Gradually the noise lessened, and the ground became still again. We would go around the house to see what had been broken this time.'

'Our gardener, being too old to be called up, continued to work for us throughout the war. He often had to get onto the roof to straighten pantiles which had shifted due to the vibration from bombs and gunfire. He said he could feel the roof lifting if he was still up there when the guns started up again.

My parents were both in the ARP in Hythe. My father was at headquarters in a house in Saltwood. My mother drove her own car throughout the war, as a casualty car, and had to tow the mortuary trailer.

One bomb dropped on the Arcade in the middle of town killing several people. I was standing in the garden at the time and saw this giant mushroom of smoke. When it dispersed, pieces of patterns and shop bills blew into the garden on a south-west wind.

I remember seeing sections of the Mulberry Harbour being towed down the Channel in preparation for the invasion of France. They looked like great Martello Towers. I also remember seeing dozens of German bombers droning in on a daylight raid over Dungeness. In the middle of the pack was one painted black and we joked that Goering must be aboard. This was on a Friday, a day one always avoided going into Hythe to shop as it was usually the day they dropped their load over the town, either deliberately or jettisoning them on their way back to France.

During the war years the population of Hythe dropped from 8,000 to about 2,000.'

DUNKIRK

'Ramsgate was at war – our lovely town was silent, sullen, anxious and only the gulls reminded us of other days. Now they flew up, startled in the anti-invasion lights and filled the night sky with troubled calls, green, ghostly and so sad.

We went to our beds thinking of invasion, air raids and the soldiers on Dunkirk beaches. An explosive gloom hung everywhere.

One morning, after a period of rain, the sun shone on a quiet calm sea. The world sparkled. We had thronged the clifftops to see what all the black specks on the horizon were. We watched a sight so unbelievable we were spellbound, and shouted our joy as we realised that they were hundreds of boats carrying our army from Dunkirk. There were tiny river boats towed by cabin cruisers, fussy tugs, elegant boats and broken down fishing vessels. But they landed and were given every comfort the town could supply. Sad, exhausted men but so grateful to be alive.

They were taken to the station. Here utter chaos prevailed. Hundreds of fearful little children were being evacuated, clutching gas masks and cases. Anxious mothers, police, tea ladies, officers and nurses. Oh yes, confusion, but Ramsgate's very great day.'

'At the Kent & Canterbury Hospital the red alert had gone out to the staff, surgeons and physicians who were assembled in my office waiting for information.

The telephone rang and at the other end was the Harbour Master

KENT DEFENCE.

Elham Emergency Committee.

Notice to the Civil Population in Case of Emergency.

PARISH of LYMPNE.

Should it be necessary for the Civil Population to remove, those who desire to do so are to assemble at The Green opposite the County Members and thereafter proceed by the route : via Lympne Hill, Hurst Farm, in a westerly direction towards Cranbrook.

Conveyances will, if possible, be provided to collect and carry the aged, infirm, and young children, and those in charge of them only, all others must proceed on foot.

All children under five years old must be labelled.

IMPORTANT.   The people are to bring all necessary clothing, boots, blankets, etc., to protect them from the weather, also their money and available food. All articles unnecessary for subsistence to be left behind.

The Exodus will be under the control of the Police and Special Constabulary, whose instructions must be strictly obeyed.

These instructions are circulated to all Householders by order of the Chief Constable of Kent. The Emergency Committee do not consider that the danger of an invasion, or the necessity of moving, is any greater now than it has been since the commencement of the War, but should the occasion arise these instructions will act as a guide to anyone desirous of moving.

By Order of the Elham Emergency Committee.

W. S. PAINE & Co., Printers, Hythe.

A notice issued to the civilian population of Lympne in 1940, when invasion was a terrible possibility. Thankfully, the plan for the movement of refugees along our roads was never to be tested.

of Folkestone. "Can you take casualties?" he asked. "Yes, how many?" "I have 600 wounded men lying on the pier," he replied. Knowing that we could not cope with anything like that number I phoned the Ministry of Health on the special line and they said they would ring back. Within minutes the reply came – that we were to do nothing, a hospital train was leaving Ashford and would take them. We were then warned to expect heavy bombing and wounded civilians. This luckily did not happen and over the next few days we received only a few strays from the small boats, including some Algerians hugging their rifles and their French loaves.'

MY 21st YEAR

'In 1940 I was working for solicitors in offices overlooking the Guildhall in London. When the terrible news of Dunkirk was announced on the radio, work stopped and we were all told to go home. Can you imagine thousands of people walking through the City of London to the main line stations – in my case it was Cannon Street. Crowds of us walked up the steps into the station, and there was only the sound of feet. No word was spoken, utter silence. I felt it was unreal, like a nightmare.

Later that year after the big daylight raid on London in September – in fact, 12th September, my 21st birthday – we were once again told to make our way home. All transport had stopped. I started from my office at 3 pm and arrived at my home in Welling at 9 pm, having walked all the way on broken glass and debris left by the raid. I began my trek home via the City of London, over London Bridge, along the Borough and into the New Kent Road, past the Elephant and Castle, then on through the Old Kent Road through Deptford, New Cross, Lewisham and Blackheath. By this time most of my walking companions had left me to go to their homes. Many lorries went by overflowing with people getting a lift but none seemed to be going my way. I walked across Blackheath and then along Blackheath Road to Woolwich and on up Shooters Hill. By the time I reached this point it was dark and the raids had started again. I just kept walking, with gunfire, shrapnel and searchlights all around me. It was so dark and I felt as if I was the only person left alive.

When I finally reached my home my parents were in the garden shelter. As I went in my mother, in tears, said, "Here's your dinner and your birthday present – Happy 21st birthday!" In the envelope were 21 £1 notes, a fortune. It was a pretty unusual 21st birthday celebration.'

BATTLE OF BRITAIN DAYS

'Where were you when the war broke out? I was in Godmersham church with my father. During the sermon a note was handed to the vicar and it was announced that war had been declared. Walking home with my father some minutes later the Ashford siren sounded "Air Raid". By the time we had decided what to do, the "All Clear" was heard.

Not much happened in the village for some time except a steady stream of people going off to join the Services. The evacuation of Dunkirk, however, brought the war to Godmersham. The sight of the long Red Cross trains carrying wounded, slowly trundling their way to London, made us all aware that there was a lot more to come.

The Battle of Britain was not far off. The first aircraft to crash locally was a Spitfire. This came down at Pope Street and attracted a good crowd. The pilot baled out, landing on Godmersham Common. Soon the sky over the village was filled with aircraft as each day the huge German formations made their way inland. When aircraft came down it was all too often our own fighters.

One of the most spectacular crashes was an ME 109 which dived vertically from a great height, plunging to the ground at the boundary of Godmersham and Chilham Parks. Soldiers, serving locally, dug down to a great depth to find the pilot but it was decided eventually to leave him there. A service was conducted over the spot by the Army chaplain.

Nearer to home, one Wednesday afternoon, a Hurricane crashed on the side of the home of the Fields, then living at the top of the hill on the Canterbury Road. This aircraft plunged into the garden making a large crater, and one wing badly damaged the bungalow. The wreckage burst into flames and caused a lot of damage to the sheds making up this smallholding. I think I owned the only mobile fire fighting equipment in the village, a truck carrying two five gallon drums of water and a stirrup pump. This was the only time I used it. Even so, it was not used for very long, as the fire was hot and when ammunition started to explode we withdrew to a safer distance. I must mention Chilham Fire Brigade who arrived soon afterwards and performed sterling work.

The RASC had arrived in the village soon after Dunkirk and stayed until the invasion. We soon became used to seeing huge dumps of ammunition under almost every tree.

The RA installed a searchlight battery at Eggarton and this stayed for a very long time and was there when the V1s arrived. Members of the battery, at times, attempted to shoot down V1s with their Lewis gun with very little success.

Most mornings Col Armitage would walk round to the shop and have a chat with my father. The main topic of conversation was always the war. The Colonel was convinced that elephants could solve most of the British Army's problems.

Who remembers the VE night celebrations? A huge bonfire on top of the mound and later the village lads setting fire to the dry grass. Was I one of them? I expect so. Who called the fire brigade?'

'For days and weeks we had become accustomed to the fighting going on above our heads and it was difficult to realise there were men risking their lives, indeed fighting for their lives. It just seemed a huge panoramic stage with players wheeling and diving, shining in the sunlight. We knew there might be danger for us, of course, but on the whole it was something to watch and point at. On this particular Sunday, I had cooked the meal and we had our usual visit from Mavis, the Bromley schoolgirl evacuated and living with her grandmother next door. Her father, an engine driver, mother and small brother Norman had come down for the weekend. My husband had been on duty with the Home Guard the night before and after eating, we went upstairs to rest on the bed. There had been planes in the sky all morning, we thought hardly anything of them. The noise kept getting worse and we drowsily wondered if we should be getting up when a piercing scream of plane engines and a tearing noise came, which we could no longer ignore. Surely a plane had come down outside the house!

We rose quickly and ran downstairs to the neighbours standing outside. The German plane was down in the field across the farm road. Walter ran to get his Home Guard rifle and put his tin hat on, Tom Masters, the next door lodger doing the same, also Mavis's father. Mavis's mother, who knew I was three months pregnant with my first child, advised me to stay with the children. There were four airmen in the shot-down Heinkel bomber, one dead and one who died on his way to the casualty clearing hospital in the village at Benenden School. I heard afterwards that Mavis's mother bandaged one airman with strips torn from her petticoat. While this was going on, there was still terrific noise in the sky with the victorious English plane doing a victory roll over the bomber.

The German plane had ploughed right through a hedge making a terrific gap and coming to rest in the middle of a grass field. Walter said that one airman was trying to use the guns to shoot at the men running to the plane. Luckily the guns had jammed – although Walter had taken his rifle he had not loaded it! Very soon

197

the ambulance came, the village people and the policeman took over and when the military arrived, the soldiers mounted guard over the wreckage. The Heinkel was down in the field for months before eventually it was dismantled and taken away.'

'In 1940 my father was working as a fruit foreman with a gang of about 18 women. His job was to move the large 50-rung ladders for the women to pick cherries. He was employed on a farm at Rodmersham.

At lunchtime one of the women collected a little tea from each person, put it into a cloth bag and placed it in a billy can of boiling water. It made one of the best cups of tea I have tasted and with bread and cheese made a good meal. The Battle of Britain was at its height then, and when the planes were overhead we children went under cover. This meant hiding under the large steam engines which were parked opposite.

I remember seeing the dog fights in the sky: planes on fire and airmen bailing out of their damaged craft. When the All Clear sounded, we collected the shrapnel and spent bullets, which were often still warm. One German plane was shot down at Blue Town, Milsted, where it landed on the woodman's cottage. There were acres of woods but it had to land on his home – fortunately he was not hurt.'

THE BOMBING OF CANTERBURY

'In the blitz of June 1942 I can mainly remember seeing the red glow over the city and then going to work the next morning and seeing the devastation. Dozens of fire engines worked for two or three days after that and we used to make tea at our office for the firemen.

During our lunch hour I went to look at the remains of the Langton girls school. I particularly noticed how the main clock had stopped and that the school gong hanging below it was still perfectly in place. I also went to the cathedral area and saw the ruined library with many leaves of books scattered everywhere. Most of the precious manuscripts had been sent to safer areas beforehand and the stained glass windows had been removed sometime before the blitz. I think the sheer joy of seeing the main part of the cathedral standing up above the smoke and smell of all the other burning buildings made us all very grateful for the work of the cathedral fire-watchers who had literally picked up and thrown to the ground many incendiary bombs which had landed on the lead roof of the cathedral, thus saving it from destruction.

During the daylight raid of October 1942 I was in the centre of Canterbury shopping and went into Lefevres. The Mayor of Canterbury, then Charles Lefevre, was getting everyone into the centre of the shop; many children were frightened and crying as this was a far noisier raid with more high explosive bombs being dropped. It was over quite quickly and after the All Clear I went to our office, which this time had been badly damaged. The next day we spent collecting our records and moving them to another building to continue working – our office being the Collector of Taxes we were very busy with war damage payments etc.'

LIFE AT THE RODNEY

'My father had bought the Palm Bay Hotel in Cliftonville in 1940 but we were not destined to stay there for long. By Christmas we had had a visit from an Army officer to tell us politely but firmly that the War Office had requisitioned our home for the duration of the war as it overlooked the sea. My father argued to no avail but was told he would be recompensed at the end of the war, and we were on the move again. We moved into a smaller pub in the village of Garlinge and here "our war" began. As we were only minutes away from Manston Airport – the first on the German list to be bombed as it is so near to the French coast – we knew we were in the flight path. We were told we were all going to be evacuated to Staffordshire and all the local schools would now be closed for the duration of the war.

My father had had enough of being pushed around and put his foot down. No way was he going to let his family be split up! He said we were all going to chance it; if we were going to be killed by a Jerry bomb at least we would all go together. We were at once bombarded by Local Education Officers, the police and even the local MP, but he would not be moved and said he would personally be responsible for our education. So we said goodbye to all the other kids and "lost" three years schooling.

Life now became a lot of fun, at times frightening as the air raids were many and often prolonged but there was so much to occupy the three little King girls at The Rodney. One of the bars was a long ballroom with a stage and band etc and now was full every night with noisy soldiers who were billeted under canvas in Dent-de-Lion park. They got drunk, they sang and danced and three little girls could watch them, unnoticed themselves, through a crack in a kitchen door as they pranced around the ballroom in a drunken line banging Dad's tin trays like drums and screaming songs like *MacNamara's Band* until they got thrown out at closing time. There was no point in putting us to bed as we should not have got to sleep.

The soldiers were raucous and bawdy in the ballroom but how different it was in the Saloon Bar. There were the usual chaps and "bar fly" ladies any saloon bar has in any pub but we had our young handsome RAF officers and they were marvellous. To my young eyes each one of them was a hero. We got to know them so well personally. One of them was called Hutson, I remember, and he was a commercial artist in Civvy Street. He painted and drew all of us and we loved him. One night it was his turn and he did not come back. As the Battle of Britain went on there were so many evenings when we dreaded them coming in as so many had "bought it", or even worse had just not come in and were missing. They had become part of our family so it hurt.

We had just started off at The Rodney with a bar staff and a cellarman but of course as the war went on they were gradually all called up for the Services and as my father was a very old man, Jackie and I became the cellarmen. This was in the days of old, large wooden beer barrels and "hogs heads" which had to be attached to beer pumps leading up to the pumps in the bar. Bungs had to be knocked out and in and barrels humped up onto rails and when empty turned on their sides to drip into ullage bags – a filthy job. The day we found a large frog in the ullage was the day I decided I would never drink beer and I have not.

So here we were in what had now become known as Hellfire Corner and bombs and air raids were happening all day and, even worse, at night. Often weeks went by without us getting into our night clothes at all. So many families had been bombed out leaving them only in their pyjamas that my father issued orders that we should be fully dressed in the event of an air raid. We also had "hurrying away cases" sitting just inside the front door with a change of knickers and pyjamas, our identity cards, our ration books and our gas masks etc. Thank God we never had to use them.

Uncle Alf, my father's brother, had been bombed out – a direct hit – while taking a bath quite early in the bombing so my father issued another edict that no one in the family was to take another bath for the duration of the war, to avoid being left naked and clothesless like poor Uncle Alf. We were allowed an all over wash in the bathroom and the only one of us three tall enough to put her foot in the wash basin was Jackie. However, one day she was standing like a stork washing her leg when a bomb dropped outside the door and she fled screaming downstairs to Dad in the bar, to the amusement of all the customers. For weeks she was teased unmercifully by the locals, "Have you washed the other leg yet, Jack?"

As the bombing got worse with raids every night my father decided that the safest part of the house was the Saloon Bar as it had a central chimney breast and he and I had noted when out on our walks that bombed buildings tended to have the central chimney breast left standing. So we never actually used the Anderson air raid shelter carefully built in our garden but, so as to "Dig for Victory" as we had been encouraged by the government, my father grew mushrooms inside it quite successfully and tomatoes on top.

While all the private cars had been taken off the roads and there was a curfew after dark, we took to walking in the afternoons along the heavily fortified seafront. We had all looked forward to coming to live by the sea, as being little London kids we had not seen the sea very much, but of course by the time we had arrived in 1940 all the back was cut off by concrete blocks and rows of barbed wire. Also a lot of the beach was mined so there was no way any of us actually walked on the sand but we could walk along the cliff tops and chat to the soldiers who were manning the ack-ack guns and the huge searchlights in the sunken gardens at Westbrook.

Most of the houses on the seafront were, of course, empty with blind, boarded up windows and overgrown gardens. My father asked me as we were walking along by what had been Westgate golf course, "What would you do if suddenly you saw German soldiers swarming up over those cliffs?" It was quite on the cards that we should be invaded from the French coast so this was possible. After a little thought I decided that if confronted by the enemy I would throw pepper in his face and thus blind him. To this end I carried a small drum of pepper in my pocket when out on future walks. We had been told to be prepared and I now was!

One cold morning in the snowy winter of 1941, Dad, Jackie, Daphne and I were walking along Northdown Road in Cliftonville and we were quite alone, not another soul in sight, when my sister Jackie suddenly saw a little mouse running along in the gutter. We all stopped to look and Dad said sadly, "If you should tell someone when this old war is over that you saw a little mouse in an empty Northdown Road they will never believe you."

We had our share of bombs and though we never got used to it, it had its humorous side, living as we did in a pub and having to keep up the morale of the customers. One evening, there was not a raid on and my mother was getting changed to go into the bar. On her way downstairs with a large cut glass vase in her hand and only the dim blue blackout light on the stairs, she trod on one of the cats and came hurtling down the staircase, throwing the vase over the bannister as she fell. It landed with a crash outside the Saloon Bar door and when she marched in very aggrieved because no one had come to see what had happened, she found an apparently empty bar. All the customers, my father and staff were on the floor or hiding under the tables as they were sure we had had a direct hit. My mother was not amused but they were all in hysterics when she explained.'

CHRISTMAS 1943

'Dover was a Hellfire Corner in the Second World War. The town was heavily bombed and shelled between 12th August 1940 and 26th September 1944. A total of 10,056 buildings were destroyed. Shell attacks and air raids totalled 3,059 with 464 bombs and 2,226 shells, causing 216 deaths, 344 serious woundings and 416 slight injuries amongst civilians. Many troops were killed also, including American soldiers.

I worked for the Commanding Officer up at the castle and, toward the end of the war, the Germans shelled us for three weeks 24 hours a day. As I fell asleep over my typewriter, the CO had my bed taken down to the castle and at last I got some sleep. Incidentally, the 2nd Canadian Division finally put paid to those guns.

I was appalled at the way Dover had been shelled and bombed. The roads had big holes in them. Eventually, though, when it got near Christmas 1943 I started to think about parties. I wanted a Christmas tree, so one Sunday afternoon a few fellows and girls set off to Guston. A lot of people had left Dover, so we thought that if there was a Christmas tree in someone's garden we could have it. We did find one in a back garden and we were about to dig it up when a fellow came in and wanted to know what we were doing in his back garden.

Eventually they went out again and chopped one down in the Marines' place. They were furious about that, so Moss took it out in the lorry when the Marine CO came down to find it. Normally, we used to ask them down for our parties, but not that Christmas! The tree was put in a box and mutilated a bit and I had to think of something to put on it. So I bought a pound of mothballs, painted them pink and silver, put a hot pin in them and hung them on the tree. Then one of the fellows came back off leave, bringing some lights and fancy things to put on the tree. I wrote a short play and eventually we had a smashing Christmas, 1943.'

DODGING THE DOODLEBUGS

'It was a lovely sunny June day in 1944 and we were living at Pinks Farm, Rodmersham. I was playing with my two brothers in our conservatory when we heard a loud burst of machine gun fire. Father, who was a Special Constable, had told us that if we heard firing we were to take cover so as I was the eldest I took charge and hurried them indoors. We had only just got under the table when there was a huge explosion, breaking the doors and windows, and the soot came down the chimney, covering the cat asleep on the mat and us as well.

When everything was quiet I remembered my mother and father. They had been picking cherries in the orchard, where a huge ball of smoke was rising into the air. In the confusion we all ran into each other and quickly realised that we were all safe. We walked to the wreckage of the plane and my mother said, "The poor pilot". In the orchard there was utter chaos, with dead sheep and chickens with their feathers burnt off.

It was the next morning that the radio news reported that London had been hit by these new pilotless craft. British pilots had tried to divert them from their targets in London by using the wings of their own planes to force them into open fields. In the orchard I had noticed a terrible smell, and this I later learnt to be the rocket fuel.'

A German plane brought down in an orchard at Bicknor in July 1943. Although strictly out of bounds, wrecks such as these attracted souvenir-hunting children. (South Eastern Newspapers Ltd.)

' "Mummy forgot to switch off the aerial." Fifteen years after the war ended we drove past the radar station where I had worked as a WAAF in 1944 and there was the great aerial – like a metal bedstead for a giant – solemnly rotating round and round for all the world as if no one had remembered to tell it the war was over.

The radar station was near the railway level crossing and the white windmill on the outskirts of Sandwich. The Battle of Britain was long over but there were regular night air raids, and day and night there were the doodlebugs coming across the Channel – over 2,000 fell in Kent, I am told, and about as many got through to London during that summer of 1944.

The station comprised this large rectangular radar aerial and a series of low, flat-roofed brick buildings just off the road. For 24 hours a day the WAAFs manned the big plotting table and others gazed at the radar screens in little darkened cubicles. When an enemy aircraft was detected – and it was our job to spot it first – the Fighter Direction Officer would come and sit beside you and together in the darkness the two of you peered at the little twelve inch screen. He was speaking to his fighter pilot or squadron, directing them onto the target and the WAAF's job was to track the "echoes" and decide which echo amongst the myriad of echoes and clutter on the screen was the one we were engaging and which one was our fighter plane, and to mark their progress continually. The Flight Director was usually a fighter pilot in his early twenties, grounded for some reason, and the WAAFs were 18 to 20 year old girls in the main. In my case I had been doing this job in various stations in the South for over two years. I can recall that when the raids were on it was very hectic and tiring, particularly on one's eyes concentrating on those "blips" and after about 20 minutes we were usually given a short relief. We rested with special goggles on to save our night vision before going back to our sets.

It was certainly a friendly place and I don't remember being particularly frightened when raids were on but, having my mother living in Central London, I do remember the worry and stress and sense of responsibility in trying to defeat the raids. In my time there it was mostly those ghastly doodlebugs but we did manage to shoot down a lot of them.'

'Christopher was with his mother, helping on the allotment. He was about six years of age and his mother was a very large lady, well endowed bosom-wise.

Whilst happily occupied on this particular afternoon, the siren sounded out over the town of Ashford and in the sky appeared the dreaded doodlebug. Now, the sign that a doodlebug or flying bomb was about to fall was that its engine stopped. Panic ensued. Christopher's mother did no more than throw herself on top of her son.

He maintains even now that he thought the bomb had dropped directly on top of him that day!'

LIFE GOES ON

Coping with air raids, the blackout and rationing, life still went on for families in Kent – children grew up and teenagers fell in love, and women learned to turn their hands to anything to 'make do and mend'. Soldiers and airmen became familiar companions, but the uncertainty of life was apparent to all, particularly the brave airmen whose toast was, 'Here's to the next man to die!'

RATIONING AND THE BLACKOUT

'Blacking out homes was difficult; many windows were taped to stop splintering and masses of black material was bought to make extra thickness for curtaining and sometimes frames of wood covered with lino. It was also difficult to travel at night, with no lights anywhere. Buses and cars had headlights partially covered by black paper, and torches could only show a slit of light. If you travelled by train it was difficult to know at which station the train had stopped – no lighting was allowed and there were no names on the platforms as these had all been removed. One hoped that a porter would call out the name. The trains were always full of soldiers and very dimly lit.

Rations were very small, especially meat, tea, butter and cheese. Sweets were also rationed. We *never* had bananas and if oranges were available the word would soon go round and long queues appeared. Alternative foods appeared, such as whale meat and snoek, and dried egg powder. Special allocations of cod liver oil and orange juice were made for babies and men who did heavy manual work had an extra meat ration. No one ever went really hungry but food became somewhat monotonous. Many people grew their own vegetables and those without a garden were given council allotments.'

A CHILD'S VIEW

'Whilst my father was away in the army, we went to live in a flat opposite my grandparents' home and like many grandchildren, I spent much of my time with them. As the air raids were on, we quite often had to take cover under the Morrison shelter in the kitchen. My grandfather didn't think much of this shelter and decided that, as the part of a building most often left standing after bombing was the staircase, he would clear the coal out from the understair cupboard and this would be our shelter. It was very cosy as we all settled down in our hideaway with all mod-cons but the thing I shall always remember was the lingering smell of coal dust. This smell even today brings back war memories.

Everyday things were in short supply, or unobtainable in the shops so we never wasted anything. We were all experts in "recycling" and the habits I learnt then I have been unable to break. Every scrap of wool or material was kept to be made into new garments. My mother's dresses were cut down to make clothes for me, which sounds quite bizarre but she always managed to make them look pretty and I was delighted with my cardigan made of left over knitting wool – a true Jacob's coat of many colours.

Meat rationing was the one thing I knew which would get my grandmother angry. She was a very quiet, gentle lady but the butcher to which she was allocated made her see red. It seemed to her that although she would save her coupons for a special joint, he always produced the toughest old beast when she came in the shop. Offal was supposed to be obtainable without coupons but she contended that the animals grew without "insides" for the duration of the war as offal was never available.

I was very proud of my ration book with my name on it, not realising how difficult it was to make the meagre rations eke out to feed two growing children and that my mother must often have gone short to give us extra. I used to go down to the sweet shop with my ration book and pennies to buy my two ounces of sweets. The most popular were the very tiny sweets which you could make last a long time, like rainbow drops, satin cushions, dolly mixture or jelly babies. I admit, I still occasionally have a bag of dolly mixture even today. In the window of the shop were "dummy" sweets and packets of Rose's chocolates which I had never tasted; I promised myself that after the war when rationing had ended, I would buy myself a whole quarter pound – which after a long wait, I did.

Our pleasures were simple and often involved making things. In those days, milk bottles were sealed with cardboard discs. If these were washed and the centre flap removed, then two of them placed together could be wound with wool until full, cut between the two discs and tied with a long piece of wool and hey presto, you had a pompom. Small nails evenly spaced round the edge of a wooden cotton reel and you were ready to make yards and yards of french knitting. Odd scraps of cardboard cut into squares or circles and strung with thin string were then woven with raffia to make table mats.

When at last Peace came, my world very suddenly expanded. From being a restricted, protected and often disrupted life with little colour, all at once "the lights went on" and for the first time in my memory, people everywhere were happy. I was allowed to stay up on VE night and we went up to Buckingham Palace where the King and Queen appeared on the balcony. Trafalgar Square and Piccadilly Circus were ablaze with light and soldiers were climbing the lampposts. We walked for miles, it was a night never to be forgotten, the only shadow being that my father was about to depart for Germany and would be there for the following two years.

The celebrations went on for weeks, or so it seemed. We had a street party where by amazing efforts the mothers pooled their resources to give us children the time of our lives. Everywhere was decked with bunting and Union Jacks and we all had paper hats. To round off the day, a massive bonfire was built in the middle of the road. This was an amazing sight and burnt especially well as it caught the tar alight and left a hole in the road next day. But no one seemed to care – at last we were at Peace!'

'Not long after the war broke out children from Chatham were evacuated to Whitstable. I was very disappointed as we were supposed to have three evacuees but they ran out three doors up the road. I cried for ages as I thought they would be the next best thing to the brothers and sisters I always wanted. These children came from the poorest part of Chatham and as far as I can remember didn't know very much about beds, knives and forks or washing. I remember one of the ladies up the road being in a panic because she had lost her evacuee. All the neighbourhood were out looking for him. Eventually he was found under the bed. He didn't know he was supposed to sleep in the bed; at his home Mum and Dad and the youngest slept in the bed, as the next baby was born the older one moved out of the bed and slept under it!

The children of Whitstable were never evacuated and after a few months the powers that be decided it was stupid for the children of Chatham to be evacuated to Whitstable so they were all taken off to Wales. We were sorry to see them go as by then we had got used to their different ways and grown to like them.

We moved a little way out of the centre of Whitstable to Gorrell Road at the end of 1940. I wasn't quite so scared of all the bombs there as there were more open spaces and not so many houses to fall on me as there had been in Argyle Road. My Dad was too old to be called up and so joined the LDV, "Look, Duck and Vanish", which later became the Home Guard of Dad's Army fame. He and Mum also used to have to take their turns in fire watching. Obviously the adults living in the same house weren't allowed to fire watch on the same night; someone had to look after the children.

The day Canterbury was bombed all the road were out discussing where the bombing was. The following morning my cousin and his friend went to catch the bus to go to Simon Langton school in Canterbury. They got as far as the top of St Thomas Hill before the bus was turned round. They were both indignant, not at not getting to school but at not being allowed into Canterbury to collect all the bits of shrapnel etc. They came home, changed out of school uniform and rode their bikes back into Canterbury. The tales they told me about the damage scared me silly and it was at least a year before I went there again. My cousin thought I was really stupid as on the Saturday he wanted to show me all the destruction.

Going to school by train every morning from Whitstable to Faversham we used to moan at Adolf Hitler because never once, as far as my memory serves me, was the train held up by bombing. In the evening when we wanted to get home it was a totally different story. We often wondered why he laid in in the morning. It was very scary coming home in the train and knowing that somewhere had been bombed during the day but not knowing where. Everybody would be hanging out of the window to try to see if their home was still standing. Once again I was very lucky.'

'We were at war. Every newstime my brother and I had to sit in total silence while the grown-ups hung on every word which issued from the large brown bakelite radio which sat in the middle of the red runner on the oak sideboard in a small semi-detached house in Aerodrome Road, Hawkinge. From the tension exhibited by our parents, we knew it was serious, but we had no idea of the impact it was about to have on our lives, or the lives of millions of others.

For us, this much heralded war added interest to our lives. Dad came home with long pieces of wood which he made into frames which slotted into the windows. He then tacked blackout material over them. No light must show outside, and we were pleased to creep round the garden giving the verdict on his efforts.

The whole family went round to the village school and queued up for gas masks. Frank, being three, was allowed to have a Mickey

Mouse mask, but being a year and a few days older, I had to put up with a very ordinary mask. When it was put over my face I felt trapped, unable to breathe properly, and cut off from everyone. It couldn't come off fast enough. A baby, thrust into a thing which looked like a cage for dead birds, began to cry pitifully, and I joined in.

Our house received a visit from the local policeman, who came to advise us to evacuate. Dad had a disability which meant he was not forced to join up, so Mum said we were not going anywhere. The family was not going to split up. In that case, we were informed, we must leave the vicinity of the aerodrome whenever the warning sounded at night. The policeman's words alarmed me, and I knew that I wanted to get away, whether or not everyone else went. I ran upstairs, lay under my bed and thumped the floor, but Mum refused to take me, or to allow me to go.

Our neighbours moved out, and service people were installed in their houses, and in other houses in Hawkinge. One night, the siren sounded. Recalling the policeman's words, I was out of bed in a flash. Reluctantly Mum and Dad dressed, and Mum made sandwiches. I didn't know how she could bear to waste time doing that when it was not safe in the house! Eventually, she was ready, and my brother and I were plonked at either end of the old pram. A blue oil cloth bag containing the savings books, a bottle of water, a bar of chocolate and the sandwiches was dumped between us, along with Mum's best hat, and we trundled off into the night.

On the way up Chapel Street, we were joined by my grandfather, who had moved up there from Dover. Unfortunately, Mum's hat fell off the pram and got trodden in the mud. A little further on, a black dog hurtled out of a gateway barking loudly. And all the time, we listened. With relief we gained the shelter of a barn in a field.

Once inside, I felt safe, till Grandad struck a match to light his pipe. Lights must not be shown or every German would home in on them! I yelled, and could not be comforted, till Grandad said he would do without his smoke.

The steady note of All Clear started the tired trek home. Nothing had happened, and after one or two similar excursions, my parents ignored any night time warnings.

In any case, Dad had made us a shelter of our own in our back garden, about five yards from the fence round the airfield. It was a big hole with earth steps down into it. Over it was a roof which he made by criss-crossing the hole with timbers, covering them with sheets of corrugated iron, and piling soil over the top.

This was 1941, and there was plenty of activity on our airfield. Spitfires and Hurricanes came and went, and a few Lysanders and the odd amphibian. Our bedroom window looked onto the airfield, and we spent many an hour with our noses glued to it. The road, passing by the front of the house, had become a bicycle path for air force personnel going on and off duty, and for other vehicles going to and from the buildings which lay beyond the houses down our road. For a short while, a barrier separated our road from the rest of the village, and we had to get permission to pass it.'

LOVE AND MARRIAGE

'My father was posted to a camp in England, he didn't go abroad. At weekends he used to bring home four or five of his soldier friends who lived up North, and couldn't get home for just a weekend. We had a huge lounge, and the soldiers used to sleep in a row on the floor. My funny memory of this is taking a cup of tea in to them in the morning, and seeing them lying there with no teeth in! I had hysterics the first morning and asked my father whether he had a nice young chap he could bring home. He said his friends were all his age, but a few weeks later he came home and said he'd invited a young soldier called Peter to stay for the weekend. This was much more my cup of tea, and he came every weekend after that, and we started going out together.

By this time the war was almost over. My father was de-mobbed but Peter was sent to Africa, where he served for about 18 months. We wrote regularly, and I used to meet the postman on my way to work. One morning he was smiling all over his face and handed me what looked like a hard football. My name was painted on it and we just didn't know what to make of it. I took it back home, and in the evening my father struck it with a hammer. Inside was a coconut! I didn't know they grew in a shell. I'd only seen them covered with fibre.

Clothes and food were in short supply, and we had coupons for food, clothes, furniture etc. When you had used all these up, you couldn't buy anything else until your next lot of coupons were due. Working in a shoe shop, my mother kept me well shod (a lot of black-marketeering went on in those days). If my mother did a good turn for someone, they might hand over some clothes or food coupons and we did very well on the whole.

After 18 months, Peter came home to England. Although we had been apart for so long, and hadn't really known each other all that time before he went to Africa, we continued going out again, and became engaged. When we decided to get married, I can still hear my father saying, "Thank goodness for that, it will help with the sleeping arrangements."

Preparing for the wedding was quite a headache, but by this time my mother was working in a grocer's shop, and a lot of the customers contributed eggs, sugar, margarine etc towards the wedding cake.

Peter had brought home some lovely white silk material, and my grandmother made my wedding dress of this, and it was really beautiful. I often think of my best friend, Joyce, who was our chief bridesmaid. She wore a pair of beautiful nylon stockings! No, she hadn't been out with a GI but her father was a very wealthy businessman and there was nothing Joyce wanted for.

When we set up home and the war had been over for some time, we were still rationed, but having babies helped. They got their rations on a Ration Book so the family as a whole were quite well fed!'

MAKE DO AND MEND

'My maternal grandmother, with whom we lived to keep her company during the emergency, spent many hours at her old fashioned sewing machine to keep my sister and me decently clothed. My problem was that the resulting garments, lovingly constructed from cloth which was already well worn, ripped only too easily and I often returned from play with a torn skirt. There was, of course, no suggestion that girls might wear trousers when climbing railings!

Although we took with us our modern appliances, such as the Acme wringer, my grandmother's mangle dominated the scullery. It had enormous wooden rollers. My paternal grandmother's equally large mangle stood in her back yard and, apart from its usual purpose, was used by my grandfather to expel the fermented juice from his rhubarb when he was wine making. Surplus eggs were laid down in "isinglass" and fruit was bottled. We were self sufficient in most vegetables.

Home-made toys were plentiful but rubber balls were not. I remember begging a friend not to throw my ball while she was near bushes but she paid no heed and my ball was lost for ever, despite frantic searches. I am sure that whoever found it was overjoyed.

We were aghast when one of my aunts squandered a quarter of a clothing coupon on hair ribbons for my cousin. Another cousin wore a kilt made from a scarf. As a baby she had been dressed in garments sent by my uncle from South Africa, where he was training with the RAF. The ship had been damaged and her garments bore the stains of immersion in I know not what! They had been a long time in the journey but fortunately he had bought large. Another uncle was in

America and his wife was the lucky recipient of a blue and white striped dress. Happily for my sister, it was a bit tight for my aunt and had to be passed on. We were thrilled one Christmas to receive, also from America, a spoonful of peanuts each.'

'Through the WI I learned glove making and skin curing, so was able to cure the skins of my rabbits and also lamb skins which were available from newborn fatalities. These were made into mittens for the little girls. Rabbit skins were made into fur collars and gloves, which were appreciated by all the family, especially when cycling. No more frozen hands. I also learned how to make baskets using material from the hedgerows, and to do rushwork. Rushes were used for chair seating, floor mats and baskets. Some items I found I could substitute – leaves from the garden, sedge from streams, and various rushes could be collected locally. With a little practice and ingenuity there was no limit to what one could make.'

'Clothes rationing exercised our ingenuity. We could get army blankets and I remember making a warm dressing gown from one of them. The silk parachutes, unpicked and bleached, made useful underwear. When my winter coat showed signs of wear and looked shabby, I, like many others, took the coat apart, brushed it and turned it inside out – the same model but a little more nap on the cloth.'

'During the war a call was made for dried nettles to be used for medicinal purposes. Living on a farm, I had the use of the top floor in the oast house, which had a slatted floor once used for drying hops. So, armed with gloves, we went round the village pulling up nettles in gardens and fields and filling bags with them.

The fresh nettles were spread on the floor of the oast house until they were dry and then packed tightly into bags. It took several bags of fresh nettles to fill one bag of the dried material, which was labelled and sent off to an address in London. The money we received per bag was given to the Red Cross.'

THE FINGER OF SUSPICION

'It was the spring of 1940. Our bungalow looked across the valley to Steed Hill on the North Downs. It was reported from there that flashing lights were seen in the early morning, so the police were called upon to investigate. My mother and I lived there alone at the time and knew nothing of such activities. The local constable called and was very courteous, investigating what could be causing these flashing lights. He came again at the time of day the lights were seen and discovered that the early morning sunshine was coming through an angle of the bay window onto a clockface on the chest of drawers, across to the mirror of the wardrobe door and out at the opposite angle of the bay. Mother getting up and dressing caused the flashes!'

'HERE'S TO THE NEXT MAN TO DIE'

'During the war our pub, The Three Bells at Swingfield, became popular with the American airmen stationed at Hawkinge aerodrome. They liked to watch the locals play dominoes and darts and would bet on the outcome of the games. They liked to bet on anything, but never joined in the games themselves. There was one thing about them that particularly annoyed my father. They devised a game of tossing pint beer glasses over the top of the pub. Apart from one night nearly seriously injuring someone, the glasses fell on the ground and smashed. The Americans would say that they'd pay for replacements, but that wasn't the problem. Glasses stamped with the Imperial Pint measure were in very short supply during the war.

The Americans never talked about their missions, and because they drank in groups one soon noticed if anyone in a gang was missing, but it was taboo to ask where the missing airman was. The Americans' last drink was usually accompanied by the toast, "Here's to the next man to die".'

DOING OUR BIT

Working on the land and in heavy industry, fighting fires, or going into the Services, women played a full role in the war effort, their work essential to keep agriculture and industry alive. There were those men who took on dangerous responsibilities at home too, such as the members of the guerilla Special Auxiliary Units.

ON THE LAND

'I was 20 years old and had only been married for a few months. My husband was in the RAF and already on his way to Burma; he was to be away for five years. So I joined the Land Army and started work on the farm. At first the men made fun of me, all older men who had been farm workers all their lives, but soon they became my friends when they realised I could do the work.

I had a herd of cows, three bulls and calves in my charge. I started at five in the morning and worked to very late at night for a payment of £2 per week. I was in lodgings a mile from the farm to start with so I rode a two stroke motorbike to work, but after a few months a farm cottage became vacant and the farmer offered it to me. It was a one up, one down with a lean-to which was the kitchen. Outside the back door there was a shed with a copper to boil your clothes and next to it was the toilet, which was just a bucket with a seat and a hole. At the top of the garden was a well for all the cottages to get water from. Of course, there was no bathroom. You heated up the water in the copper and bathed in a tin bath.

I was up at four, using sticks to light a black cooking stove to boil the kettle for a cup of tea. Then it was out to the farm to get the cows in for milking, which was done by hand, and the churns had to be ready for the lorry at half past seven. With the milking done it was home to breakfast, which was a slice of bread and dripping and a cup of tea. Then back to the cowsheds to turn out the cows and clean them out, and take the small bull for his walk (the other two ran with the cows). The next job would be to get out the tractor and go out to the field to cut the kale.'

'I joined the Land Army and after passing my medical was posted to a hostel on the Romney Marsh. I arrived at Appledore railway station, was picked up by car and taken to Brenzett, where I met about 40 other girls green as grass just like me. Nearly all of them were Londoners.

It was tough going at first, up at half past five each morning and cycling miles following a threshing machine pulled by a steam roller. We did all kinds of land work – bean cutting, picking up spuds, sheep dipping, haymaking, stooking, bale carting and then back to threshing.

Hostel life was great fun. The rules were very strict and we had to be in by ten at night – but we used to let the odd one in via the window!'

Land Army girls were essential to the continued production of food during the war. Many of them were Londoners – 'as green as grass'.

'When the war broke out in 1939 East Kent was considered a safety' area for evacuees from London, but by early 1940 we became a danger zone: all our evacuees had left, and in our village we settled down to war. We became fire-watchers or joined the ARP or the WVS and my friend Mary and I also became members of the Emergency Land Corps, which meant we were put on a list and were available for farmers to hire for seasonal work. Mary was a retired farmer's daughter and was full of knowledge. I only had a vague idea of such jobs as hop picking, potato picking and apple picking, but had great faith in Mary and she never let me down.

After a few days helping a smallholder by pruning his raspberry canes we started our first big job – hop picking. The village was surrounded by big hop fields, but we were engaged to pick in a small local field owned by an elderly farmer and normally picked by local villagers. He was short of workers and he was pleased to employ us. It was a very traditional hop field and had been run in the same old way for years.

The first morning seemed to me to be a very early start; it was quite chilly and the dew was still on the hops. We were dressed in

215

our oldest macs, scarves and boots. On arrival we were taken to our allotted rows, given our tally-sticks and told to start picking. I think it was the last farm to have this type of tally-stick, difficult to describe but very simple to work.

Each group of pickers was given a number, which was also on their tally-sticks. It was made from a piece of wood, about twelve inches long and roughly two inches thick, which was split into two, leaving about two inches at the end of one piece. The shorter piece was given to the picker and a hole was pierced in the longer piece and, threaded by a length of twine, was hung on the tally-man's belt. At the end of the day when the tally-man came to count our full baskets (each basket holding about four or five bushels) the picker handed him her half of the tally-stick which was fitted into his half making one stick again, and the tally-man then scored across the thick side of the whole stick with a file, once for each full basket, and handed the short stick back to the picker, keeping the long piece hanging on his belt. Thus both sticks had exactly the same number of marks: simple and foolproof. The number of bushels was entered in a book in the farmhouse each day.

At the beginning the Battle of Britain was being fought overhead as we picked. By rights there should have been an air raid shelter for us, or at least for the children, and there had been a half-hearted attempt to dig a trench for them, but it had soon filled up again, and anyway the children preferred being with their mothers, cheering our planes on! When the planes were too close we used to lie down under the rows and put our empty baskets over our heads. I could just see our house from the field and lay there watching it, ready to run back if necessary to help my mother. The farmer's wife, who was an eccentric to say the least, used to come down to the field and run through the rows calling out "Don't stop working, it's playing Hitler's game. I am not hiding away!" but we all ignored her advice.

On the Saturday after we had finished, we all put on our "town clothes" and went up to the farm to get our pay. We had to wait outside the farmhouse, while everything was checked, and in turn received our due amount and then off we went rejoicing. The children who had picked were particularly happy, as the money they had earned provided them with best clothes which they could choose for themselves!'

'In 1939 I was seconded from Folkestone Technical School to the Ministry of Agriculture and Fisheries. I worked with all WIs from the Isle of Sheppey down through Harrietsham to Rye and west of that area – to help them with Fruit Preservation to shop retail standard.

The fruit was picked by WI ladies and the farmers were paid for it.

I drove round the villages in a travelling van loaned by America with an American canning machine in it. Later there were three canning machines, with helpers who were trained as I had been, to operate the machines. The machine sealed the lids on the cans containing fruit in syrup or tomatoes in brine, and then the cans were boiled in a machine like a wash-boiler. The cans were cooled – in the stream at Wingham – and then taken into the WIs to be labelled. One fruit was worked on at a time. The WI were paid for the fruit, sugar and calor gas by the shops who then distributed and sold it.

The season started in June and went on till the end of October. They worked all the hours God sends to harvest the soft fruits, cherries, plums, tomatoes, peas, beans and made chutneys. We had a very good London representative of the Min of Ag & Fisheries to check the quality, a Mrs Coolin, who was very fair. Mrs Strachan of Ash was one of my helpers. No expense was spared for equipment and petrol, tyres, etc.

The fruit preservation centre at Barham village hall in 1942. Such labours were invaluable in times of rationing – Barham WI alone produced 22,759 lbs of jam by the end of the war.

I also helped train WI members in practical classes to make the best use of their rations and the contents of parcels that many received from their American connections and how to use soya flour in various ways.'

THE AFS

'At the outbreak of war in 1939 I was working at Littlewoods Stores in Ramsgate. Subsequently the store closed and I volunteered for the Auxiliary Fire Service. My father was a full time Air Raid Warden, my brother waiting to join the RAF and I was engaged to Frank who was serving in the Fleet Air Arm.

In 1942, aged 20, I was accepted into the AFS as No 878641. We had no uniform to start with – that came later. My duties were in the control room as a telephonist and on occasions I was engaged on mobilising. This entailed keeping maps of the local and surrounding areas up to date using pins and flags to show the deployment of appliances and crews. It was vital that this was done accurately to show at a glance where appliances were and what was available at any time. We worked in eight hour shifts – 2 pm–10 pm, 10 pm–6 am and 6 am–2 pm in the control room under the fire station in Effingham Street, Ramsgate. We had 48 hours on duty and 24 hours off. Whilst on duty we were housed in billets at Liverpool Lawns and Northwood Road.

During a particularly bad night raid on Canterbury or Manston when Ramsgate gas works were hit, I was off duty, but feeling my help might be needed I ran from my home in Cecilia Road to the fire station. When I arrived, far from the heroine's welcome I'd expected I was told off for wearing my tin hat on the back of my head with the strap across my throat. This was the way I always wore it – it was so much more becoming than the regulation, and protective, position! I think it was the same night that I spent my shift sitting under a very large, thick-topped table in the watch room manning a telephone. I often wonder if that table, my make-shift air raid shelter, is still there.

When we came off duty that night, the whole town seemed to be covered in grey ash and I got home to find Mum had uncovered the old kitchen range in the scullery and was cooking on it. With the gas works out of action there was no other way. I know whenever there was a raid whilst I was on duty, I used to wonder what I would find when I came up from the control room – and even if I would still have a home to go to.

I often think of the worry my mother must have had. Her husband an Air Raid Warden, daughter in the Fire Service and son in the RAF

– not knowing from one day to another if we were going to come home in one piece, or even come home at all. Of course, both my brother and I were only in our early twenties and, strange as it may seem in these days, the whole thing was an exciting adventure to us.'

THE WAAF

'I have very clear memories of days and nights spent in an underground bunker near Dover, as a WAAF, in the 1940s. The radar stations all round the coast gave warning of approaching enemy aircraft, enabling "plotters" far inland to show their tracks, record the height at which they were flying and enable the RAF to be off after them, or the AA guns to do their work.

The science of radar was fairly new, and surprised the Germans when it came into operation. Electro-magnetic waves located the enemy aircraft and bounced back to the stations which had emitted them, and quite unscientific operators could record direction and height. But the transmitters and receivers were newly devised and, left to themselves, might make wrong recordings, on account of the unevenness of the terrain, or metallic deposits of any kind within a certain range of the station. Therefore it was advisable to fly aircraft on known directions and at known heights and to compare these known factors with the tracks recorded by a radar set, in order to prepare a diagram of likely errors and thus to be able to correct them. It sounds simple, but a lot of statistical work was involved, and long days and nights of watching and calculating.

As a simple radar operator I had been fairly content with my lot, until one day I took a cup of coffee to the CO in his office and rather impolitely looked at some charts there, and said cheerfully, "Ah! co-tangent curves!" With a look of astonishment he enquired what I knew about co-tangent curves, and it was only what I had learned in a sixth form maths class. But that was apparently more than most radar operators knew, and within days I was transferred to HQ and shut in an office with lots of graph paper and a telephone – the first to plot charts on and the second to communicate with research workers at various locations around the coast.

Events and developments brought me after a while to Dover, where I was busily recording data concerning the established radar stations known as "the chain". I liked working, even long hours, because it saved me from being hustled into a shelter every time a shell was fired over from the French coast by the German gunners there.

219

So I kept my head down, plotting charts and preparing information for the real researchers. One night I was doing this, quietly and contentedly, until one of a group in a huddle some yards away got up and said, "How long have you been here?" "An hour or so," I said. "Have you overheard our conversation?" "No, is it interesting?" "Very – I think you had better sign the Official Secrets Act." This sounded quite terrifying, but it wasn't – just a formality. In return for my signature, I was given an idea of the secret which I had to keep – the imminence of the V2 rocket attack – and then I was allowed to help to devise means of plotting the trajectory of such a high speed weapon, in order to give some warning to the public. It proved to be a nearly impossible task, and one from which I was quite soon released on being promoted to commissioned rank and sent for officer training.

Eventually this phase came to an end, and I was launched as a fully fledged signals officer and returned to my native Kent, to a station in Walmer. Here the work was quite different and concerned maintaining radio communication with other stations on the coast, in order to make a radio path for bombers ordered out by "Bomber" Harris, against the unfortunate cities of Germany. In time these operations were moved to France, Belgium and Holland as the Allied armies advanced on the Continent. So my Kentish wartime, with its memories of white cliffs, glimpses of the French coastal road and the gun emplacements there, gave way to more humdrum work at Overseas Aircraft Control at Gloucester and Uxbridge, more global, but far from home.'

WORKING ON THE DOCKS

'My husband went into the army in 1940 and after his training was sent overseas. I went on munitions. I became very ill and was discharged, but was later recalled and went welding at Sheerness dockyard for four years. I had to wear an identity disc round my neck with a number on. Hundreds of women took over men's work and I wonder sometimes how we managed to do it. We clocked in by 7 am, having walked three miles. A bell would start to toll slowly as it got nearer to 7 am, then a little faster, then very fast, and you should have seen us run then. If you were late, the punch on your card would show up and if you had three late marks in a month you were in trouble with your chargehand. I had an hour for lunch, then clocked off at 6.30 pm. This was seven days a week. Once a month we went in groups to give blood, had a cup of sweet tea, then went back to work.'

THE SPECIAL AUXILIARY UNIT

'One of the best kept secrets of the war was the formation of the so-called "stay behind units", or Special Auxiliary Units as they were later officially called, dotted about from Essex to Hampshire, those areas most vulnerable to invasion. These units were quite separate from the Home Guard; in fact its members, all volunteers, would have been classified as guerillas, with no protection under the Geneva Convention. If captured, having no official accreditation, its members would have been shot.

I was one of the volunteers, and our headquarters in this part of Kent was at Bilting, commanded by Colonel Peter Fleming, a Guards officer with considerable experience in intelligence work. Peter, incidentally, was the brother of Ian Fleming, who you will know as the author of the James Bond series of spy novels.

These units were made up of six men acquainted with the local area and trained at headquarters in the use of explosives and sabotage techniques. My cell was at Huntstreet, in a deep hole in Capon Wood, fitted out with rough bunks and stocked with a tank of water and rations for ten days. Explosives were stored in another hide some way off.

On occasions we stayed overnight, taking part in night training with a unit of the Lovat Scouts. My overnight absences were explained by my Home Guard activities, and my wife did not find out the truth until long after the war. And although my sons often searched for the hide, and even ferreted for rabbits quite close to it, they never discovered it until many years later when the roof rotted and eventually collapsed. Looking back, I sometimes wonder why I ever volunteered!

Looking back to the early days of the war, with the Germans only 30 miles away, we seemed oblivious to the dangers that could lie ahead. In the glorious weather of the summer of 1940 the work proceeded as usual; the binder cutting the corn while, overhead, on those August mornings, waves of bombers with their fighter escorts regularly passed on their way to London with little opposition. But later in August and September, when our own fighters came into the area, we saw quite a few aircraft come down – and some bombs, too, from German aircraft which turned back from London, dropping their loads on the way home. Winchcombe was fortunate on one occasion, being straddled by five bombs, all blowing craters in the fields either side of the house.

Although during 1940 there were occasional visits by Army units on exercises, the war seemed somewhat remote in our quiet little community. After Dunkirk, though, there existed the real possibility of invasion, and one of the things I remember was the erection, all over our open fields, of 15 ft poles with their ends buried deeply in the ground, so that we looked like a hop garden that had lost a lot of its poles. The idea was to wreck gliders, should they ever arrive carrying German troops.

Later on, a prisoner of war camp was established near Ashford, and farmers were able to employ prisoners to work on the land. I had a gang for a day or two hoeing wurzels. They arrived by truck at 7.30 am and were collected at 4 pm. There were Germans and Italians, the former being much the better workers.

The war brought many changes to agriculture, and when Belgium was overrun a new crop came to East Kent – flax. It was essential for all forms of webbing, parachute harness and so forth, and I was employed by the Ministry of Supply to help grow it. I spent six months learning how, and was allotted most of East Kent as my area. I had to see that the right quantity of seed was delivered, that the seed beds were right, and to organize pulling at the correct time. Flax is pulled from the ground, not cut, by a special machine. Three of these machines were rescued from Belgium to be copied, but somehow the copies weren't exactly efficient and were a real headache at harvest time.

I had a team of six Land Army girls as drivers of Ford tractors – the old models with steel wheels. The wheels had to be fitted with wide wooden rims, held on by bolts, but after a bit of trundling along hard roads they were inclined to work loose. I would often get a frantic call from one of the girls to say one had fallen off and would have to go and search for her, usually many miles away via roads without signposts. I thus got to know East Kent and the Romney Marsh area well.

It was an interesting job, and I met many farmers during the two and a half years I did it. After the war, of course, the demand ended, and the East Kent flax industry died.'

HIGHDAYS & HOLIDAYS

BESIDE THE SEASIDE

Generations of children have eagerly awaited the day out or the family holiday at Margate, Ramsgate or Cliftonville, or any other of the Kent seaside resorts that came to be such a special part of our lives. The smell of seaweed, sand between our toes and the seaside landlady – who needed foreign shores when our own was so inviting?

AN OUTING TO SANDWICH BAY 1900

'A day we all looked forward to in our village of Northbourne was our annual summer treat of a day at Sandwich Bay at the sandhills. Lord Northbourne very kindly lent his horses and corn carts to take us there. Each waggon had two horses and the men walked proudly by the side of the horses with their whips resting on their shoulders. Boards were put across for us to sit on and believe me, you certainly needed a cushion as well before you got to the bay, after bumping over those sandhills. But how we loved it and I think our mothers did too. By the time we arrived at the bay it was lunchtime. Everyone was given a meat pasty and we sat on the sand and ate it, after which all the children made for the water. The horses had their annual paddle too, the men taking them in to cool their feet. Some didn't think much of it at first but soon got used to it. How happy we all were, and after a good tea we loaded up for home, tired out.'

BROADSTAIRS IN 1914

'When we went on the sands we wore all our clothes including shoes, socks and hats – but not gloves. Many people from London also wore gloves. We all wore blue bathing costumes, and my hair was put up under a mob-cap, not very waterproof. We undressed in a wooden bathing machine which was then drawn down to the sea by a horse. We went down little steps into the sea. Ladies were fully dressed to sit on the sands. They wore beautiful big hats and very few went into the sea. If I paddled my clothes were tucked into my knickers. All girls paddled like that. We had fun on the sands with donkey rides, sand castle competitions, sand services and digging holes. We could also sit on the sands and watch Uncle Mack and his minstrels free; adults paid sixpence.'

MEMORIES OF MARGATE

'We had been looking at some bathing costumes from years gone by and a Sheppey lady of at least 90 remembered "when I was a girl and we went to spend the day at Margate. They had them bathing machines with horses then. You paid from high water mark to high water mark. If the tide was in you had to dress very quick. When the tide was out you had time to tie your corset right.

I remember the smell in them machines like yesterday, there was no windows. Damp clothes, seaweedy smells and horses . . . very strong the horse was. And on the beach you had to take great care where you sat down. There were plenty of machines . . . and horses. But they were wonderful days." '

'Many years ago when I was a child before the First World War, nobody would be allowed to undress or dress on the beach. We had bathing machines (changing rooms built on a carriage) which were drawn by horses following the tide in and out.

We also had pierrots (a type of clown) at Margate and their concert party folk who performed on incredibly small stages and for a few pence one could sit on a deckchair and enjoy their really good performances. For the children there was a Punch and Judy puppet show and how the youngsters enjoyed condemning old Punch.

Paddle steamers came to the end of the pier from the Thames via Southend and hundreds of Londoners poured into the town for a day's enjoyment. On one of these days I was a seller for the first "flag day". We sold paper flags on pins in aid of nurses and it was called Alexandra Rose Day. For this event we were expected to wear white dresses.

We had two railway stations from which steam trains left for London. These trains started from Margate; one train went direct to London and the other took the south coast route via Ashford. The coastal train left the Sands station (which was situated where Dreamland is now) and travelled to Ramsgate harbour, steaming first through a tunnel in the cliffs. Air vent chimneys can still be seen at odd intervals along the way today. I can remember the occasion when a train came out of the tunnel too quickly and nearly ran into Ramsgate harbour after hitting the buffers. Thereafter the trains had to halt near the end of the tunnel and wait to be signalled on, to travel at a slow speed, almost walking pace. Motor cars were very scarce. Our transport was by tram, horses and bicycles. The trams were open topped and when it rained we had to get under cover by using the waterproof aprons which were attached to the seat in front. I remember the day when we had such a fierce gale that two trams had to travel together along the seafront in order to move along. One of our horse transports was by the "brake". These had enormous wheels and we had to climb a short ladder to reach our seats. Private transport was a "landau", a carriage that was pulled by a horse. It had a hood similar to the one found on a baby's pram. When it rained it was great fun to put it up and sit beneath it with no windows to look through.

Westgate was a private estate and to keep that status it had to be closed at both ends for 24 hours once a year. There were four gates, two at each end of the through roads. These were manned and had to be opened and shut to allow people and traffic to go through.

If you went on an outing you had a charabanc, a motor driven vehicle which was open to the elements with its canvas hood, again similar to the baby's pram, folded at the back. When it rained this cover was handed from seat to seat until it reached the windscreen. On its reaching the front we nearly always found that it would not fix on to the slots and often the occupants of the front seats held it in place and the side shields would flap in the breeze. One had to be tough to go on these outings!'

'Margate in the early 1920s was so enjoyable. It always seemed to be lovely sunny weather and the highlight was to go to the beach. There was a children's playground where parents could leave their children with a nurse in attendance. Then there was Punch and Judy, and the Toffee Man who made toffee in a hut on the beach and would throw pieces to the children. Some, of course, ended up in the sand but that didn't put the children off.'

'As a young child, between 1927 and 1939, I came on holiday with my parents and brothers and sisters to stay at Garlinge, near Margate. We stayed with a family in Caxton Road, and the lady of the house supplied us with what was called "cooking and attendance". My father would go out each morning early to buy meat etc for our meals and groceries would be bought about every other day. We would then take them back to our landlady and she would cook our meals for us – breakfast, dinner and tea.

We sometimes enjoyed a ride on a break-cart which left the Clock Tower at Margate at about 11 am. It was pulled by two horses and took us for rides through the countryside, usually around Pegwell Bay, or to Manston where a stop was made at The Jolly Farmer pub. There were also evening mystery trips by coach from the Clock Tower via Minster lavender fields or Manston aerodrome.

There was a concert party on the sands at Margate and they sold song sheets of popular current tunes. There were also sand sculptures to be seen on the sands by the Clock Tower. You could have a donkey ride on the sands, the donkeys coming from stables behind Dreamland. There were fireworks at Dreamland every Thursday evening.

We also used to look out for a character called Lobby Ludd. One of the daily papers printed a silhouette of this character and details of the area of the seafront and the times he could be seen on that day. You had to have the newspaper under your arm and if you recognised him, go up to him and say, "You are Lobby Ludd". If you were right he would give you half a crown. I don't think we ever found him!'

WHITSTABLE IN THE 1920s

'The highlight of my year, as a child, was our family's annual six week visit to my grandfather, who lived in Argyle Road, Whitstable. These visits took place in the halcyon days between the wars, and the sun always seemed to be shining. The centre of Whitstable is very little changed since those days and it is easy to recall earlier times.

Our first trip was to my aunt's toy shop to buy buckets and spades, then on to the shoe shop to buy paddlers – a form of rope-soled sandal with white cotton uppers and white cotton tie-ups. These were very necessary because of the shingle beaches. We also had to be equipped with new swimming costumes – always starting off navy blue, with short sleeves and legs (sometimes to the knee) and white edgings. Of course, after a few dips they became very washed out and the bindings became pale green! In later years – about 1928 onwards – very smart two-coloured costumes were the rage, with brightly coloured tops (sleeveless with narrow shoulders) and black from the waist down, topped off with rubber swimming caps in bright pink, orange or yellow. We were the cat's whiskers, or thought so.

Days were simple – errands in the morning, or swinging in the garden, while the washing, housework and cooking were attended to, then the beach in the afternoon, where we had the use of a hut belonging to my mother's girlhood friend.

I can remember, as a four year old, walking down to the beach with my sister and father one rather chilly morning to sail my boat. We prevailed on him to let us paddle and were fully engrossed, when I leaned back on the breakwater, only to find it wasn't there! I'd chosen the part where the groyne was stepped down and over I went, fully dressed in coat and hat, into about two feet of water on the other side. I could hear my father saying "Now where's that child got to?" and my bubbly reply, before I was hauled out, dripping wet. It seemed a very long walk home, and very public too.

We were quite content amusing ourselves on the beach – bathing and sand castles (on the small strip of sand) when the tide was in, cockling and investigating moored boats and a very sinister wreck when the tide was out. There were usually a few friends and relatives to swell the party and all the huts were occupied. We always stayed until tea-time and if we weren't going to the "pictures" afterwards, would stay – playing cricket, hide and seek round the huts and balancing on the breakwaters – until sunset, or, if the tide was right, until the barges left harbour, as many as four or five, with enormous red-brown sails – a sight I still remember as being very special, as they glided out at high water.

The summer milestones then were the same as now – the carnival, regatta and fireworks. Before the war the carnival was a very boisterous affair with streamers everywhere and confetti, and there were several floats which belched smoke and sprayed water – no worries about pollution in those days, and what fun it was. The streets were filled with young people for a long time afterwards, and many girls had confetti stuffed down their necks and were well and truly "jumped". The regatta was quite an affair, too. It didn't mean a great deal to us landlubbers, but we enjoyed the greasy pole, and the fight between the sweeps, armed with bags of soot, and the millers, armed with bags of flour.

Sundays were very special – chapel in the morning with all the relations, then a walk in the afternoon with usually a band concert in the castle grounds, complete with a box of chocolates supplied by my father.

The town was always full of visitors and while running errands for my mother for shrimps and other delicacies I used to see how many times I could get my photo taken by one of the photographers working up and down the High Street. We also had to keep a look out for Lobby Ludd, though what I should have done if I'd seen him I don't know, not having the appropriate newspaper available!'

HOCKEY AT FOLKESTONE

'From 1920 onwards I came every Easter with my parents to Folkestone for the annual Hockey Festival. I would look out for the first primroses on the railway embankment as the train sped southwards; they were such a joy to see and flowered so much later where I lived in Harrow.

Of course, we spent most of our time watching hockey, but my sister and I spent many happy hours between matches exploring

Caesar's Camp, the Warren and Hawkinge Woods. We also enjoyed watching the London Scottish Regiment take on local teams at roller hockey on the skating rink on the lower promenade.'

KENTISH DELIGHTS

'From the age of three until I was 13 and evacuated on 1st September 1939 to the deepest rural reaches of Somerset, summer holidays were spent on the Kent coast. A confession at this point – one year we defected to Gorleston in Essex. This disgraceful episode was not repeated and the next year we were back at Westbrook or Tankerton, Sandgate or Westgate, Cliftonville or Broadstairs. We spread our favours very widely. The only criterion which seems to have been applied was that the chosen resort should be close to a larger, more popular resort. I think, with hindsight, that a degree of snobbery came into play; Margate was thought to be slightly downmarket but Westgate or Cliftonville perfectly acceptable. The one exception to the large resort rule was Folkestone. The Leas were the attraction there and my grandparents promenaded with great regularity – my grandmother protected from the sun by a Japanese parasol which, now, I possess. She wore, also, gloves and a hat!

The preparation for our exodus from the metropolis seems to have taken weeks. The first priority, of course, was finding the accommodation. Invariably, this was a furnished house, as close to the beach as possible, which was rented for a month. The ladies and the children were installed for the whole period; the men joined us as and when business permitted. To complete the household there was a dog, for most of the period a snappy Sealyham bitch called Gypsy, and, most importantly, my aunt's "treasure". She went by the name of Lily, a simple soul, who appeared, to my childish eyes, to be delighted with the change from the city to the seaside even though she still had work to do. Albeit, she had time off to listen to the band, sit on the beach and eye the local lads.

The real excitement started when the trunks were assembled, ready for packing. They had a unique smell, which persists to this day. Once the trunks were packed, roped securely and labelled, Carter Pattersons were summoned to start them on their journey to Victoria station where they were handed over to the Southern Railway Company and conveyed to the chosen resort. Presumably, a local carrier picked them up from there and delivered them to "Sea View", "Bay View", "Mon Repos" or whatever. They never failed to be waiting for us when we arrived.

Now came the hardest part to endure – waiting for the day when the taxi drew up at the door and we were off to Victoria station. Usually, by this time, I was sick with excitement, literally!

The smell of the station is unforgettable. The train itself was a mixture of steam, coal and leather (the latter, the straps which raised and lowered the windows). All this was part of the holiday.

I cannot remember what the countryside looked like between Victoria and the coast. Once we were through the suburbs I was looking for the sea and imagining I could see it round the next bend. And then we were there and I was running along the platform and, on one occasion, right into a lamppost, almost knocking myself out.

Soon, we were installed in our temporary home and I was agitating to go to the beach but little girls had to wait until an adult was available to take them. Usually, it was my grandfather and we made a preliminary exploration of the nearest stretch of beach. Sometimes it was sandy, sometimes pebbly. There were advantages and disadvantages with either. I hated sand between the toes but, also, I hated having to wear sandals because my soft, city feet could not cope with walking over pebbles.

The days ahead stretched on, seemingly without end but, of course, they did. In between, what pleasure there was. The paddling and, for some members of the party, swimming from which one emerged to be wrapped in a towelling cape and rubbed very briskly. The English Channel is never warm! If still cold, we would retreat to our beach hut for hot drinks brewed on a primus stove.

A great deal of the holiday was spent on the beach but there were trips into town and visits to band concerts and children's entertainments on the pier. I cannot recall that the adults went out in the evening but, as they were all great card players, I imagine they amused themselves with whist, rummy etc.

At this distance in time, I cannot differentiate between the resorts. They all run, one into another – a wonderful mixture of sun (did it never rain?), sea, sand and pebbles. Memories are revived by a few black and white photographs. But I do not need reminders. Those holidays on the Kent coast are indelibly stamped on my mind and are revived every year when we take our grandchildren to Seasalter, Tankerton or Whitstable and hope that the tide will be in and that they will not make too much fuss about sand between the toes.'

RAMSGATE IN THE 1930s

'I was born in Ramsgate, a small Victorian town, in 1922 and so was growing up in the 1930s. One of the highlights of the year, to which we youngsters all looked forward, was the "Summer Season". School was over and the holidays began, with long days on the beach, swimming and sunbathing. Most days my mother packed a picnic lunch and my father joined us for a swim before returning to work.

We had a small square striped tent which was set up with a number of others at the back of the Westcliff Beach, for which we paid one guinea for the season; in this we left buckets, spades etc with no risk of them disappearing. We were like one big happy family.

In the early 1930s each summer a small concert party headed by George Thomas would arrive, giving evening shows at a small theatre on the East Cliff. The cast would consist of a comedian, pianist, maybe an instrumentalist, soprano and baritone and two dancers – all working very hard taking part in sketches, songs and dance items. Several times a week there would be matinees at the bandstand in Ellington Park.

On the main beach in Ramsgate was a small outside theatre with Harry Gold and his Yachtsmen and as the name implies the cast wore naval outfits and entertained the crowds, some seated and some standing. The weather must have been good as there was no means of cover. On the roof garden of the Pavilion, Al Tabor and his band played for light music concerts and dancing.

What fun we had, so much to do – simple entertainment with family and friends. These artists returned year after year and so became a familiar part of life, as were the crowds of holidaymakers who came by coach, train and steamer from London.

If you felt like a short train ride to Broadstairs, there was Uncle Mack and his Minstrels at the end of the jetty, or Punch and Judy on the beach. When Uncle Mack died he was missed by thousands and there is a memorial to him on the sea front.

Then as the 1930s progressed, Billy Merrin and his Commanders, a band from the Nottingham Palais, was another attraction of the Summer Season. Their arrival heralded concerts on the West Cliff bandstand in the afternoons and dances in the West Cliff Hall in the evenings – how many romances began there? We girls had crushes on the male soloists. It was all so exciting, yet simple and carefree. We even learned the Palais Glide.

On Thursday evenings there was a firework display in Ellington Park, preceded by community singing – we could be heard for miles around.

So each summer passed – September came, tents were packed up, swimming and beach wear put away. The entertainers went back to London and Nottingham and we went back to school with happy memories of those precious days.'

'After lunch on Sundays we would often take the train to Ramsgate, to visit my grandparents. In summer, at the risk of getting a faceful of soot, we would open the windows and smell the lavender fields at Ebbsfleet and watch the pickers at work, cropping the lavender by hand.

Ramsgate was a wonderful place for a child, and when we tired of the sands there was plenty of traditional seaside entertainment on offer, from the two sets of donkeys offering rides (either towards the harbour or to the East Cliff), Punch and Judy, bandstand concerts, the "Merrie England" funfair and the "Jolly Boys" concert party on a little stage on the beach, to the more grandiose evening entertainment at the Pavilion. On the seafront there was a little zoo, with one tatty lion, a few small bears, and some very rude monkeys! The best treat of all was to catch the train from the seafront to Dumpton Gap. As it went through tunnels in the cliffs, panoramic scenes lit up, transporting us to the jungle or the Himalayan foothills in an instant.

All too soon our Sunday would be over and we'd take the train back to Canterbury, past the lavender and those ever-increasing slag heaps at Chislet.'

CLIFTONVILLE EVERY YEAR

'Cliftonville was our annual holiday destination when I was a small girl in the early 1930s. We always had ten days at the beginning of September, after the corn harvest was finished and before apple picking started in earnest, Father being a farmer near Sittingbourne.

A lot of our friends went to Sheerness, which was only about nine miles from home, but we went 40 miles to Cliftonville, and we thought it quite an adventure. We drove down in the Morris Cowley, Father preferring this, he said, to the Morris Oxford, and we always had a tourer as we didn't fancy being cooped up in a saloon. The one I remember best was a two seater, registration no. KR46. It had a hood which pulled up over the driver and passenger if it rained, but I had to sit in the dickie seat and get wet. There was no Thanet Way in those days, so our journey took us through Canterbury. The Cowley wasn't always enthusiastic about getting up Boughton Hill (Mother and I had to get out and walk up on one occasion), but once we were up we amused ourselves seeing who would be first to spot the cathedral towers through the trees. Another landmark was the Cherry Brandy House at Sarre. Excitement mounted as we arrived at Margate and saw the sea. Not that we liked Margate – being so close to the station, Mother said, made it "trippery", and also she said the

On the way to the sands at Cliftonville in 1931. On the left is the huge display of photographs taken by the professionals every day along the front.

sands were dirty. At Cliftonville the tide came right up to the cliffs twice a day, so the beach was scoured.

We stayed in one of the hotels overlooking the Lido. It wasn't as luxurious as the large Cliftonville Hotel just along the road, which had a glassed-in verandah all along the front with potted palms growing in it, but all the same we thought it was quite nice. I have no recollection of the food but it must have been acceptable, as the same people returned year after year, and indeed some became life-long friends. Our bedrooms had washstands in them, with jugs and basins. The jugs were filled with cold water, while hot water was brought around at appropriate times in an enamel jug, and left at the door. We had chamber pots too. Mother used to feel sorry for the chambermaids – she said it must be a nightmare trying to get rid of all the sand we washed off ourselves after a day on the beach. I believe baths were available if we made arrangements and paid an extra shilling, but I don't remember anyone using them. We were all expert at keeping ourselves clean with a minimum of water, and anyway, we would have baths as soon as we got home and got the copper fire going for the hot water.

There was so much to do in Cliftonville. The Lido was new and offered all sorts of entertainment, such as talent shows and organ recitals, and we always enjoyed watching the swimmers in the pool, though we ourselves preferred the sea. Another favourite venue was the Oval, where we used to see the "Fol-de-Rols" and "The Roosters". I feel sure we saw Arthur Askey there before he became famous, and lots of other entertainers who went on to become celebrities. In the evenings it was our practice to put on our best frocks and after dinner walk along to The Bungalow for a little light refreshment, and at least once during our stay we would walk along the cliffs to the Captain Digby at Kingsgate.

For me, however, the highlight of the holiday was the beach. Usually we went to Walpole Bay, either walking down the steps or the Gap. Once down, there was a sort of board promenade built up over the sands under the cliffs. We could get refreshments there, and usually after our dip we would go up for a Horlicks. The beach photographers kept very busy taking pictures of all us holidaymakers, and these were displayed in glass cases. We always enjoyed looking for ourselves. Once on the sands the grown-ups would hire deckchairs. There they were – the ladies in their second-best frocks, three-quarter length coats, cloche hats, shoes and stockings, the men in their second-best suits with waistcoats, trilby hats or caps and highly polished shoes. Most of them chain-smoked cigarettes. Father smoked Players, which I thought was a good thing as I liked collecting the cigarette cards.

The beach, to me, was a magic place. There would be crowds of people – families staying in the countless boarding houses in the side streets, and better off folks from all the big hotels along the cliff top. It was alive. The sea was never cold and I couldn't wait to get on my cotton bathing costume (orange at the top, and black at the bottom) and white rubber helmet. None of us had more than one costume, so after the morning swim we would hang it to dry on a deckchair until it was time to go back to the hotel for lunch. Then we'd hang it out of the window and hope it would dry to put on again in the afternoon. Sometimes we would go along to Palm Bay. At certain tides we seemed to get lovely waves to ride on, and Father and I enjoyed ourselves enormously. Father was a good swimmer, but Mother wouldn't venture in except to paddle without getting her frock wet. At low tide there were all those exciting rock pools.

You never knew what you were going to find – a hermit crab, a sea anemone or a limpet clinging to the chalk.

There were ball games on the sands, too. French cricket was a great favourite. The sands were kept free of seaweed by men with horses and carts, who loaded it up and took it to local farms to be ploughed in, so there was plenty of room for games at low tide. Digging was popular too. We used to build forts, houses and boats, and it was a great thrill to sit in your boat and watch it being surrounded by water as the tide came in. I had the largest available seaside spade so that Father could use it, and a galvanised bucket that was a smaller version of the real thing. Father insisted on the galvanised pail, as he said it would last. Indeed it did, for we were still using it for chicken corn 40 years later. I didn't dare say so, but I would have loved a brightly coloured tin bucket with pictures around the side, and a crab in the bottom. It would have made my happiness complete.

The time came in the mid 1930s when Mother said we were to go further afield, and we set off for Bournemouth, and later to Devon and Cornwall. They were pleasant in their way, but to me they never held the enchantment of the busy, bustling, exciting Cliftonville seafront of my childhood.'

THE OTHER SIDE OF THE COIN: THE LANDLADY'S STORY

'Before the last war Ramsgate was a popular, thriving holiday resort. Thriving in the summer that is, but with the bulk of jobs dependent on the holiday trade it was a depressed area during the winter and what work was available was poorly paid.

During those years thousands of holidaymakers, mainly Londoners, flocked to the seaside, with easy access on the Southern Railway and by charabancs, so, with no mills or factories etc, "letting" was the way our Mums could make a bit of extra cash.

After Christmas, an advertisement was sent up to the *London Evening News* for B & B, and our Mums sat back and waited for the bookings along with their deposits to come rolling in. My mother was always fully booked as many families came to us year after year for the same week or fortnight, so it was only a case of filling in the gaps. The practice was that if you got too many lets, you passed them on to the neighbours, at one shilling per let, who then wrote to the would-be-visitor and explained that they had been "passed on".

My parents moved their bed down to the parlour and we children had mattresses in one corner of the living room, with a curtain fixed across to allow us some privacy. That way we could let off three bedrooms. I lost my bedroom from about Easter to September every year. Some friends of mine had boards put across the bath for their beds.

We never had a holiday as we were told that living by the seaside we did not need one. I don't think that the visitors were any better off financially than we were, and after paying for their stay they seemed only to come down with a week or two weeks' housekeeping money. We charged twelve shillings and sixpence for Bed and Breakfast, and for a little extra did something called Bed and Attendance. This was when they preferred to buy in their own food, and my mother cooked it for them in the evening. One family took this last idea a bit too far, as the father and son spent every day fishing in the mud on Minster Marshes, and one day laid six muddy, smelly tiddlers on the draining board and expected us to cook them. No way!

Every morning started with taking up jugs of hot water for washing and shaving to each room, which had a jug and basin on top of a marble topped washstand. The breakfast was prepared. Plates and plates of bread to cut (no sliced bread in those days), bacon, eggs etc. In fact, a full English breakfast with unlimited pots of tea. Our own standard of fare improved at this time, because our Mum bought best back bacon and gammon rashers, which we had as well, instead of the usual "streaky".

Afterwards, as if by a signal, doors would open all down the street and the visitors would stream out, like a mass exodus, on their way down to the beach and the many resort attractions, on foot of course. They were allowed to come back later in the day for a wash and brush up, and, before going out again in the evening, the ones having the "attendance" had their evening meal.

My parents always waited up for them and offered a cup of tea before they retired. This was lovely for us children as we lay behind the curtain supposedly asleep but listening to all their grown-up chatter, a lot of which, I am sure, was not meant for our young ears.

In the main we had good people although we heard many hair-raising tales from neighbours. Sometimes we had courting couples, who had separate rooms of course, and my mother made it very clear from the start that she did not have any "hanky-panky" under her roof.

Saturday was "changeover day". One lot went, and the new arrivals were expected. After breakfast the ones that were going paid their bills and, with fond farewells, toddled off until next year. We children hung about the door and, if we were lucky, were handed a shilling which we were allowed to keep. Once I was given half a crown, and thought I was rich! Our people always paid their dues, but other neighbours told horrific tales about people popping out, saying that they were going to the shops, never to return, leaving empty battered suitcases behind!

When they had been waved off and had disappeared out of the gate, pandemonium broke out. Beds were stripped, rooms swept; all spit and polish. There was a frantic effort to wash, dry and air sheets to all be put back by the afternoon. Wet days were a nightmare. I suppose, looking back, we did not really have enough linen for this enterprise.

Anyway, by some miracle, when the next folk came struggling along with their suitcases all was well and the kettle was on ready to offer them a nice cup of tea. The older boys shared the use of an old rickety barrow, and moved them from the station and pushed their luggage the half a mile for threepence a case. While all this was going on, we older girls had to take the younger children out of the way so we congregated outside with our brothers and sisters in their prams and pushchairs like proper little mothers.

At the end of the season my mother took us children, with her letting money, to the school outfitters and rigged us up from the skin out! Vests, liberty bodices, etc, full school clothing, nightwear, shoes, etc, and always a nice warm winter coat.

I am sad to say that I don't think she ever had much out of it for herself, but, oh, the bliss when I got my own room and bed back.'

' "Apartments – Bed & Breakfast – Board Residence." These cards put in the window were known locally as "Poverty Cards". From May to September in the 1930s many houses in Margate displayed these cards. In our house it was "Apartments and Bed & Breakfast".

Apartments consisted of bedroom and sitting room with the 'visitors', as they were called, going out after breakfast and buying food for mother to cook for lunch. Fridays were hated because they usually wanted a load of fish and chips cooked.

Letting was hard work, with no hoovers, washing machines and other labour saving devices. For the Bed & Breakfast clients, breakfast was provided by Mother for the princely sum of three shillings and sixpence per night. It all amounted to a lot of hard work for very little money. However, letting was done by most people in Margate. Although my father had regular work as a carpenter, wages were low in those days, so what Mother earned by doing a bit of letting helped with the rates, a ton of coal for the winter, and hopefully a little bit to put by for a rainy day.

Letting had its share of dramas, tragedies and comedies. One young couple knocked at the door one Saturday evening and booked for a week. During the week a very irate Mayor of Luton called at our house looking for his daughter, who had eloped with her young man the previous Saturday.

August Bank Holiday was then the first Monday in August, and was considered the height of the season. An elderly man and his wife arrived on holiday on the Saturday, and the said gentleman departed this life in his sleep that night. Fortunately Mr Gore, our local undertaker, soon had the matter in hand and the poor chap was discreetly removed.

My husband's mother was also one of the band of Margate landladies. My husband had three brothers, and one dinner time one of the boys came home, washed his hands and unfortunately dropped the cake of soap in one of the waiting saucepans of potatoes. I gather from my mother-in-law those particular visitors never came again!

On leaving school I was to become a waitress and chambermaid for the season. Saturday was the highlight of the week when I received any tips, generous or otherwise. One of the less generous was when I was told by the departing guests that there was something in the wardrobe for me. Upon rushing upstairs I found two coat hangers. On another occasion I was informed there were some beer bottles in the sideboard, and I could take them back and get the money on them.

That was the 1930s and that way of life is long gone. However, I still have memories of Saturday nights spent shelling peas, stringing currants and top and tailing gooseberries. These were put in individual basins with the visitor's name scribbled on bits of paper placed on top.'

ROYAL CELEBRATIONS

Jubilees and coronations were celebrated with enthusiasm in towns and villages across East Kent, some local people making the trip to London to watch the pageantry unfold before them.

GEORGE V's JUBILEE 1935

'During my last year at school I have a vivid memory of being taken with a group of schoolchildren accompanied by two teachers to take

238

our places in the Mall for the Silver Jubilee procession of George V and Queen Mary. It was a blazing hot day and I had never seen such crowds. We waited for what seemed like ages, eating our sandwiches and drinking tepid orange juice from waxed cardboard containers. Then we heard the sound of music in the distance and along came the soldiers in their colourful uniforms marching with the bands, their musical instruments glittering in the sunshine. At last, what we had been waiting for; the handsome horses, the open landau and the surprisingly small but commanding figure of George V. Beside him sat Queen Mary, upright and regal. Her dress, her arms, her neck and her forehead were covered with the most magnificent jewels, and on her head she wore a beautiful tiara. The jewels shone so much in the sunshine they looked alive. It was over all too soon and we had to make our weary way home after a very exciting day.'

'Jubilee Day was fresh, fair, warm and beautiful as only a perfect spring day in England can be.

Every house in Godmersham had its tribute in the way of flags, streamers, festoons and all that ingenuity could devise. One household, having left it too late to procure any of the stereotyped decorations, had to make good with flowers; and with jam pots tied to the gate and filled with white and red tulips and bluebells got from the wood managed to achieve the prettiest decoration of them all.

The village had decided that their permanent memorial of this great day should be a copper beech. The tree, having been purchased in a large tub, could be sunk straight into the ground without any disturbance to its roots, near the village hall and in full view of the road.

The remainder of the day was spent at the Great House, to which every member of the parish had been invited. Various amusements and competitions had been arranged, one of the most popular being a cricket match at which the ladies snatched a dramatic last minute victory from the gentlemen.

Races and sports for the children took place on the wide, spreading lawns, and there were side-shows for all who cared to go in for them. Coconuts might be shied at and no money asked, competitions essayed for which there was no entrance fee, treasures hunted for and no charge made.

Tea was a splendid affair, all sitting down to a lavish spread for which so many and such enormous hams had been carved up, so many meat pies broken into, that, even after everyone had eaten all they wanted – and some of the younger ones perhaps a little more – there was enough left over for a substantial supper.

The richly decorated cakes set out on the children's tables exceeded all expectations, every child carrying off a sugar ornament which some at once ate, but which others kept on their mantlepieces and regarded as among their greatest treasures. The children received yet another gift, for each, down to the very latest arrival, was given a mug.

After a short rest more games followed and then, at eight o'clock, an hour towards which all minds had been turning, three generations of happy people gathered round the house to hear the message from the king. The message ended, the King's health in locally brewed ale, or home-made lemonade, was drunk, and then came supper, when everyone once more broke bread together.

And lastly, after dancing on the green, all went home through the fragrant evening air with the crescent moon setting over the Down and nightingales singing in the wood.'

'For the Jubilee all the Dover schoolchildren took part in a display at the Crabble Hill Athletic Grounds. We were dressed in red, white and blue pixie suits – top, shorts and a pixie hat. I remember I was in red.

Day after day we rehearsed in the playground at Barton Road school, all marching and making various patterns, flags etc. We marched to our positions and then stood stock still.

On the great day these hundreds of children gathered together and crowds of people came to watch. One child was chosen to speak a verse through a microphone, though I don't remember now what it was. Later the schools were taken to the cinema to see the film of the display, taken from the air and showing clearly the patterns we had made in red, white and blue – very patriotic.'

THE CORONATION OF GEORGE VI 1937

'One of the highlights of my life was seeing the procession of the Kings and Queens of Europe and many foreign dignitaries driving down Whitehall to Westminster Abbey. They were followed by the exquisite gold coach carrying King George VI and Queen Elizabeth to Westminster Abbey to be crowned.

The adventure started at eight o'clock on the evening of 11th May 1937. My mother, sister and I met under the clock at Charing Cross, with sandwiches, flasks and warm rugs.

We chose Whitehall because we knew that the nearer we were to the Abbey the more likely the route would be lined with very tall guardsmen. This proved correct, for lining Whitehall were sailors who were much shorter with their flat caps, and were kind enough to move slightly from side to side to allow us a better view. They had been supplied with hot drinks and chocolate during the night.

The theatre audiences were walking home, many in evening dress, maybe going to pre-Coronation parties? The buskers entertained us and the whole atmosphere was electric. There was a warm, friendly feeling. Sitting on the pavement we were of all nations. We seemed to understand each other although speaking in many languages.

There were bright clothes of many countries as well as coster-mongers, Pearly Kings and Queens. We enjoyed dancing, singing and of course, the inevitable salesmen selling muffins, chestnuts, hot dogs, flags, balloons and periscopes made of cardboard, which really did not work because by the time we had adjusted them the coach had long passed by.

We slept a little and took it in turns to walk about until it was not possible because the pavements were so full. We were allowed to use the road until it was time for the barriers to be put into position. Dawn was breaking! At 5.30 am or thereabouts we saw a short but commanding figure walking up the centre of Whitehall. The long white hair and flowing cape belonged unmistakably to David Lloyd George, quite alone and apparently deep in thought. A family near us called out to him in Welsh and he came across and talked to the crowd for a while.

Gradually the parade started. There were peers and peeresses of the realm wearing robes and sparkling jewels, orders and tiaras. Some were walking and some were riding in cars. Ministers of the Crown, Ambassadors and Governors, plumes flowing in the breeze, decorations shining, were followed by the Lord Mayor of London and his entourage. Then came Mayors of London and the provinces, representatives of the Services, Railway, Ambulance Service, Fire Services, the Police Commissioner and other officers on their lovely grey horses.

The bands were all playing as they took up their places en route. The pipers' marching feet and swaying kilts added to the colour and excitement.

We could hear shouting and cheering getting louder and suddenly there they were! Kings and queens and princes – many of whom in a few years time would have to go into exile, perhaps never again to rule over their countries. A special memory!

There were Queen Wilhelmina, King Zog of Albania, the sad figure of King Leopold of the Belgians, his arm still in a sling following the car crash which killed his beloved Queen Astrid, the young and then handsome King Farouk, King Haaken of Norway and I believe Prince Olaf, the King and Queen of Denmark and the small but very regal figure of Haile Selassie of Ethiopia.

241

Then came louder cheering for our own Royal family – Queen Mary, the princesses, so small that we could hardly see them, the Princess Royal, the Kents, the Gloucesters, Lord Louis and Lady Edwina Mountbatten, each family procession flanked by Household Cavalry. There was that wonderful music of horses hooves and the glint of the movement of their gleaming breastplates. Each coach was drawn by horses with shining coats, manes flying so proudly, and surely enjoying the cheers of the crowds.

Gasps of delight rose as the golden coach came into view. The King and Queen were each wearing a smaller crown, not yet the Coronation crown. As they passed into the distance, the crowd quietened, most people had tears in their eyes, so emotional was the experience. Or were they tears for the terrible events that were to change the world in a few years from then?'

'When suggestions were put forward for the celebrations in May 1937 at Stone, it was agreed that an ox should be roasted in the recreation field. The legs of the ox were tied together and it was put on an iron rod and the fire lit underneath. Although the fire was lit at 4 am and the roasting went on until 3 pm, the meat was *very* rare. The organiser was hoping to sell all the meat, but I'm afraid a lot was left unsold and a loss was made instead of the profit hoped for.'

'We had a good procession at Smarden for the Coronation. We at the butcher's shop had two black bullocks leading the procession and two motorbikes with a pig in one sidecar and two lambs in the other. I remember grooming them and getting them ready.'

THE CORONATION OF ELIZABETH II 1953

'The weather on Coronation Day in June 1953 was very disappointing, wet and miserable, which put paid to many planned celebrations.

Television was just beginning to become popular in the homes of the general public and my memory of the occasion is of people being glued to their new novelty with friends and relations invited to join with them to watch the proceedings in London.

We were living at Aycliffe, Dover and a small fancy dress parade was arranged amongst the local children. My daughter, then aged five, went as the Queen of Hearts (one of several!) and recalls being highly indignant because I nailed her jam tarts to a small board so that they would not fall off. She maintains it was to stop her from eating them, but whatever the reason it doesn't say much for my pastry!

Parties like this one at the Mission Hall, Seabrook, Hythe were held all over East Kent in 1953 to celebrate the Queen's coronation.

Incidentally, the green on which the parade was held and the adjacent houses have now fallen victim to the Channel Tunnel approaches.'

'It was a damp and cold morning when we arrived at the village hall to cut masses of sandwiches. I don't remember how we acquired all that food in those days of shortages!

I remember that I dressed up as a Beefeater and entered the fancy dress competition; so did another WI member, she was part of "a bicycle made for two!" We won the first two prizes, which were a new crown and a new half-crown. In the afternoon there were sports events for the children in the meadow, whilst the grown-ups watched the Coronation events on the television set specially installed in the chapel room. Another set was installed in the old Legion hut. It is all quite a long time ago, but I can still remember that (after a couple of gin and oranges) I danced with the Reverend Watts, late that evening in my wellington boots, under the coloured lights which had been strung up in the Jubilee tree. This was in the middle of our village and the side road was closed off to

243

traffic. My son was seven years old, and I can remember how thrilled he was to be allowed up until midnight on that eventful occasion!'

'Plans were laid long before the great day with the village of Crundale joining in with Godmersham's celebrations. A marquee was erected by the old village hall, decorated with a mass of bunting and flags, of course, and a big bonfire built on the top of the Mount with the Godmersham Park estate workers and many villagers helping.

Sadly, the day dawned very wet, but all the activities continued. All the children and some adults were invited by Mrs Tritton, the owner of the Godmersham Park mansion, to go down to the house and watch the Coronation on the TV – quite an experience as most of them had never seen television before.

After that some sports were organised for them, followed by a splendid tea party in the marquee. All the children were given a Coronation crown coin.

Later on in the evening, in spite of the continuing rain, many trooped up to the Mount to see the lighting of the bonfire – not an easy task as everything was so wet – but it did get going and finally a very damp and bedraggled collection returned home at the end of a very special day. The same spot on the Mount was where the Mafeking Bonfire had been lit and we're told that the fire on that occasion got out of hand. The local fire brigade was called but they were all so tight that they never managed to get to the scene! Nothing like that this time round.'

ENTERTAINMENT THROUGH THE YEAR

In the days before television, and even radio, people got together within their own community and organised their own entertainment. Clubs and societies flourished in even the smallest of villages and there was something for everyone, from sports to concert parties. Goal running was a local sport which attracted a wide following. There were also the annual events, from Easter to Christmas, to look forward to and celebrate. Some, of course, are still part of our lives but others, such as Empire Day, once celebrated by children throughout the country, have passed into history.

NEVER A SPARE MOMENT

'Woodchurch was typical in the range of activities we could choose from. Cricket has been enjoyed on the village green throughout the past century and the football club is still keenly supported. Goal running matches took place between local villages until the start of the Second World War. The British Legion met monthly in their hall and organised many events. The Gardening Society also contributed to activities, and the Women's Institute has been very busy since 1927. Whist drives have always been popular, and the National Farmers' Union has been active for many decades. The Woodchurch Band started in 1861 and there has always been a keen interest in music. On Boxing Day the village band, with brass instruments, flutes, violins etc, went round the village playing and ended at the squire's house, Hingehurst. A Mr Tester ran concert parties known as The Cameo for many years, much enjoyed by all. The King's Messengers Church Club for the children gave encouragement to them to perform plays and become involved in many charitable events. The residents never seemed to have any spare time on their hands whatsoever.'

GOAL RUNNING

'Goal running was common between villages, as all it needed was a large rectangular area of grass, and teams of no fixed size but open to all who were willing to run. One short side of the pitch was halved and each team used its half as a base, and its "goal" was the corner of the rectangle diagonally opposite its base, which if successfully reached counted for one point. The opposing team sent a chaser to touch this man before he could reach his goal, thus scoring a "stroke". Runners always had to use their discretion when leaving their base, whether to run for a point, act as a decoy to lead an opponent into danger or to chase for a stroke. To decide the team winner, strokes and points were added together, a stroke equalling a prearranged number of points (usually about ten or twelve). Children simplified the game by not scoring points, and called the game "pot". The goal became a prison, into which anyone fairly caught was placed and from which they could only be released by one of his team making the diagonal run from its base to goal without being touched.'

MAY DAY

'When I was young and just a shy, tousled, curly haired daughter of the village blacksmith, May Day was an important day in our school at Painter's Forstal. As far as I can remember, it was a school holiday. The day and evening before was taken up in picking the white hawthorn blossom (it always seemed to be out on May Day) and twining it round our wooden hoops to make garlands, tied with ribbons. With our garlands held high and flowers in our hair, we would walk round the village in procession, collecting halfpennies on the way.

The other essential item for May Day was the maypole. For weeks we had practised the steps, taking the pole up to the playing field. We girls each had a boy partner and by 1st May we could perform the "Spider's Web" and other intricate dances. In and out we danced, holding our braids in both hands and putting red over blue, yellow under white, in time to the music. This came from a wind-up gramophone, looked after by the headmistress. The girls were all dressed in white; what a pretty sight we must have been.'

EMPIRE DAY 24th MAY

'When I was at school at Cliftonville in the 1930s, we celebrated Empire Day every year. We practised for weeks before, then the day arrived. We started with the raising of the Union Jack and singing *God Save The King*.

First came the top infants class who danced, each dance representing the four countries of the British Isles, with a flag for each. They would finish by standing close, back to back, then a child would step up onto a chair holding a Union Jack. Next was the tableau. A senior pupil would come first and sit on the dais as Britannia, reciting a verse about Britain, followed by a girl in the costume of each country of the Empire, reciting a verse about each one and carrying produce they provided. I remember New Zealand carried a toy lamb and Australia a basket of apples. When the tableau was complete we all sang with gusto *Land of Hope and Glory, Land of our Fathers, Londonderry Air, Jerusalem*, and *Ye Banks and Braes*, ending with *God Save The King* and saluting the flag. The afternoon was a holiday. Parents and other relations came and enjoyed it as much as we did. I cannot remember it ever raining on Empire Day.'

'As a school, we would attend a service in Holy Trinity church, Sandgate Road, Folkestone, before which we all marched in single file and saluted the flag. This was a large Union Jack on a pole stuck into the grass verge of a broad path leading through shady trees to the church.

Even after rehearsals at school, where we were drilled by a Sergeant Major who marched us round and round on the grass square within the confines of a large walled garden, I doubt if I ever did salute correctly. Timing the moment when you did eyes right and raised your hand, and how soon you could resume your left, right, left without having to change feet to get into step, was agonising to a child of ten.

Juniors were dressed for the occasion in blue and white striped cotton dresses with a Peter Pan collar, while the senior girls' dresses were square-necked. We all wore white shoes and white stockings, and the statutory white gloves. Hair ribbons had to be navy blue and of course our panama hats, with very wide brims, very high crowns and very broad navy blue ribbons hanging down the back, had the inevitable elastic under the chin.

The church service itself was strongly patriotic, with *Land of Hope and Glory*, both stirring and uplifting.'

'We all congregated in Radnor Park at Folkestone. The band played and all the civic dignitaries were there, as school after school marched past the Union Jack with a sharp "eyes right" to salute the

Empire Day at Alkham school. Every schoolchild once celebrated on 24th May – and looked forward to the half day holiday.

247

flag. I well remember a helmeted policeman standing with a tower of panama hats that had blown off and were awaiting collection when the parade was over. Woe betide anyone who broke ranks to retrieve a lost hat!'

FETES AND CARNIVALS

'The last Saturday in May was Fair Day at Newnham. In the lower part of Hilly Field, roundabouts, swingboats and hoopla etc would have previously been set up. The local men paid into what was called a "slate club" and that day was share-out day. The local brass band played and there was a short service in the church. After the service the bandsmen marched, playing their instruments, as far as Doddington Place with a lot of us children following. In the afternoon there would be forms in the field for the bandsmen to sit on and they played at intervals; in the evening some people would dance.

We needed money for the fair. Some of us children walked to a farm about two miles from Newnham and some from Doddington came three and a half miles to arrive at 7 am to pull weeds from the corn. We walked up and down the rows of corn until 4 pm with a break for sandwiches and a bottle of drink at noon and we were very pleased to receive one shilling.'

'The church fete at Lydd in the 1930s was a grand do and many people attended. It was held in the Grange field. All the ladies and girls wore hats, even the members of the Mothers Union serving teas in the marquee.

The marquee housed the Garden Society show, the giant vegetables and the lovely flowers. The sweet peas were marvellous. There were also exhibits from Lydd school of children's handwriting, drawings, embroidery and crafts. In the field were all the usual sideshows, plus the aerial flight. This was a terrifying experience, holding on with both hands to a handle attached to a wheel that whizzed along a steel wire, then bashing into a bale of wool or straw.

There were coconut shies, clock golf and a wonderful machine that tossed ping-pong balls into the air while people stood around with butterfly nets, the one who caught the most balls in their net being the winner. The small merry-go-round was operated by winding a handle. The baby show and the fancy dress were judged. The young things of the day played tennis on the grass court, dressed in all their whites.

At dusk it was like fairyland walking along the pathway through the trees to the field, candles in coloured glass containers fixed to the trees showing the way. Competition winners received their prizes and there was much discussion as to whether the results were fair. The young things now waltzed and foxtrotted on the tennis court, the girls dressed in frocks with low waists, the men in blazers and flannels.

This was one of the great days of the year.'

'A big village fete was held at Alkham in about 1931 when funds were raised for the building of the village hall. There was one notable attraction – a real, live mermaid! The viewer climbed steps to look down into a tank of water. At the bottom of the tank could be seen the mermaid, sitting on the sand combing her hair.'

'One of my happiest childhood memories revolves around the annual Hospital Fetes that were held in Newington during the 1920s and 1930s. All monies raised were in aid of St Bartholomew's Hospital, Rochester. Our sports ground was on the Rainham side of the village on the A2. As my parents and family lived quite near, this really was a red letter day for me. The grounds were adjacent to the Newington Red Brick Co, now the local industrial estate.

These fetes were always held on a Saturday in August. The highlight of the day for us children was the fancy dress parade. My mother and sister used to spend hours making various costumes for me over the years. On the day we made our way from the village centre behind the various floats and headed by a brass band, I think from the Chatham area. One year, 1933, Evelyn Jenner and I were chosen as maids of honour to the elected Village Queen, Joyce Chappell (we were all schoolgirls together); quite a big day for us. Another year I remember being dressed up as a rose to present the bouquet to Mrs Harcourt Vallance from Milsted, who opened the fete that year.

There were many stalls. I loved looking round them, budgeting my money that my brothers had given me (I was the youngest of the family). There were lovely home-made ice creams and various sweets, peppermint creams, coconut ice and turkish delight.

A turn on the hoopla was never very successful; my eye was on that diamante bracelet, but it was not to be, I just could not get the hoop over that stand. A ride on the swingboats, where two of you sat, one at each end, and pulled ropes to make them swing to and fro; I thought I was in heaven. The boys, of course, favoured the coconut shies.

The flower and produce tent had a smell of its own. A mixture of vegetables and fruits at one end, and home-made cakes, sponges etc the other. I loved the scent of the roses and sweet peas, and as the heat inside the tents rose on hot days, the perfume was quite over-powering. My mother and I would collect as many wild flowers as possible on the previous evening to enter a vaseful in the children's section; you can bet we were over the moon if we won a prize, but quite put out if we didn't.

The tea tent was very popular; my mother was always one of the helpers. There were sandwiches, cream cakes and sponges, with glasses of home-made lemonade for us children, with dear old Bill Castle in charge of the huge urns for the vast quantities of tea for all those thirsty throats, and all this time the brass band was still playing.

My father was usually either busy around the produce tent, or on the 'Bowling for a Pig' stand.

The Maidstone & District ran a ten minute bus service at that time from Faversham to Gravesend on Service 26 which ran through Newington, and many people passing through would drop off and enter into all the fun, swelling the funds at the same time. Practically everyone in the village was there; I don't think the local shops did much trade that afternoon.

I was allowed to stay until about eight o'clock, after that it was a dance and entertainment for adults. I was asleep as soon as my head touched the pillow.'

'One of the highlights of the tourist season on Sheppey was the Sheerness Carnival. It started just after the Second World War and was held on a Sunday in July or August and attracted large crowds who would line the pavements along its route.

My friend and I used to get a lift from our homes in Minster to Sheerness shortly before 4 pm on Carnival afternoon, and we'd find ourselves a good place to stand. Chances are we'd know some of the people standing near and could while away the time chatting till the procession appeared. Street sellers would do a good trade persuading children to buy paper wavers, tooters or furry toys, dangling from a piece of elastic.

The first sign would be the sound of one of the marching bands, St John's Ambulance maybe, and there'd be two or three more from the island or mainland. Then the police car leading the procession would appear, followed by the Mayor and Mayoress's limousine with them waving and acknowledging the crowd like royalty, and after them the many decorated cars and floats representing local businesses and organisations. The loudest cheers were reserved for our Carnival Queen and her attendants, but there would also be the Carnival Prince and Princess, the OAP queen and the carnival queens from other places on the island and nearby mainland.

Fearsome-looking Zulu warriors would walk beside the floats, rattling their tins and collecting coins for local charities. The Zulus were at various times cadets from the shore station, HMS *Wildfire*, young men from the Rugby Club or stevedores from the dockyard. They blacked-up faces and bodies, donned leopardskin loincloths and brandished spears and shields or a big juicy raw bone from the butcher's. Earlier in the day there had probably been some fun on the seafront with the Zulus "boiling" a missionary in a big cauldron, or having a soot and flour fight.

The carnival would take about an hour to pass. After it was all over we'd buy ice cream or hot dogs from a shop on the seafront and walk back to Minster along the beach and up the cliffs. I never remember a carnival being spoilt by rain. To finish off the evening there would be a fireworks display about 9 pm to entertain the crowd who'd stayed in Sheerness.'

SPORTS DAY

'For 18 years, from 1896 to the outbreak of the First World War, an annual sports day was held in St Margarets-at-Cliffe. Mr Laslett of Reach Court Farm lent his meadow for the proceedings, the boys from the Gordon Orphanage came with their bagpipes to entertain, there were refreshments and the whole village turned out to watch or take part. There were races for boys, girls, men, men over 60, spinsters, visitors, on bicycles, in sacks, in wheelbarrows, with egg and spoon, with potatoes, on horses, in costume and over hurdles. There was a high jump, a long jump, pillow fights, quoit throwing, cricket ball throwing and a land crab race. They raced for silver cups, medals and prizes. Penknives were popular for the boys but many prizes were quite substantial. In 1909 the boys under 14 winner, I. Green, received a camera. The same year the tug of war teams both got prizes of 24 and 12 shillings respectively, and W. Jones, who won the mounted costume race, was given a gold hunter watch! In 1911 a half ton of coal was offered to the oldest inhabitant, but no one came forward.

As well as being able to compete in the main sports event, the children of the village had their own race and sports day each year with their own challenge cups to compete for. No wonder the whole village turned out to watch or take part.'

BONFIRE NIGHT

'The week before 5th November most of the local children at Newnham would roam through the woods collecting dead wood etc for the bonfire. A field at the back of the village, called Hilly Field for obvious reasons, was ideal for the fire at the top. We wanted money for fireworks (children were not given pocket money in our day, at the beginning of the 1900s) so we dressed up in old, long skirts and wore a mask over our faces. We then went Popeing, as it was called, and said our piece – Remember, remember the 5th of November, the gunpowder treason and plot, etc. When this was finished we knocked at the door of the cottages and were usually given a copper or so.'

CHRISTMAS

'In the early 1900s we made our own Christmas presents to give to people: bookmarks made of cardboard bound round with wool, spill boxes made of thick brown paper to hold spills, handkerchief boxes made out of large cigarette boxes which were painted and then had scraps stuck on them, and small boxes to keep pins or small jewels in which were cheese boxes woven on the top with different coloured wools.

Christmas was a great family time. Parents, grandparents, aunts, uncles and cousins all came for a time. On Christmas Eve, Dad would help us put up the paper chains which we had made earlier. You could buy penny packets of cut coloured strips to make into chains. You made the stuff to stick them with out of flour and water. We believed in Father Christmas and hung up our stockings before going to bed. In the toe of the stocking in the morning there was always an apple, an orange and a sugar mouse. We always went to the 11 am service on Christmas morning in the Wesleyan chapel in Folkestone. There was always a post on Christmas morning.'

'Christmas Day started when I emptied the stocking filled by Father Christmas, which hung at the bottom of the bed. Then there was always breakfast of cold rabbit pie, the rabbit being in the jelly from the meat, before we set off for our grandparents at Martinvale, where all the family met. There were about 15 of us. We had a roast of meat or chicken midday and the day ended with a cold meat supper. Tinned fruit was a treat, the cheapest being pineapple at about fourpence ha'penny. My mother ordered her Christmas cake from the International Stores at Alkham.'

'Christmas in the early 1920s started really in September. Mother collected ingredients for "the" puddings all the year, and about the last week in September was Pudding Time.

The big mixing bowl was got out and all ingredients set on the kitchen table. We children settled round the table with our own "bag and bowl". Big sticky raisins had to be stoned, currants and sultanas tossed in flour and shaken in the sieve to remove stalks, grit, etc. Candied citrus fruit came halved with the pulp removed and encrusted with candied sugar and the "cup" filled with a solid lump. All sugar had to be brushed and cleared before the peel could be cut into strips and chopped – Mum made candy from the sugar later on. Almonds had to be soaked in boiling water to allow the skins to be easily removed. If soaked properly the almonds popped out of the pointed end when the fat end was squeezed. These also had to be split and chopped. Spices were bought ground but the nutmeg had to be grated. Fresh lemons were there to be squeezed for juices and skin grated for zest. Ooh, the lovely smell of it all, to say nothing of the odd "tasters" of everything.

When everything was ready Mother supervised the mixing. Flour, sugar, everything in its order, all mixed with a huge wooden spoon. A dozen eggs, beer and lemon juice and all was done. The bowl was covered with a large wet cloth and was put into the front room where everyone was invited to stir and wish.'

'Christmas, for me in the 1920s, began some days before, by making the paper decorations. We made rings from coloured strips of paper by joining them together by sticky paste and arranging the rings into chains.

Christmas Day eventually came. After the excitement of waking and finding my stocking filled with an orange in the toe, next came the party in the afternoon which my Granny always gave. We would walk round to her house by the village pond, up the garden path and into the room with the table laden with good things to eat and crackers on the plates. There were eight in our family, with two lots of aunts and uncles and their children, the Hobday family and of course my Granny. Granny was a little white haired woman, who gave us pennies when we went to see her every Sunday on our way from church. After eating as much as we could and putting our paper hats on, we went into the sitting room, and there a lovely sight awaited us. A Christmas tree with real candles, twinkling and shining through the dark green branches, gold and silver decorations hanging from the tree. The presents were given out and opened with delight. After that, games were played, blind man's buff, postman's knock, pass the parcel, spin the plate, forfeits and hunt the thimble.

When we were tired of running about, next came the family concert. Everyone did a turn, from the youngest to the grown ups who wanted to. I liked singing, as most of us did, except my brother, who couldn't sing, but his conjuring tricks went down well. I remember my eldest sister Meg was a great success when she sang *The Ash Grove*. The piano was played by my aunt and Uncle Ern's skill on the accordion was enjoyed. My father always sang the last song. He had a deep bass voice and would sing old favourites – *Drake's Drum* and *The Flies are on the Turnips*, also *Sussex by the Sea*. After last drinks, it was time to go home, so we put on our coats, said "Happy Christmas" and walked back round the village, our boots and shoes making a ringing sound in the frosty night air.'

'At Christmas on the wards at The Kent & Canterbury Hospital during the war years as many patients as possible were sent home and no member of the staff had leave over the holiday, so there was the minimum of work for the nurses to do.

Instead of our coffee and tea breaks in the nurses' dining room, each ward had a coffee morning or tea afternoon and the wards vied with each other to achieve the best party. A surgeon or physician used to don a paper hat and carve a turkey for each ward lunch.

We did our best to decorate the wards with anything that was available, such as blackout paper cut into silhouettes and stuck on the walls. A few paper chains were obtained from our homes that could be spared. All wards had a large Christmas tree given them. As all forms of decorations were unobtainable during the war years, I used to contact a local Canterbury store to borrow their fairy lights when the store closed on Christmas Eve. All sorts of ingenious ideas were used to decorate the tree, such as coloured paper bows and streamers. One year I remember obtaining masses of glass test tubes and filling them with various coloured liquids from our lotion cupboard and hanging them on the tree with great effect, although the ones filled with pale yellow liquid were viewed with some suspicion.'

'There was definitely more carol singing done in those days. We'd go out for a jolly week around Smarden. The men used to go and sometimes it was in aid of Benenden Chest Hospital. There was one story going through Smarden of a group of carol singers singing at a haystack, thinking it was a house!

Oh yes, we used to hang our stockings up at Christmas. "Hung me stocking up till I left home." We had one of Mum's stockings, with holes in it. Mind you, I always thought of the Browns up the road with envy – they used to hang pillow cases up!'

Index

255